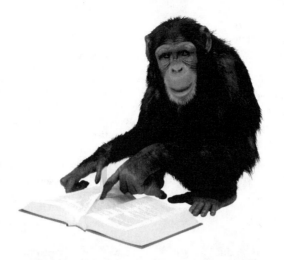

Digital Photography!

I Didn't Know You Could Do That...™

Second Edition

Erica Sadun

SYBEX®

San Francisco • Paris • Düsseldorf • Soest • London

Associate Publisher: Cheryl Applewood
Acquisitions and Developmental Editor: Bonnie Bills
Editor: Dann McDorman
Production Editor: Molly Glover
Technical Editor: Eric Bell
Book Designers: Franz Baumhackl, Kate Kaminski
Graphic Illustrator: Tony Jonick
Electronic Publishing Specialists: Judy Fung, Jangshi
Wang, Maureen Forys, Jill Niles
Proofreader: Laurie O'Connell
Indexer: Ann Rogers
CD Technician: Kevin Ly
CD Coordinator: Christine Harris
Cover Designer: Ziegler Design
Cover Illustrator: Daniel Ziegler

Library of Congress Card Number: 2001094586

ISBN: 0-7821-2965-X

For Mom and Dad, who put up with me until adulthood, with respect and gratitude, especially now that I've got kids of my own. And in memory of Mamma, who will sorely be missed and who always had her head on her shoulders just right.

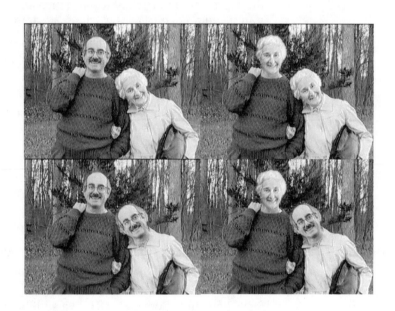

Acknowledgments

This book could not have been written without the generosity and skill of others. I am deeply grateful for the assistance offered so freely by so many kind people. No book is ever truly the work of one person. I would like to thank everyone who has given of their time, help, advice, and information. I humbly beg the forgiveness of any person I have overlooked.

I wish to thank, in particular, Sherry Bonelli formerly of Sybex and Neil Salkind of Studio B. I cannot express how marvelous it was to work with both of them. In fact, all of the wonderful folks at Sybex and Studio B made this a project of particular joy and pleasure. I would also like to thank Bonnie Bills, Liz Burke, Amy Changar, Siobhan Dowling, Maureen Forys, Judy Fung, Molly Glover, Nancy Guenther, Christine Harris, Don Hergert, Tony Jonick, Chuck Larrieu, Lucienne Loh, Kevin Ly, Dann McDorman, Keith McNeil, the amazing Dan Mummert, Jill Niles, Laurie O'Connell, Ceola Richardson, Ann Rogers, Kara Schwartz, Marilyn Smith, Colleen Strand, Jangshi Wang, Kris Warrenburg, and Nathan Whiteside. Sybex is truly a kinder, gentler publishing company. The entire production team did a fabulous job. Thank you.

I also want to thank all of the companies and Web sites that have graciously granted permission for their software and services to be included in this book. In particular, Adobe generously allowed me to package PhotoDeluxe on the CD-ROM that accompanies this book.

In addition, thanks to those people whose outstanding courtesy helped this process enormously. These include the simply incredible Mike Wong of Lexar; The Altamira Group, especially Carolyne Walton and Sid Fish; Steve Berezin of Berezin 3-D; Ceiva and Richard Attenberg; Jeff Kelling of FotoTime; JP Wollersheim, Bridget Thornton Padilla, and Lisa Marshall of PhotoLoft; Rachel Branch of Sony; Abe Schoener of eFrames; Chris Johnson and Lylia Lammens of PhotoPoint; Tara Poole of Shandwick, International; Avi Shmidman; Bill Martin; Patty Thompson, Peter Hanisch, Patrick Sagisi, and Mark Dahm of Adobe; the good folks at Ulead; ClubPhoto; eFrames, especially Abe and Michelle; Jackie Zide of Manning, Selvage, and Lee for eMemories; Dick Paulson of EZ Prints; Ofoto, especially Jeremy Pepper; Photo-Channel, especially Joseph Bach and David Bremner; Dawn Weissman of PhotoPoint; GatherRound.com's Mollie Lupinacci; Marc Holmquist of

PhotoDex; Laura Shook of Cerious Software; Dennis Curtin of Short Courses; Travis White of Ulead; Michael Bartosh and Bo Turney of Apple; Jenny Menhart of Ahead; Kris Konietzko of TSI Communications WorldWide; Alan Williams of Adobe; Gerald of Seattle FilmWorks, aka PhotoWorks; Shelly Sofer of MGI; Stephanie Xavier and Molly Fitzpatrick of Access Communications; Kari Day of Real Networks; Sean Wright of Dell, Inc.; JASC; CompuPic; and PhotoIsland.

Contents

Preface to the Second Edition

How times change. A year ago, my friends and family were interested in, but somewhat bewildered about digital photography. This year, practically everyone I know is looking to jump onto the digital photography bandwagon.

Hardly a week passes without my parents seeking advice for some friend or another: "The grandkids are coming next month to visit the Schnurrs (or the Bloggs, or the Goldsteins, etc.) and they want to buy a digital camera before they get here. Which model should they get?" When technology hits the retirement community, it hits hard and fast, particularly when it is targeted towards grandkids or golf.

The digital camera has become the small businessperson's best friend. With a digicam and a Web site, more and more people are moving their local shops online. Specialty stores, in particular, profit from the wide exposure that the World Wide Web offers. Digital photography can quickly put inventory online and in front of a huge audience of shoppers.

Within the last year, most barriers that kept digital cameras from home use have fallen away. Prices have dropped, optics have improved. For just a few hundred dollars, consumers can buy a camera with excellent zoom and superb picture quality. And now, you can take your digital pictures to Wal-Mart or the corner drugstore and walk away with prints in an hour, for about the same cost as film. You'll never know the difference in the prints.

The biggest difference between this year and last is how so many people now understand why digital cameras are so exciting. You can snap lots and lots of pictures without guilt—there's no film to waste. You only print the pictures you like, and you can improve them before you print. You can share your pictures over e-mail and the Web. You can create lasting keepsakes like personalized ties and coffee mugs. You can save your pictures to CDs and DVDs and play them back on your TVs. The potential truly is unlimited. Digital photography has brought picture-taking into a whole new realm of possibility and product.

Introduction

In 1995, I saw my first consumer-grade digital camera. It was too cool for words. I fell in love immediately. I knew I simply had to have one of my own. So, in early 1996, I went out and spent far too much money. I bought myself a new technological friend. Here it was—shiny, gadget-filled, and very expensive—and I didn't have a clue what to do with it. I don't mean to suggest that the answer "take pictures" escaped me. After all, I had been shooting digital images since the early 1980s. But I didn't realize how much that little device might change my life. I had never thought of using my camera to remember where I parked my car, to give slide shows in foreign countries, or to see what my ear really looked like. Yet within the first few months, I had done all that and a lot more.

Digital cameras are selling like hotcakes because people sense the awesome potential of filmless systems. Digital cameras are more than just cameras with chips inside them. They offer a different way of thinking about pictures and new ways of sharing them with friends and family around the world. Does your 35mm camera usually sit on the shelf except for during vacations and special occasions? You'll probably find yourself using your digital camera far more often.

In 1999, a major stumbling block was cleared. Prior to that time, many people rejected digital cameras because they couldn't create "real photos." Now dozens and dozens of photo-finishing companies offer digital photo processing that produces prints on real photographic-quality silver-halide paper. Depending on the quality of your digital camera, you can order prints that look as good as 35mm prints.

In the years since I bought my first Casio (a 320×240 pixel model that cost $1,000), I've stumbled across many wonderful projects for digital cameras. These have ranged from the playful to the serious, and from the home-based to the business-intensive. I think you'll enjoy trying these projects with your own camera.

You don't need a special make or brand of digital camera for the projects presented in this book—any digital camera will do. They work equally as well on my Nikon CoolPix 800 (which sold for over $300 when I purchased it) as they do on my father's Little Tykes digital camera (which cost $12.50, including shipping). A handful of projects do require a video-out port or an onboard LCD screen, which are features that are not included on the Little Tykes model.

How This Book Is Organized

Digital Photography! I Didn't Know You Could Do That… Second Edition contains descriptions of more than 60 individual projects. These range from snapping high-quality photographs, to sending pictures by e-mail, to placing clown noses on your nearest and dearest. Each project contains step-by-step instructions and important how-to tips. Whether you're reading this book from cover to cover or skipping between projects and pages, you'll come away knowing exactly what you can do with your digital camera.

I've organized the projects into the following categories:

Composition, Lighting, and Posing: Some Tried-and-True Advice Learn how to take excellent photos, light your scenes, set up a portrait studio for under $20, and pose your subjects. This part contains plenty of photos to illustrate how you can take better pictures.

Manage Your Digital Camera Learn how to power your camera, add image memory, transfer your pictures to your computer, and use filters and lenses. The types of batteries and memory you use for your camera can make the difference between capturing that special moment or missing it because you ran out of power or storage.

Enhancing Your Images with PhotoDeluxe Acquire the essential Adobe PhotoDeluxe skills that will help you improve and manipulate your images. Many of the projects covered in this book make use of this software, which comes absolutely free with this book!

Just For the Fun of It: Digital Photo Projects Learn how to create photo fantasies, warp images, morph between photos, create photo montages, and much, much more. You'll have a lot of fun with the Web site–based and PhotoDeluxe projects covered in this part.

Fix Your Digital Photo Problems Learn how to correct image flaws such as poor contrast, low light, red-eye, and so forth. You can even get rid of unwanted background elements and improve your subject's complexion.

Cool Picture Projects   Use your digital photos to create animated slide shows, coloring book pages, calendars, and more. These projects are easy and put your photos to good use.

New Viewpoints: Postprocessing Your Images   Get a different view with your photos. You'll learn how to stitch together panoramas, assemble three-dimensional pictures, and blow up images to poster size.

Digital Camera Crafts   Learn how to create craft projects with your digital images. From fashion wear to window decals, digital photo projects are fun, easy, and make great gifts.

Digital Camera Versatility   Discover all the weird, wacky, and wonderful ways your digital camera can help you remember, document, and see things. The ideas in this part range from the serious (taking shots at the scene of an accident) to the silly (playing Face Bingo).

Some Day My Prints Will Come   Explore how to make prints from your digital photographs. You'll learn how to print your photographs at home on your own printer, as well as how to prepare your digital photographs to send to a photo-finishing service for producing silver-halide prints.

Share Your Pictures   Learn how to distribute your photos over the Internet. You can send photos by e-mail, create and share online photo albums, and use a digital photograph frame to send pictures to those without Internet connections.

Digital Photo Sampler   Throughout the book, you'll see many digital photographs illustrating the projects. However, the black-and-white pictures cannot do justice to the full range of color and tone that you can capture with your digital camera. This 16-page color insert, which presents photographs that show how you can use your digital camera to produce fun, interesting, and artistic images, will give you an idea of the visual and emotional impact that color images can convey.

In addition, you'll find an appendix and a glossary at the back of this book. The "Field Guide to Online Finishing and Album Sites" appendix lists the top online digital photo finishing and album sites. Use this handy reference to decide where and how you'll post and process your digital snapshots on the World Wide Web. If you're unfamiliar with any of the terms you see in this book, check the glossary for the definition.

Free, Free, Free

The CD-ROM that accompanies *Digital Photography! I Didn't Know You Could Do That...* Second Edition is absolutely jam-packed with demos and shareware that you can use with your digital images. But the best part is that it contains a licensed copy of Adobe's PhotoDeluxe software. Yes, you read that correctly. PhotoDeluxe, a $49 value, is included free with this book.

With PhotoDeluxe, you'll be able to see, manipulate, and edit your images with wonderful control and precision. Make sure to read through the "Enhancing Your Images with PhotoDeluxe" part of this book to learn more about how to use this powerful photo-editing software.

In addition to PhotoDeluxe, you'll find quite a few commercial demonstration software packages. These packages "expire" after a period of time, usually ranging between 15 and 30 days. Take advantage of this free time to test the programs, kick the tires, and see if they are worth your monetary investment to purchase a license. These are truly excellent packages that you'll probably want to make part of your digital photographer's toolkit.

Finally, you'll find a number of shareware programs. Unlike PhotoDeluxe and the commercial demos, these packages are not free. Instead, they allow you to try the product before you buy it. Shareware only works when people take personal responsibility and pay for the software they actually use. Be responsible. If you like the software, send the requested fee to the developer. This helps keep shareware alive and available for the rest of us.

Composition, Lighting, and Posing: Some Tried-and-True Advice

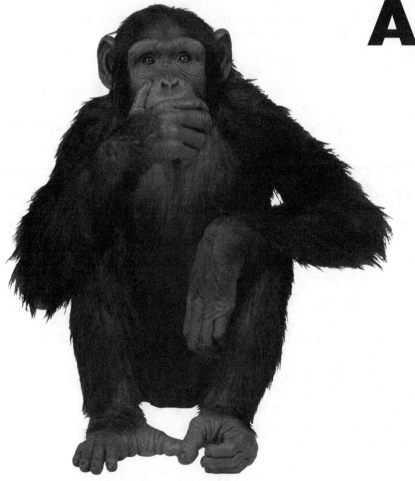

Whether you're using a traditional film camera or a fancy new digital one, the composition, lighting, and posing play important roles in your photos. The time-tested techniques and tips described in this section will help you create better, more professional snapshots while taking advantage of the special features provided by your digital camera.

1 Compose Your Shot with Care

Do you remember that joke about Mozart (the one in which he's busy decomposing)? In photography, composition doesn't mean creating music. Instead, it refers to the way that the photographer places all of the visual elements of a picture. Good pictures don't happen by accident. Good pictures result from planning and following the basic rules of composition—the better the composition, the better the photograph. If you think that you take pretty good pictures now, you'll be astonished how quickly your snapshots improve when you apply the basic rules of photographic composition.

Get Closer...Much Closer!

Do you know the single worst mistake that amateur photographers make? It's distance. People shoot pictures from too far away. They think they need to capture the whole scene instead of just the real point of interest. This one bad habit makes many bad photos.

You can easily improve your photos with one quick fix: Move closer. The closer you get to your subject, the better your photos will turn out. Some people operate under the mistaken impression that you need to take pictures of an entire landscape or an entire person—including all the hair, limbs, clothes, and so forth—in order to create a memorable shot. On the contrary, your photos should focus on a point of interest. For example, when your subject is a person, think of the eyes as the most important part of your photo. The more you concentrate on a person's face—and, particularly, a person's eyes—the better your photo will turn out.

Consider the three photos below. With each photo, the camera moves in toward the subject. See how the pictures improve with each step? Getting closer creates snapshots that focus more narrowly on the subject while creating a sense of intimacy between the subject and the viewer.

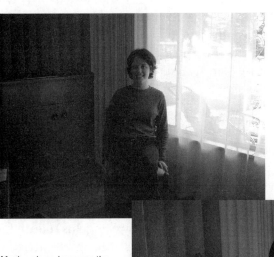

From too far away, the subject is completely lost in the picture. The real center of interest occupies only about one-sixth of the total photo.

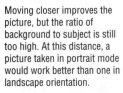

Moving closer improves the picture, but the ratio of background to subject is still too high. At this distance, a picture taken in portrait mode would work better than one in landscape orientation.

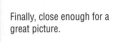

Finally, close enough for a great picture.

Use the Rule of Thirds

Way long ago, in ancient Greece and Egypt, philosophers noticed a strange feature of beauty. Many things we find attractive incorporate a natural ratio of approximately 3:2, which they called *Phi* (rhymes with *tie*). This ratio came to be known as the golden ratio, or even the divine ratio. The ancients used this ratio to create art and architecture to mimic the beauty one finds in nature. The idea is this: Things that are split into thirds, with some feature placed about two-thirds of the way across the scene, look good. It's as simple as that.

Artists and, later, photographers picked up on this ratio to form the rule of thirds, which we use in composition. This involves placing visually interesting points along imaginary lines at one-third and two-thirds of the way across a picture. But the adherence to using Phi goes further than that. Even the most common print sizes (3.5×5, 4×6, 5×7, and so forth) approximate the golden ratio between their width and their height.

You can improve your photos by using this rule of thirds. Just imagine two pairs of lines. One pair runs horizontally across your picture at one-third and two-thirds of the height. The other pair runs vertically, again at one-third and two-thirds of the width. When framing your image through the viewfinder or on your camera's LCD screen, place the most important features of your picture along one of these lines. Whether you shoot your pictures in landscape or portrait mode, this rule will improve your picture's composition.

N O T E   Most digital cameras now ship with both a traditional viewfinder and a liquid crystal display (LCD) screen. While some people prefer using the viewfinder to "point and shoot," others like the convenience and preview features of the LCD screen. Whichever feature you use, remember to frame your pictures carefully before pressing the shutter release.

If you're not comfortable "imagining" the lines, you can actually place them onto your camera's LCD screen. Simply cut out some transparent plastic, draw your lines on it, and apply it to your camera's display. Plastic used for making viewgraphs or transparencies works particularly well for this purpose. If static electricity doesn't keep your plastic attached to the LCD screen, use a little transparent tape to apply it.

The illustration below shows the differences between images composed with and without using the rule of thirds. Notice how both portrait and nature shots improve when this rule is applied.

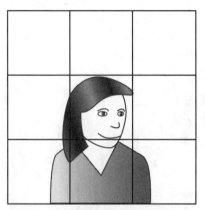

Composed without using the rule of thirds, a picture is not visually interesting.

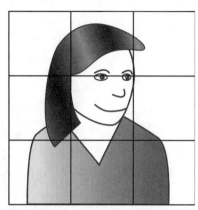

Positioning the eyes on the top line improves the picture

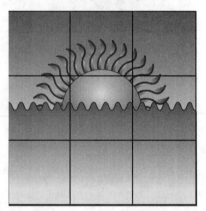

The horizon rests directly in the middle of the picture.

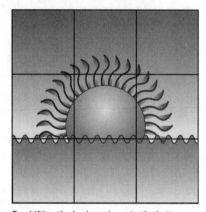

By shifting the horizon down to the bottom line, the rule of thirds improves the picture.

NOTE When using the rule of thirds, it does not matter on which of the lines you choose to set your visual focus point. Use any of the four lines or four points (where the lines intersect). Your photos will improve.

Simplify Your Background

One of a photographer's biggest goofs is to allow the background to be too cluttered with objects and people. Busy backgrounds distract the eye from your main subject, drawing attention away from what you should really be looking at. Contrast the pictures below. See how the picture works better with less happening in the background?

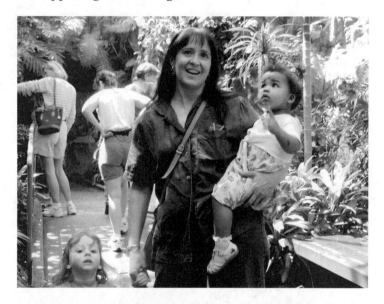

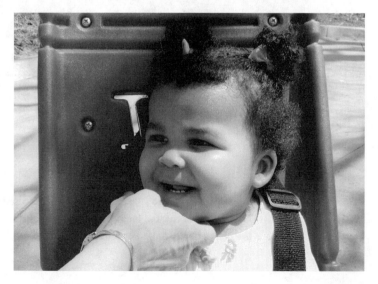

You can easily solve the busy background problem. Consider these hints:

◆ Avoid busy scenery. The simplest solution is the most obvious. Take pictures away from cluttered areas. Choose a plainer backdrop for your snapshots.

◆ Move the camera. Sometimes you can avoid visual clutter by adjusting your viewpoint. Try walking around your subject with your camera until you find a more flattering angle.

◆ Move closer. The more subject the picture contains, the less background your picture shows.

◆ Drop down. By shooting up at your subject, you can sometimes avoid a lot of eye-level clutter.

◆ Take a portrait. Turn your camera 90 degrees and shoot in portrait mode rather than in landscape mode. Portrait shots limit the amount of background and show more of your subject.

Frame It!

Shooting your picture through a natural frame can add elegance to your pictures. Natural frames include windows, doors, and tree limbs, as well as other overhanging features. Adding a frame to your picture can make it look better. This works by directing the eye toward the subject. The picture on the next page shows an example of a "framed" shot.

WARNING   Watch out for your depth of field—make sure that both your frame and your subject stay in focus! Frames don't work well if either they or the subjects slide into fuzzy obscurity.

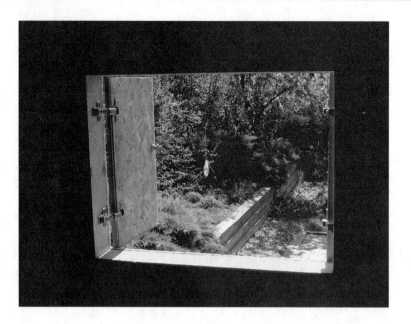

Choose the Best Camera Angle

Did you know that your point of view could dramatically change the way that you perceive a subject? When a camera shoots down, we tend to think a subject looks smaller and humbler. When the camera looks up, we think the subject looks bigger and stronger. These camera angles mimic the way that we have learned to look at things and people during life. Consider the viewpoint of an adult looking down at a child or a child looking up at an adult, and you can understand how the direction of a photo can resonate with personal experience. You can take advantage of the way that we naturally interpret these angles to add meaning and effect to your pictures.

Shoot 'em Down

You can make your subjects seem smaller and more appealing by shooting down. This angle can make a young girl look more demure. It can make a child seem more childlike or an adult less imposing. Downward angles emphasize eyes and cheeks, while minimizing chins. Large cheeks and small chins correlate with the way we view children. The picture below shows a person shot at a downward angle.

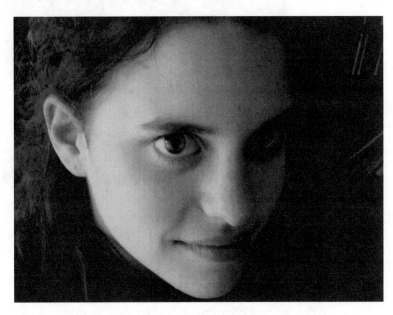

NOTE You can use a downward angle for good or for evil. Many political photographers shoot down when they want to humiliate or minimize a politician or public figure. Because we identify downward shots with an adult viewpoint, these pictures can make people look less important.

Downward angles also make pictures feel more closed and complete than other angles do. When taking photos of the outdoors, a downward shot where the horizon appears high in the picture will produce a feeling of limits and claustrophobia. You can also use a downward angle to hide an ugly, overcast sky, as in the example on the next page.

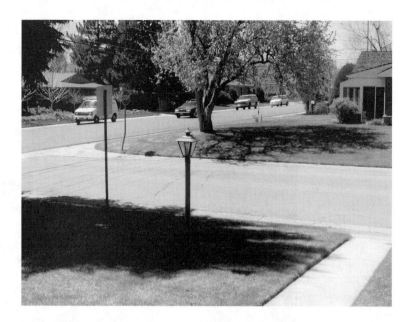

Shoot 'em Up

You can make your subjects appear bigger, more imposing, and more demanding of attention just by lowering your camera and looking up. Use this camera angle to flatter your subjects and make them seem more important. You need not limit this technique to photos of people. Take an upward-pointing picture of your dog to show how strong and fierce he is. Take a picture from the bottom of a statue to emphasize its height and majesty. However you use it, remember that the upward angle lends prominence and strength to both the subject and to your photos. This technique particularly emphasizes the chin, lending a sense of power to your subject. The picture on the next page shows a person shot at an upward angle.

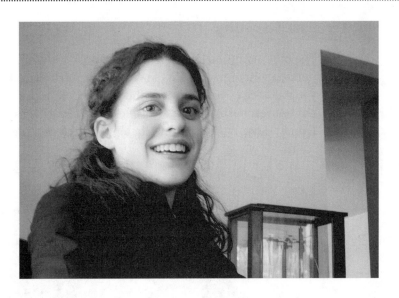

Upward angles open up pictures by lowering the horizon, as in the example below. They lend a feeling of spaciousness and freedom without limits or restrictions. When shooting outdoor photos, use an upward shot to draw in the sky and capture the full magnificence of nature.

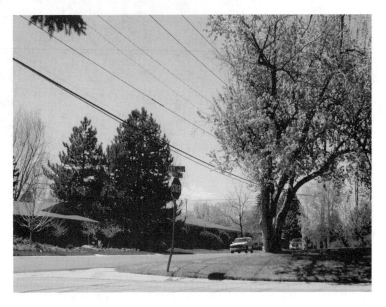

Straight Shooting

The most common shot—the straight-on, neutral shot—forms the bread and butter of photography. This shot creates plain and undistorted portraits of your subject, as you can see in the picture below. Use this angle when you're not trying for artistry or special effects. It's straight, it's honest, and it's simple. It may be boring, but it works for almost all of your photography needs.

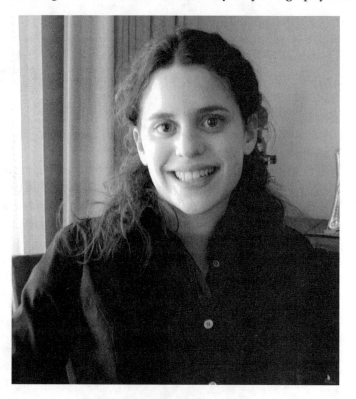

Horizontal or Vertical Orientation?

As you've probably noticed, photos tend to come in one of two orientations. In the vertical portrait shot, the height exceeds the width. In the horizontal landscape shot, the width exceeds the height.

Horizontal and vertical compositions create different effects. Vertical photos capture individuals and small groups best, at the expense of the background. Horizontal shots, in contrast, are best for large group shots and general photography both of people and nature. The following pictures show how using a vertical shot improves a photo of a person.

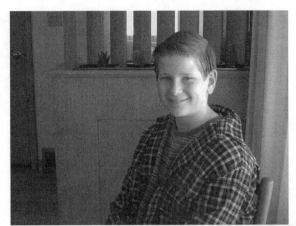

Horizontal composition includes too much background for a portrait.

Vertical composition captures more of the individual.

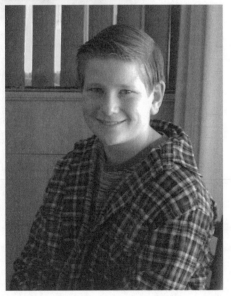

Because of its more generalized nature, the typical camera creates horizontal shots by default. To take a vertical picture, just turn the camera on its side and shoot. Many tripods allow you to mount your camera for either vertical or horizontal shots.

Face Your Subject to the Center

The way a person faces, called a *leading look,* can direct attention into the picture or out of it. Looking out of the picture produces photos that don't quite work, as you can see on the next page.

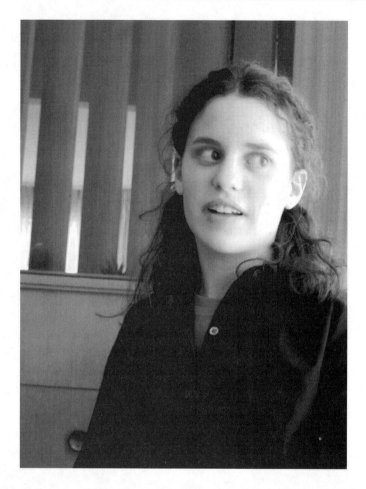

Ask your subjects to look toward the center of your photographic frame, or move the camera and your composition until their pose *does* work.

Avoid Unwanted Background Elements

Sometimes, we forget to look at the background. We become so fixated on our subject's great expression or adorable pose that all sorts of unwanted visual details pop into our photos, unannounced. Often we don't notice the other elements until too late, when the moment has already gone, and then we're stuck with the pictures with little "problem" items all over the place.

You can learn to break out of the whole subject-fascination trance and avoid the pitfalls of unwanted elements in your photos. Start by thinking before snapping your photos. Take a good long look at the whole picture. What items don't belong? What can you improve simply by moving an item—or yourself—to another location? It's easy to get rid of unsightly details. The problem is noticing them in the first place! The pictures below show the difference between just shooting a photo and noticing the background first.

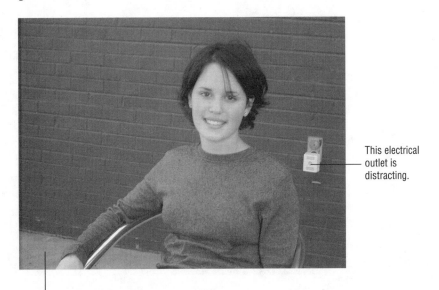

This electrical outlet is distracting.

The photo will work better without seeing the contrast between the brick wall and the ground.

The photo is greatly improved without the background elements.

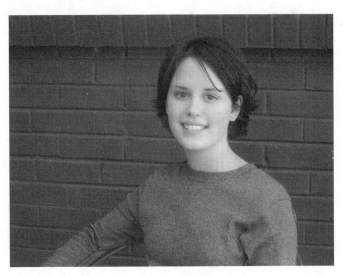

The worst offender for this sort of photography is the classic "tree growing out of someone's head" shot. By concentrating on your subject, rather than the background, you may end up with a telephone pole, sign, or tree sprouting from a head. Remember the basic rule: Stop, look, and if necessary, move! Only then should you snap.

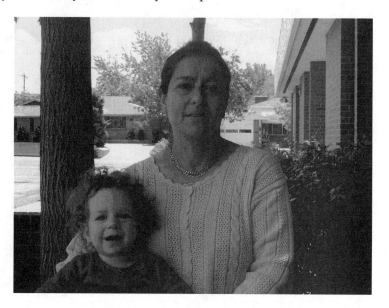

NOTE In some cases, you can fix background problems by using photo-editing program tools. See number 32, "Remove and Replace Unwanted Elements," and number 33, "Alter Photo Backgrounds with PhotoDeluxe Tools," for some suggestions.

2 Use Light Effectively

As a digital photographer, you need light. For obvious reasons, without light, you cannot take pictures. And without good lighting, you cannot take good pictures. Good lighting makes the difference between drama and melodrama, between splendor and ordinary, between memorable and dull.

Sunshine can be your best friend, or it can be your worst enemy. While you're letting it fill your camera with brilliant colors and images, remain wary. Learn to tame and control it. Make it do what you need it to do. Natural sunlight creates the most dramatic and colorful scenes. It can also fool your camera. It can make your pictures harsh and unflattering. It can bleach images to near-whiteness or hide your subject in an artificial dark.

You can improve your digital photography by learning to use light effectively. By following simple guidelines, you can ensure that your pictures turn out the best they can be—whether you're shooting indoors or outdoors, or in bright light or near dark.

Avoid Backlight

Backlight occurs when the sun (or, for that matter, any other light source) shines too close to your subject's back. Backlight tricks your camera into thinking it is taking a picture of a very bright object. Your camera adjusts its light levels too high. Instead of picking up the light levels from your subject, it picks them up from the scenery. While the scenery appears beautiful and well lit, your subject looks awful—usually as a silhouette against a bright and colorful background.

To avoid backlight, keep the sun behind you and in front of your subject. This allows your camera to properly interpret your exposure settings.

You may need to physically move yourself and your camera to find the proper lighting. If you can't reverse direction completely, such as when you are taking a picture of someone standing outside a famous monument, move in a circle around your subject until you find a happy compromise.

Some digital cameras automatically "handle" backlight, usually by turning on the flash. You can, too. Set your camera to use its flash and ignore the ambient lighting. The pictures on the next page show how the flash will compensate for backlighting. However, even though using the flash will fill in your subject, this method does not produce particularly wonderful pictures. Your subject's features will appear "flatter" than in natural light. Instead, try to avoid backlit conditions completely whenever possible.

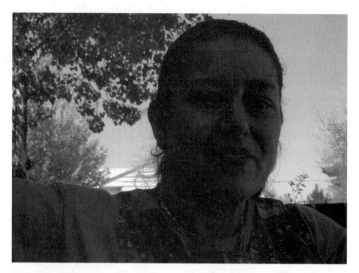

With the sun behind her, the subject's face is dark.

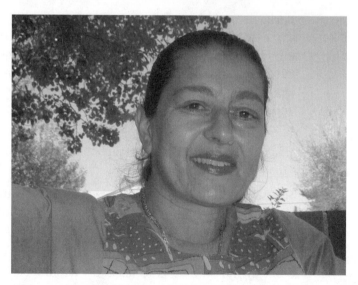

When you cannot avoid backlighting, use the flash to fill in your subject's features.

Use Indirect Light

A face full of sunshine is about as flattering as mud. Sunshine fills a face with harsh, unpleasant shadows. People look haggard, tired, and old. Every wrinkle is brought into full prominence. Shadows on the neck add an extra chin or two. Add squinting eyes into the mixture, and you have the lighting environment from hell.

Fortunately, there's a quick fix: Move your subject into the shade. Look for a tree, an overhang, or a trellis. Wait for a cloud to cover the sun, or shoot your pictures on a hazy or overcast day. Although most people think they need to take pictures in the brightest sunlight possible, you can snap excellent photos under covered patios or shadowed overhangs, as shown below.

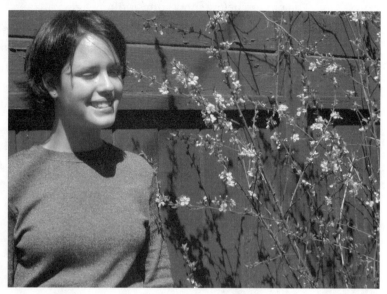

Squinting in the direct sunshine

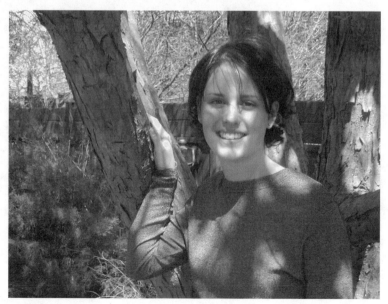

Cooler in the shade

Unlike direct sunshine, indirect light creates soft and beautiful pictures. It flatters your subjects rather than batters them. Indirect light means exactly that. Instead of light streaming directly from the sun onto your subject, it bounces off the walls, the ground, and the scenery around you. You still get plenty of light, but it's a different, more playful, and far more flattering light. The picture below shows how indirect light can create a great portrait.

When you cannot avoid full sunlight, use your flash to fill in some of the harsher shadows. Set your digital camera's flash to its always-on setting and take your pictures. Although indirect lighting produces better pictures, your flash will counteract some of the worst shadows. On the other hand, when you have good indirect light available to you, turn that flash off!

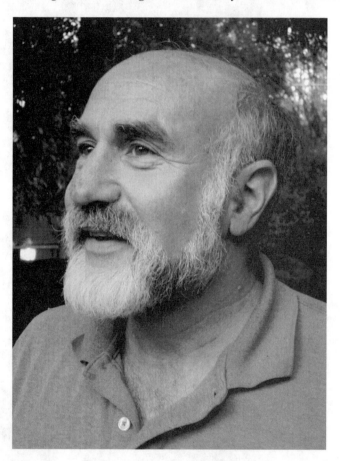

Pick a Good Time of Day

Contrast the warm, soft colors of sunrise and sunset with the harsh noon-day sun. When you take out your camera, consider how the time of day will affect the light. Choose a time that matches the mood you need. At mid-day, sunlight is strongest and most direct. Light appears to be at its whitest, colors at their most true and vivid. At sunrise and sunset, the color of light deepens and changes—often minute to minute. Colors are redder, kinder, and more dream-like.

Use these changes in light to your best advantage. If you plan your photo shoots in advance, consider how the time of day will affect your images. Do you want to create a romantic portrait? Perhaps you should wait until late afternoon or early evening. Are you seeking a dramatic landscape showing a lot of detail? Midday should work better. And don't forget those great sunset shots. When the last rays burn over the horizon, turning the clouds to fire, don't miss having your digital camera in hand and ready to shoot.

Step to a Window

Sunlight streaming through a window creates the most dramatic light of all. As it gently caresses your subject's face, get ready to snap terrific por-traits. Nothing comes close to the beauty of the classic "sitting by the win-dow" shot. The picture on the next page shows an example of this type of photo.

Use all sorts of windows. Consider photographing a child playing by a slid-ing glass door. Take a picture of another passenger while inside your car. Go to public galleries such as museums or libraries where windowed light is plentiful. Place your subject next to the stained glass in a chapel. Be cre-ative. Use a window with sheer curtains blowing in the wind. Examine the light streaming through Venetian blinds in bars of brightness and darkness. Have your subject look outside through the window or just sit, lost in con-templation. The possibilities are endless. Wherever you find a well-lit win-dow, you can create beautiful and exciting pictures.

WARNING When shooting your camera directly towards a window, don't forget to turn off the flash!

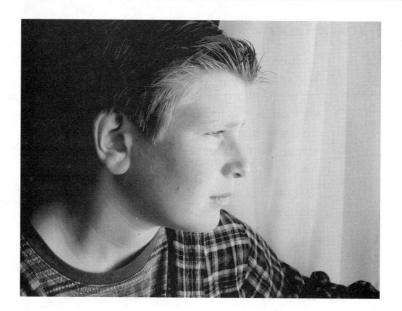

Create Unnatural Light

Did you know that you can create your own portrait studio for under $20? You just need a few simple things. Most of them are probably lying around your house. The rest you can easily pick up at a local camera or hardware store. Don't let a small budget keep you from taking terrific pictures.

The Right Equipment

Here's a list of the basic equipment you need to put together your home studio:

A sheet   Any sheet will do, although flat works better than fitted. You will use this sheet to create a uniform backdrop. In general, the more neutral the pattern, the better. The focus should remain on your subjects rather than the cute linen dinosaurs behind them.

Duct tape   Duct tape is the home handyman's best friend. Let it become your friend, too.

Photographic-quality floodlight bulbs   You'll need one or two floodlight bulbs. I use General Electric's PhotoFlood bulbs. They cost about

$4 each at my local camera shop. I prefer to use the ones with blue coating, as the plain ones create light with a distinct yellowish cast. The blue bulbs avoid this problem, albeit with some loss of luminescence.

Aluminum clamp work lights   You'll need one or two lights for your bulbs. You can pick these up at your local hardware store for under $5. Make sure to choose work lights that can handle the heat from your floodlight bulbs.

Various props   Props make a more interesting portrait. You can use chairs, stools, hats, fake flowers, stuffed animals, and so forth.

Your Setup

Once you've done your shopping, follow these steps to get your studio up and running:

1. Pick a quiet part of the house. Try to find a room that doesn't get much traffic.

2. Duct tape your sheet to the wall. (You may want to check with your spouse or parent before you do this.) Avoid damaging your walls where possible.

3. Screw your floodlight bulb into the work light and clamp it near an outlet. (If you can't get close to an outlet, use an extension cord.) These lights get very, very hot. Keep them away from children and any flammable objects!

4. Bounce your light off a wall or ceiling. This creates a softer and more indirect light.

5. Pose your subjects with your various props.

6. Get set, aim, and shoot!

WARNING   Photographic floodlights get very hot. Use extreme caution when placing them to avoid fire hazard. These lights can burn fingers. Keep children away from your studio when the lights are on and until they have cooled off and been put away properly! Never leave these lights on and unattended.

The picture below shows an example of a home studio setup.

Backdrop held up by duct tape, under $5

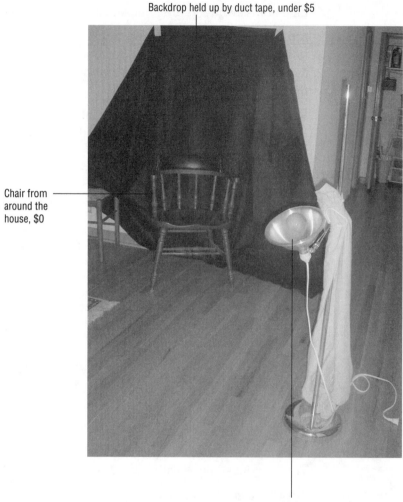

Chair from
around the
house, $0

Lighting, under $10

Tips for the Home Studio

When you're ready to start taking pictures in your new "studio," keep these tips in mind:

◆ Turn off your flash. Flash photography in these conditions can flatten the faces of your subjects, removing features. Instead, set your digital camera to suppress the flash and let the indirect light from the flood-lights create more "natural" lighting. If you can't figure out how to turn off your flash, tape a small piece of tissue over it. This will soften the flash instead.

◆ Move away from the wall. Sit your subjects at least a foot or two away from your backdrop. This softens shadows and de-emphasizes the backdrop.

◆ Turn off fluorescent lights. If fluorescent bulbs normally light your home studio, turn them off. These lights can create weird, greenish overtones in people's faces.

◆ Use extra sheets. If your studio's walls are dark, duct-tape a light-colored sheet to a nearby wall. Bounce your floodlight off the sheet rather than off the dark wall. That way, more light will travel to your subject.

Shooting in Low (or No!) Light

You can take surprisingly good digital photos in low-light conditions. Of course, your most important tool for working in the dark is your camera's built-in flash. Your flash will trigger when light conditions drop below a certain threshold. Also, some cameras allow you to take long exposures, so you can take pictures in near darkness. Keep in mind how to combat the constant enemy of flash photography—the dreaded red-eye effect—and you will be ready to start snapping your shots in the shadows.

Come to the Dark

Why not take a picture in complete darkness? I recently attended a party high up in the Colorado mountains, far from any city lights. Our host walked us back to the car, using a flashlight to guide our steps. Just as we reached the car, I decided to test my camera's flash. I had our host turn off his lantern, and I took a picture of him in the complete darkness. With only a flash to light up my shot, I was able to snap the fairly nice portrait shown on the next page.

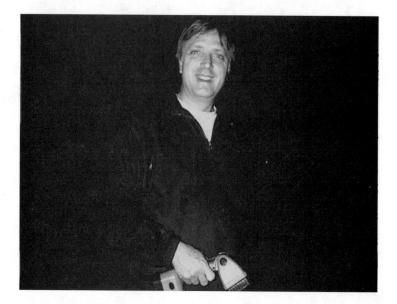

Of course, most photo opportunities don't take place in total darkness. You may take a picture indoors during a party. You may be sitting outside during twilight. If, for whatever reasons, the ambient light is too low, use your camera's flash to help you capture the moment. Your pictures may not turn out as artistic or beautiful as those shots for which you've planned dramatic lighting, but you will not have missed the chance to capture images of a special event or person.

To use your flash, keep your camera set to automatic mode. This mode allows your camera to determine when and if a flash will be needed. Because most of us want to take pictures on the spur of the moment, it's best to leave your camera in automatic mode most of the time. When you're ready to work with lights and poses, that's the time to turn off the auto-flash feature. Until then, leave it on. You never know when a special moment will come by.

Most digital camera flashbulbs have a limited range of effect. Often, this runs to about 10 feet. As you move farther away from your subject, the light from the flash will fall off dramatically. Keep this in mind when you attempt to take shots of large objects or groups of people. However, if you get too close to your subject with a flash, your camera may overexpose, washing out fine details. Instead, if your camera supports zoom, step back a bit and use your camera's optical zoom feature to get closer.

Another feature of digital flash photography is that it does not usually brighten the whole scene uniformly. Some parts of your picture may appear darker than other parts. Typically, the center is lit more directly than objects on the periphery of the scene. If I were to let my physicist husband explain why, he would probably go on a bit about inverse-squares, sines of the angle, and other rules of physics. But all you really need to know is that your flash and your camera's sensors do not always produce uniform lighting in your images. The pictures below show the difference a little distance can make in a flash photo.

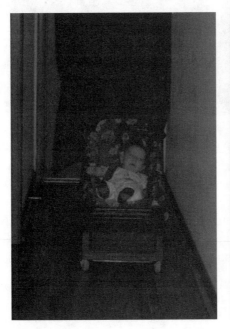

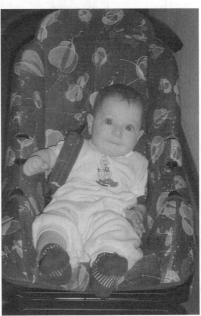

With a flash, the center is brighter, and the rest of the scene is in shadows.

Moving closer lights up the subject.

Combat Red Eye

Often, flash photography causes that eerie effect known as *red-eye*. Not to be confused with conjunctivitis (or pink-eye), red-eye occurs when the light from the flash bounces off your subject's retina, as shown on the next page. This causes the pupil to appear red rather than black. Let me suggest four ways to deal with this problem.

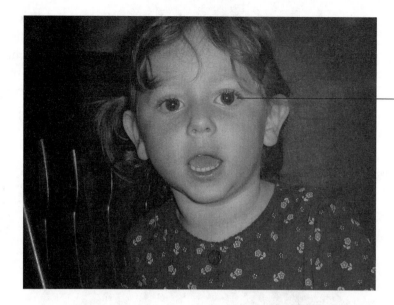

It may not be apparent in this black-and-white print, but these eyes are glowing red.

First, most digital camera manufacturers now ship their products with a built-in solution called *red-eye reduction mode*. In this mode, the camera actually flashes twice. The first flash causes people's pupils to quickly contract. This allows less light into the eye, and thus produces less reflection when the light flashes a second time to actually take the picture. Check the instructions that came with your camera to see if it supports red-eye reduction mode and, if so, how to activate it.

Be aware, however, that red-eye reduction mode puts a higher drain on your batteries (due to the double flash), and it causes a slight delay in taking the picture, usually one or two seconds. When you're trying to take action photos, you may want to turn off this feature. It can be hard to capture the moment when time passes between when you press the shutter release and when the camera actually takes the picture.

Also, red-eye reduction mode sometimes causes people to blink. After the first flash, some people will close their eyes, so that the second flash, which accompanies the picture, creates a lovely image of your subjects with their eyes shut. (Of course, if their eyes are shut, you don't need to worry about red-eye.)

A second solution is to move the flash away from the camera. This creates a wider angle between the light, your subject, and the camera. This wider angle means that the light bouncing off someone's retinas ends up somewhere on the other side of the room and not in your camera. In just one step, you've gotten rid of red-eye. Unfortunately, few digital cameras support external flash systems, and those that do aren't the type you can slip into your pocket. The gain you make in reducing red-eye is offset by the inconvenience of carrying around an external flash system.

The third solution—and, incidentally, my favorite—is to simply take more than one picture. People's irises are not so flexible that they bounce back immediately from a flashed picture. The second and subsequent pictures will capture your subjects with more constricted pupils and less red-eye. This may not eliminate red-eye completely, as will widening the angle between the camera and the flash, but it should reduce it enough to create better pictures.

The fourth, and most obvious, solution is to bring more light into the scene. Turn on some lights or move to a brighter room. The more light, the less pupils dilate. Unfortunately, this solution is not always the most convenient one.

N O T E   Did you forget about red-eye when taking your pictures? To a certain extent, you can fix these pictures later in your photo-editing program. This is discussed in number 31, "Repair Red-Eye."

Long Exposures

I love those long-exposure photos, where the headlights and taillights of cars form streaks of light along a cityscape. Many new digital cameras support special slow-exposure modes that allow you to create this effect in your own pictures.

You will need a tripod (or some reasonable equivalent) to take this sort of picture. Consider the images shown on the next page. In one shot, I tried to snap an image relying only on the steadiness of my hand. For the other shot, I used a tripod. Clearly, the longer the exposure, the more crucial it becomes to steady your camera.

Make sure to take your picture on a street with some regular traffic. Waiting for a car to come by can be excruciatingly boring, and you might miss the one car that finally appears. Always start the exposure before the car comes into view. This permits you to obtain long, colorful streaks. Also, I prefer to snap slow pictures on streets without (or with few) pedestrians. This way, I can focus the scene on the beams of light rather than any passerby. Keep in mind that composition is just as important in long-exposure shots as in short-exposure ones.

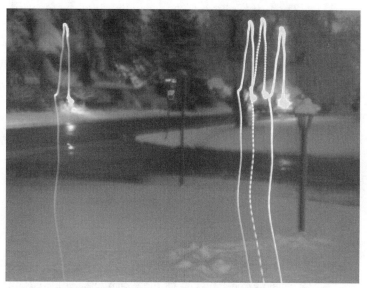

An unsteady hand ruins a long-exposure shot.

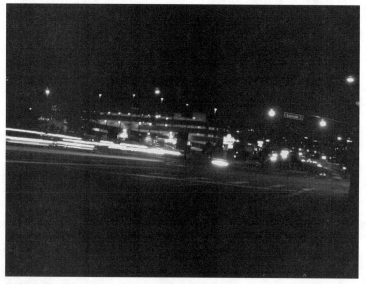

Using a tripod creates a better long-exposure picture.

Exposure Compensation Tips

Have you ever wondered what that little button on your camera labeled +/– does? This button provides you with something called *exposure compensation.*

Your digital camera takes an average of the light of your scene before snapping a picture. This helps it figure out how to set the exposure. When your camera detects high levels of light, it reacts in one of two ways: It either takes a quicker exposure or uses a smaller lens opening, both of which let less light enter your camera. When your camera detects a low light level, it either takes a slower exposure or steps up the lens opening to allow more light in.

Digital cameras use two techniques to determine how to set exposure levels. The first, called *segment metering*, divides the image into a number of segments. The camera's light meter evaluates each segment and determines how to set the exposure for a given scene. This technique is only now coming into widespread use. The second, more popular system is *center-weighted exposure*, which places a greater emphasis on the light values measured at the center of the image. This assumes that the object you wish to photograph lies at the center of the scene. Pointing your camera at a dark object might cause the rest of the scene to overexpose and bleach out.

No matter how your camera sets exposure levels, keep one thing in mind: Picture data in overexposed images cannot be recovered. No photo-editing program will be able to undo the damage that overexposure causes. By using your exposure-compensation button with care, you can prevent losing your precious photos to overexposure.

For example, the exposure-compensation button can help compensate for a backlit situation. This may wash out the background, but it allows your camera to receive the proper amount of light from your subject. Similarly, if you're shooting a picture of a bright object in a dark background, you might want to reduce the exposure compensation. This can bring out the details of a pretty pair of candles on a dimly lit table.

N O T E   Techniques for operating exposure-compensation buttons vary by manufacturer. Consult your manual to see how this button works on your particular camera.

When you're unsure exactly which exposure-compensation settings to use, try taking a lot of pictures with a variety of settings. You can always free the memory used by any bad pictures. If your camera has an LCD screen, it may be able to show you how successful your exposure compensations have been. Just to be sure, it's best to play with various settings, increase the number of pictures, and hope that you have taken one or two good ones.

3 Understand Depth of Field

To better understand focus, you need to learn about depth of field. *Depth of field* refers to the zone in which all elements appear in focus. Any objects in this range look sharp and clear in your photo. Objects outside this range appear fuzzy and out of focus. An example is shown below. Notice how the first flower, falling within the proper range, remains in focus, while the second flower looks blurry.

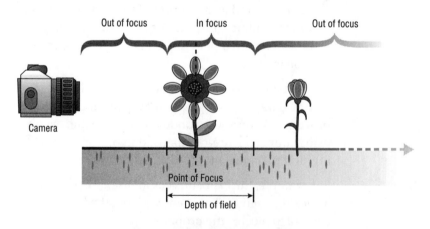

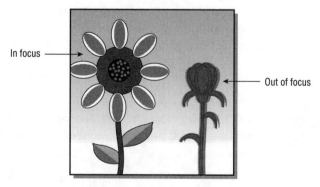

Using zoom or wide-angle settings can affect your depth of field. With zoom, maintaining correct focus becomes more exacting. When you move the camera, even a little, your subject may appear out of focus because of the limited depth of field. In contrast, wide-angle settings offer a much larger in-focus range. This makes your camera much more tolerant of small camera movements and shakes. Also, your subjects can move in a larger range closer to or away from the camera before the camera must refocus.

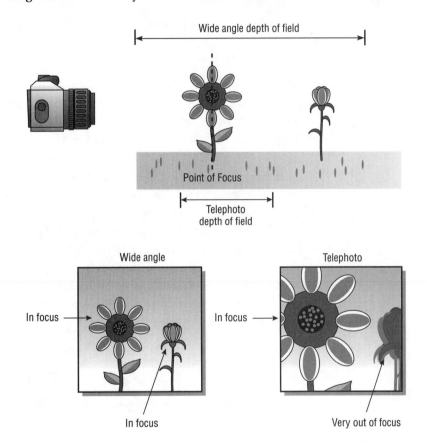

The distance that your focal point is located from the camera can also affect the depth of field. The nearer the focal point, the smaller the depth of field. More distant focal points offer larger ranges in which objects remain in focus. You obtain the greatest depth of field by focusing on objects in the far distance, such as clouds or mountains.

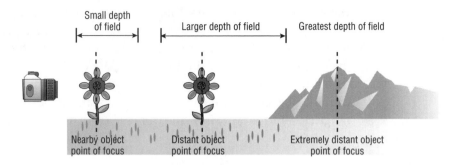

Small depth of field | Larger depth of field | Greatest depth of field

Nearby object point of focus | Distant object point of focus | Extremely distant object point of focus

N O T E   While a distant focal point offers a very large depth of field, nearby subjects will still appear out of focus. Don't assume that the "greatest depth of field" means that all distances fall within your field of focus.

The aperture levels on your camera also affect the depth of field. The iris on your camera opens and closes to let in various amounts of light. This works just like the iris in your eye, dilating to adjust for light levels. The wider the opening, called the *aperture*, the more light flows through to your camera's detectors. Smaller apertures let in less light. Even inexpensive cameras, like my old analog video camera and my new JVC-505 digital camera, may allow you to set these aperture levels manually. The smaller the aperture, the larger the depth of field, and vice versa. Closing down the aperture works much like squinting your eyes.

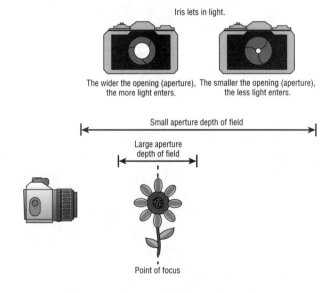

Iris lets in light.

The wider the opening (aperture), the more light enters. | The smaller the opening (aperture), the less light enters.

Small aperture depth of field

Large aperture depth of field

Point of focus

The range of the depth of field in front of and behind the focal point is not equal. The range of focus behind your focal point is always larger than the range in front of it. Keep this fact in mind whenever you set your focus and arrange your subjects. As a rule of thumb, about two-thirds of your field of focus lies behind and about one-third in front. When in doubt, always focus a little closer than farther away.

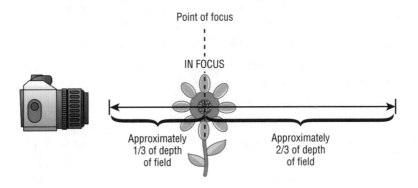

4 Achieving Natural Poses

Have you ever noticed how stiff and uncomfortable some people look in photos—those fake smiles and awkward postures? One of the most important techniques a photographer can develop is putting people at ease. A relaxed subject helps make a portrait more flattering and memorable. Create a relaxed atmosphere when taking your pictures. Not only will your pictures improve, but your subjects will come back again for more!

Lighten the Atmosphere

These techniques may help lighten the atmosphere and relax your subject:

◆ Talk to your subject. As you get ready to take your pictures, start a conversation. Talking helps many people forget about posing and produces better and more natural facial expressions.

◆ Make 'em laugh. Tell some jokes or silly stories. Laughter shakes people right out of their stiffness and into photographically pleasing facial expressions.

◆ Give 'em something to do. Props are great photographic tools. When people are busy doing something—anything—they tend to focus on the task and stop thinking about their facial expression. Children may enjoy playing with a toy. Adults will tend to focus on a task and forget about the camera. Show someone working on a hobby, doing a household chore, or otherwise occupied.

◆ Take *a lot* of pictures. People can keep that silly, stiff smile on their face for only so long. The more pictures you take, the more those muscles will tire. Prepare to throw out a lot of early shots. Eventually, the awkwardness will disappear.

◆ Move 'em around. Why not go to another room? You can go inside if you're outside or outside if you're inside. Each time you change locations, you get a fresh start and new facial expressions to work with.

◆ Catch them at an off moment. This can be tricky, but it's frequently worth the trouble. Some of your best pictures will be those that were shot when the subjects didn't know that you were taking their picture. The more memory you use in your camera, the more likely you'll be able to snap an extra picture when no one expects it. Use the biggest memory cards you can afford. Sometimes these shots turn out badly, but sometimes they produce treasures.

NOTE   You can learn more about memory cards for your camera in number 10, "Your Camera's Memory."

Remember that the best images aren't always the ones that show smiles plastered on faces. In portraits, you may want to see the truest person looking out.

Take Flattering Photos

The simple truth is that some people photograph better than others do. Some are natural models; others aren't. Whether you're dealing with a double chin or a prominent nose, you can help your subjects look their best by keeping a few tips in mind. Here are some common problems and some suggestions for minimizing them:

Double chins   You can minimize the prominence of double chins in your photos in two ways. First, ask your subjects to hold their chin up slightly. Second, shoot from a bit above the subject. Raise your tripod and shoot slightly down to de-emphasize the neck. The pictures below show the contrast between a flattering and unflattering shot.

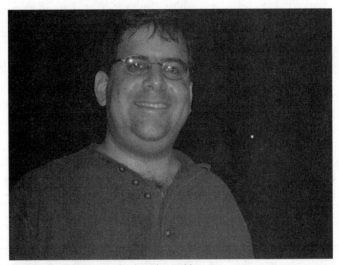

Shooting from below emphasizes those chins.

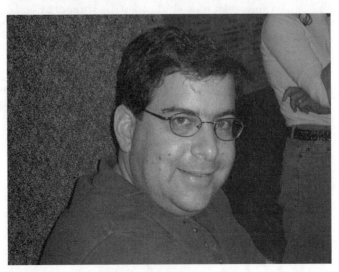

Shooting from above proves more flattering.

Weak chins   In the case of a weak chin, you want to lower your tripod to slightly below your subject's face and shoot up. This changes the emphasis toward the top of the face and away from the bottom.

Wrinkles   Wrinkles show their worst in bright light. Keep your lighting as diffuse as possible. This minimizes the shadows between wrinkles and flatters the subject.

Prominent noses   If a nose presents a problem, avoid profile shots. To de-emphasize a nose, have your subject face the camera directly. Keep the camera level with the face and avoid shooting up or down.

Unflattering eyeglasses   In the case of thick eyeglasses or unflattering eyeglass frames, consider using the glasses as a prop. For what I call the "professor shot," have your subject hold the glasses and gesture with them. This shows more of the face and avoids distortions around the eyes from both the lenses and the shadows created by the frames. This may not work for subjects with very poor vision or those who wear their glasses constantly. The former may look "dopey" during the shoot because they cannot see. The latter will seem unfamiliar to friends and family because the glasses are such an intrinsic part of the person. In these cases, consider the next suggestion instead.

Reflections from eyeglass lenses   You can fix this problem in a number of ways. First, you can add a polarized filter to your camera to minimize reflection from the lenses. Second, you can slide the glasses up or down the subject's nose to produce less reflection. Third, you can keep the glasses in place but move the subject's head slightly to minimize the reflection. If you still cannot find a flattering shot, consider using the glasses as a prop, as described in the previous suggestion.

Blemishes   When you're dealing with facial blemishes, use diffuse lighting. Also, consider touching up the photos after the shoot in an image-processing program. An airbrush will blend away most obvious facial blemishes.

N O T E   You can reduce the impact of some unflattering features, such as blemishes, with photo-editing programs. See number 34, "Fix Facial Blemishes" for details.

Ready! Set! Pose!

It helps to have a few standard poses up your sleeve. These poses can help get the ball rolling and sometimes produce the best pictures on the whole digital "roll." When you're not sure how to start, pick one of the poses suggested here.

The Angled Pose

For this first pose, you'll need a chair. Angle the chair about 20 degrees away from the camera. Sit your subject—Lela, in this example—in the chair, completely facing the way that the chair faces. Lela's legs, arms, and head should face slightly away from you. You may cross Lela's hands in her lap or place them on her hips. Next, have Lela turn her head, but only her head, toward the camera. The rest of her body—shoulders, back, feet, and so forth—remain aligned with the chair, as shown below. Tell Lela to take a few deep breaths and smile. Start shooting.

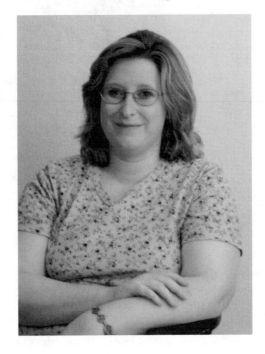

The Classic Portrait Pose

For this second pose, find a table. Place it in front of your subject (Lela again) and otherwise set up the portrait as described for the first pose, with a small angle between her body position and the camera. This time, however, when turning Lela's head, place one of her elbows on the table and support her chin with her hand. Raise your tripod and aim down toward Lela. Ask her to look up toward the camera, as shown below, and then shoot the picture.

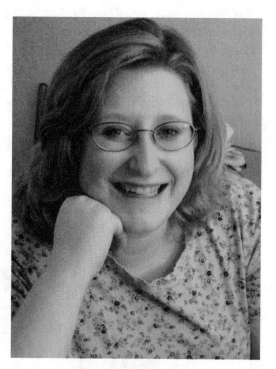

The Window Pose

For this third pose, you'll need some window-cleaner. Okay, you won't need it right away, but you'll need it after the shoot to wipe off the window. Here's how it works: Have your subject (we're still posing Lela) look out of a window on a sunny day. Place one or both of her hands on the window and have her keep her eyes focused on the outside. A good way to do this is to ask Lela to talk about what she sees. This forces her to keep her attention outside and allows you to shoot your pictures from the side, as shown next.

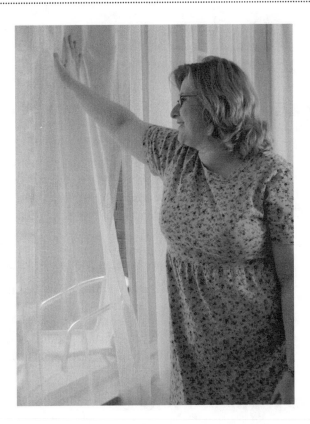

5   Tips of the Trade

Good composition, lighting, and poses will help you to produce better pictures, but there are some other things that you can do to make sure you get the best shot at the best time. Here is an assortment of tips for the digital photographer.

Take Your Camera Along—Everywhere

No matter how well you compose, light, or pose your subjects, it won't matter if your camera is not *right there with you* when the moment strikes. As long as your camera is at hand, you can capture that moment. No camera, no moment—it's as simple as that.

Take your camera with you wherever you go. Stick it in a glove compartment, a briefcase, or a diaper bag. With your camera nearby, you'll be ready to seize the moment when the right opportunity strikes.

Steady Now

The culprit for many bad pictures is unsteady hands. You can prevent the wiggles, jiggles, and bouncies that ruin pictures. All you need to do is steady your camera. Sure, you can use a tripod. Tripods are great. They provide dependable support. But if you don't have a tripod at hand, you can still steady your camera. Try one of these helpers:

◆ Rest your camera on a fence or a low wall.

◆ Steady your camera on a friend's shoulder.

◆ Use the top of a public mailbox as a camera rest.

◆ Pile up a stack of books and use them to hold your camera.

The possibilities are endless. Just remember the importance of keeping your camera still. Don't ruin a shot because your hand was too unsteady.

Take a Lot of Pictures

The more pictures you take, the more likely you will end up with a good one in the bunch. Load up your camera with as much memory as it can hold and keep an extra disk or memory card on hand to swap as needed.

Taking a bunch of pictures means you don't need to bet on any single picture coming out perfect. The worst that will happen is you get a few good shots among many bad ones. The best result will be that you get to choose from many, many wonderful pictures.

Remember to keep shooting. Take pictures from different angles and distances. Don't just seize the moment, keep seizing it. Take a lot of pictures!

N O T E   You can read more about memory cards in number 10, "Your Camera's Memory."

Don't Be Shy

Shy photographers rarely shoot great pictures. One secret to great photography is to boldly take pictures under all sorts of circumstances.

Unless you've got the camera out and you're taking pictures, you cannot catch that perfect moment. You'll miss that kiss, that laugh, that smile, that tear, and so forth, unless you're willing to jump in and photograph it. Don't be timid. Learn to let your camera out and into the best times in life. You'll be glad you did.

Watch Your Thumb

Don't put your fingers in front of the lens. No, I mean it. It sounds silly and obvious, but you would be surprised how easily you can ruin a shot by sticking your thumb where it shouldn't be. And dangling bits aren't limited to your digits. Keep that lens cap, that wrist strap, that handbag, and that power cord out of the way, too. Sometimes, we are so intent on other matters that we forget the simplest things. Watch your thumb…

…I mean it!

Manage Your Digital Camera

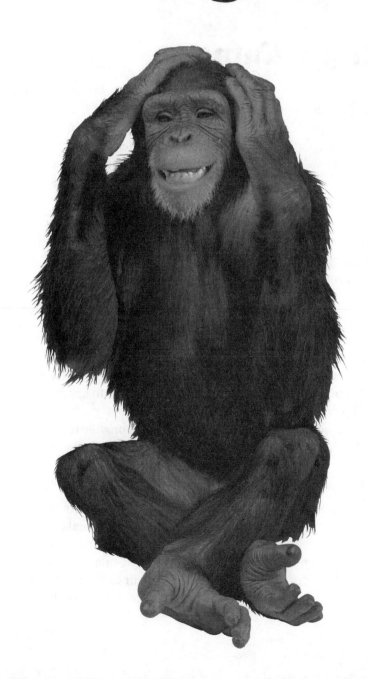

Know your digital camera, and it will serve you well. Today's digital cameras offer so many power, memory, and lens solutions that you can easily become overwhelmed. Here, you will learn the ins and outs of choosing and managing your digital camera.

6 Choosing a Camera

The question I'm asked the most is, "Which camera should I buy?" There are so many excellent digital cameras on the market today that I find this question hard to answer, particularly with any single model, let alone a manufacturer. Instead, I recommend that people evaluate their needs and budget and choose a camera after thinking through a number of points.

For instance, how you will use a camera directly influences the camera type you should buy. Will you use it primarily outdoors or in a studio setting? For family shots or for business? Consider how rugged you need your camera to be. Is waterproofing important? The answers to each of these questions will affect your choice.

Pixel Resolution

When you shop for a camera, you'll find the phrase "Megapixel" bandied about. This refers to how many image elements your camera can produce in a single picture. A one-megapixel camera creates images with approximately one million pixels. This offers basic-quality consumer-grade pictures, and should cost below $300. Middle-grade cameras provide two and three million pixels. These cameras cost between $300 and $1000. As of today, better quality cameras offer four-megapixel resolution, typically running over $1000.

Pixel count greatly influences image print quality. As a rule of thumb, you can always make big pictures smaller but you cannot effectively make small pictures bigger. The more pixels you print per inch, the better any image will look. 300 pixels per inch (ppi) produces the best-quality images. For a 4×6 picture, that comes to 1200×1800 pixels. If your camera does not support that resolution, don't despair. Even 100 or 150 ppi images look pretty good when printed to commercial grade silver-halide paper by a photofinisher. That comes out to 400×600 or 600×900 pixels—less than even one megapixel. More pixels just give you more flexibility and quality.

If you're aiming to put pictures on the Web, you can think even smaller. Web resolution typically ranges between 60–80 ppi, with 72 ppi as the most common resolution. Even an inexpensive (below $100) camera provides sufficient image resolution for Web-based imaging.

Portability

Many people consider portability to be a prime element of camera selection. Small is good. People like to stuff a camera into their pocket or handbag, pulling it out to capture that special shot. Many manufacturers now cater to this, producing cameras that are ever smaller and more powerful.

Ruggedness is another aspect of portability. Water resistance, and even waterproofness, allows you to take your camera into less civilized terrains. If camping, hiking, and snorkeling are up you alley, look for a camera that can take the punishment you're bound to inflict on it.

A last element of portability concerns battery life. Many cameras balance weight and price with battery duration. When you take your digital camera out to the hillside or on vacation, make sure that it can support long-life batteries.

Optics and Adaptability

Optics are a key element to think about, whether you're buying a digital or a traditional camera. The better the optics, the better your pictures will turn out. Look for high-quality lenses and hardware on your unit. In general, you will pay more for higher-quality components. In the long run, you'll be happy you did. These pay back for themselves in terms of peace of mind, general satisfaction, and excellent pictures.

I'm obsessed with built-in zoom. Zoom is probably the single feature that people most use on their cameras. The better the zoom, the more flexibility you'll have while taking pictures, both in terms of composition and depth of field. A good high-powered zoom can really sell a camera and I suggest you look for a digital unit that provides a wide range of zoom settings.

I will never buy a camera that does not provide an onboard LCD and flash. I recommend the same to you. As with zoom, these two features are invaluable. Other features I look for include a video-out port and an A/C adaptor port, so I can plug in my camera and save batteries. I like Compact Flash image storage, although I've known people who've been happy with both Smart Media and Memory Stick.

Better cameras offer lens threads to add-on filters and other components. When choosing a camera, look at the range of accessories offered. Many digital camera manufacturers choose odd-sized thread sizes (such as 14-mm for my Nikon Coolpix). When I buy standard filters, I use a step-down adapter so that the components will fit onto my camera. Although the Nikon-brand filters fit perfectly, they are quite expensive and don't offer the wide variety of the more standard sizes.

Cost and Reviews

After sorting through camera types and determining your needs, you'll typically be left with a few models to choose from. At this point, you'll want to start a full investigation. Get on the Internet and search for those model numbers. You'll find endless sites with a variety of user tests and feedback. This knowledge can prove invaluable in making your decision. I particularly like the reviews at the Digital Camera resource site (`www.dcresource.com`).

After settling on a model, take time to search around the Internet and find a good price. Some retailers, such as Sears, will price match online sites. If you're willing to take the risk, and order online, pick a dealer with a good reputation, such as B&H Photo (`www.bhphotovideo.com`) and make sure to pay with a credit card, to maximize consumer protections. If you're a bargain hunter, stop by the Anandtech forums (`http://forums.anandtech.com/categories.cfm?catid=40`) to search for a hot deal on your digital camera.

7 Batteries and Power Cells

Don't forget to feed your digital camera. It needs good, reliable power. You should be familiar with the various types of batteries and power cells that can help your camera function at peak levels, as well as how to tend and care for your batteries. Treat your batteries right, and your camera will thank you. Remember that digital cameras are power-hungry. Feed them the finest "juice" you can.

A Power-Source Bestiary

You can power your digital camera in many ways. Over the past few years, new battery types have entered the marketplace. These batteries offer alternatives and features far beyond old-fashioned AA batteries. Most digital cameras accept a wide variety of battery types. This creates a broad spectrum of, ahem, "power tools" to choose from.

N O T E   With the exception of generic batteries, most manufacturers' warranties require you to use designated proprietary power sources. Doing otherwise may void your warranty and cause problems down the road. Check that your camera's voltage and amperage requirements match your power source before you plug in and power up.

Alkaline Batteries

Alkaline batteries are a type of non-rechargeable power cell. They are the most commonly available batteries. Unfortunately, alkalines drain very quickly under the demands of most digital cameras.

You can pick up a set of alkaline batteries at nearly every Mom-and-Pop store in the country. They are freely available at drugstores, groceries, and so forth, at very reasonable prices. You can expect their shelf life to run for about five years, making for excellent backup power. Consider keeping a set on hand for emergencies.

The bad news is that alkaline batteries do not perform well in most digital cameras. They drain rapidly, and you can't recharge them. Using your camera's LCD screen means an almost-certain quick death for your alkaline cells. Alkalines are not recyclable and must be disposed of with care.

N O T E   When your alkaline batteries seem to run out of juice, you can usually squeeze out an extra shot or two. Just turn off your camera and let the batteries cool down for five or ten minutes. Turn the camera back on, and you can often take one or two more photographs before the batteries truly die.

Lithium Batteries

Lithiums are a type of non-rechargeable power cell. They provide greater power and endurance than alkalines but at a greater cost.

More and more stores have started to carry long-life lithium cells. Although they're not cheap, lithium battery prices are dropping. You can probably pick up a set at a Radio Shack near you.

Lithiums provide excellent performance in digital cameras and will not drain quickly, as alkalines do. They have an astonishing ten-year shelf life, which means that they make a superb backup power source. They give steady and dependable power output throughout the life of the battery.

Among all of the battery types, lithiums perform the best in cold-weather conditions. Other batteries fail at near-zero conditions; lithiums provide dependable power in subzero temperatures as low as –40 F. Environmentally, lithium batteries produce fewer hazards than alkalines do. They also weigh in at the lightest weight of all of the battery types.

Unfortunately, lithiums are still about five to ten times as expensive as alkalines. Also, like alkalines, they cannot be recharged.

Nickle-Metal-Hydride (NiMH) Batteries

Looking for the digital camera power source of choice? You'll find it in NiMH batteries. NiMHs (pronounced "nimms") are a type of rechargeable cell. NiMH batteries offer the best renewable power source available today.

NiMH batteries provide environmentally friendly, reliable power for your digital camera. You can charge cells up to a thousand times, furnishing years of use. You can also recharge them after a partial drain without creating a charge-level "memory," which might otherwise limit their power capacity.

However, NiMH batteries do have a few disadvantages. They may cost slightly more than the other types of power cells. Their shelf life is limited to a few weeks, usually less than a month. Also, NiMHs can be damaged by overcharging and overdischarging. Make sure to juice up your batteries on a regular basis, following the manufacturer's instructions for maximum charge time.

N O T E NiMH battery packs are a good alternative to individual cells and provide hours of continuous camera use. Some people do not like the "tethered" feel of using battery packs, while others swear by them. Packs have two big advantages. First, you can use them in concert with on-board batteries in your camera. The batteries only kick in when the power pack runs down. Second, you can leave your battery pack in your pocket, keeping it warm in cold weather. This allows you to keep taking pictures when normal batteries might tank.

Nickle-Cadmium (NiCd) Batteries

NiCds (pronounced "nigh-cads") are a type of rechargeable cell. NiMH batteries have all but replaced NiCds because of worries about heavy-metal toxicity. I do not recommend that you purchase NiCd batteries now that NiMHs are freely available (even though they have better shelf life and a greater number of recharging cycles). NiCds contain the heavy metal called cadmium, so you must take special care when disposing of them. NiCds also have "memory": if you charge NiCds before you fully empty the battery, you can limit their power capacity.

A/C Adapters

A/C adapters allow you to plug your camera into a wall outlet. Your camera's manufacturer usually provides these adapters at an additional cost (usually a large additional cost). A/C adapters work best for studio shots and when you're sitting at your computer.

An adapter provides unlimited power. It never runs out of energy unless you forget to pay your electric bill. A/C adapters help you conserve batteries and allow you to leave your camera powered on and unattended during image transfers.

The problem with A/C adapters is that without an electrical outlet nearby, you're out of luck. You may need to use an extension cord to reach the nearest outlet, or you may find yourself entirely too far away from an outlet to use an adapter at all. Many people do not like being tethered to a wall socket during photo shoots. Cords tangle and create tripping hazards. Sometimes the cords dangle in front of the lens and interfere with taking pictures.

Solar Power Packs

Solar power packs provide environmentally kind, "green" power for your digital camera. They allow you to take advantage of the ultimate renewable energy source—the sun. Okay, so "ultimate renewable" may not be scientifically accurate. Physicists, like my husband, will tell you in excruciating detail exactly when the sun will run out of energy and the universe will expand to ultimate entropy. Needless to say, this will not affect the average life of a digital camera.

Use your solar power pack for tripod shots and when wandering through the wilderness away from traditional power sources. If you plan on staying away from civilization for an extended period, solar power packs provide endless energy at a low weight. Some solar power packs will also charge your NiMH cells. You can pick up a solar NiMH charger for under $20 or a solar power pack that also charges NiMH cells for about $50. Solar power packs typically produce six-volt output, about the same as four AA batteries.

The main disadvantage of solar power packs is their bulk. Solar power packs are awkward to use. Additionally, these packs have an untested operational life and do not work indoors, at night, or on overcast days.

N O T E   Some camera manufacturers, notably Agfa and Kodak, now provide solar panels on some models of their cameras. These panels co-power the LCD screen and help save battery life.

8 Care for Your NiMHs

NiMHs are the best overall choice for your digital camera, and if you treat your NiMHs well, they'll provide years of dependable power. The following tips will help you make your batteries last.

Condition Your New Batteries

Run your new batteries through at least two, and preferably three to five, conditioning cycles. Start by treating your cells to a full charge as recommended by the manufacturer. Use the cells until you've reasonably discharged them, and then fully charge them again.

The battery manufacturers I spoke to suggested placing the batteries in your camera and taking pictures for an hour or two to produce a good discharge. You can also condition your batteries in any battery-operated device, such as a Walkman or radio.

Some battery purists recommend using special dischargers to increase the discharge and enhance conditioning. The manufacturers I spoke to said this wasn't necessary. In any case, after you pass your batteries through a few cycles of use and recharging, they will be ready for regular use. You can then recharge them after even the shallowest of discharges.

Charge and Recharge, but Don't Overcharge

Charge your NiMHs on a regular basis. It's better to charge more often rather than wait for the cells to run down—this helps your batteries last for years. Unlike NiCd batteries, NiMHs do not have "memory." Recharging after a shallow discharge does not limit the battery's ability to hold a charge. Unfortunately, when you overdischarge your batteries by running them down too much, you might reduce their ability to maintain a charge.

More worrisome than overdischarging is overcharging. When you overcharge your batteries by leaving them in the charger too long, you can destroy them entirely. Not only that, you might create a safety hazard. Some battery manufacturers now include fuses in NiMH battery packs. This allows the packs to self-destruct before they injure a passerby.

Always use and charge your NiMH batteries as a set. If you own multiple NiMH sets, do not mix and match batteries between sets. When you charge batteries at different states of discharge, you can actually damage them. Use a permanent marker to identify which battery belongs to which set.

9 Power Source Tips

No matter which battery type you use, you can extend the working life of the batteries by following a few simple rules:

- ◆ Turn off the LCD. Your LCD eats batteries. It consumes huge amounts of power when turned on. When you don't need to use it, turn it off and keep it off.

◆ Stop the zoom. When cameras turn on, many of them automatically extend the zoom lens. Leaving your camera on, but in "sleep" mode, may override this behavior and help save power.

◆ Turn off the flash. Flash photography drains your batteries. When you turn off the flash, you conserve power.

◆ Plug in! When at home, especially when transferring pictures to a computer, plug your camera in and avoid using the batteries.

N O T E   Your camera's energy-conservation mode can be your friend or your foe. While it works to save energy and preserve your batteries, it might make you miss an important shot. Often, you must wait for the camera to turn back on after conservation mode kicks in. When you're in the middle of an intense photo shoot, consider turning off energy-conservation mode.

10 Your Camera's Memory

What film is to traditional cameras, memory is to digital cameras. Without memory, you can't capture and reproduce images. Digital "film" allows your camera to store pictures.

Manufacturers offer a wide variety of memory solutions for their various camera models. Whether you already own a camera or are considering buying one, knowing about the diverse ways that cameras store pictures may prove valuable. Today's cameras support two types of removable onboard media: memory cards and disks.

Internal Memory

Many cameras provide internal picture memory built directly into the camera. Internal memory extends the camera's capability, adding capacity for "emergency pictures" when you run out of space on your memory cards.

Internal memory is common on older digital camera models, since they do not support memory cards or any of the other media now available. You'll find internal memory on newer models, too, notably the Ricoh line.

Cameras lacking memory cards rely on cables. These cables allow you to move pictures to your computer, but cable transfer is very slow.

Cameras that support memory cards usually allow you to copy internal memory directly to an onboard card. This bypasses the cable solution and speeds up transfers by many orders of magnitude.

N O T E   Some newer digital cameras now have firmware memory (or CMOS).

Flash Memory Cards

Flash memory cards, such as compact flash, smart media, and stick memory, use solid-state memory chips to store your pictures. These chips, like elephants, do not forget. They store your pictures indefinitely and without power.

You won't find a battery onboard a flash memory card. Their ATA (Advanced Technology Attachment) architecture—the same architecture used by your PC's IDE (Integrated Drive Electronics) and EIDE (Enhanced IDE) drives—allows cards to pretend to be traditional hard disk drives, complete with files and directories. Place your card into an ATA adapter, and it works with your computer's PCMCIA (Personal Computer Memory Card International Association) port. You can then read and write from your card as if it were simply another hard drive.

Compact Flash

Compact flash (*CF*) *cards* are built from banks of flash memory and a controller embedded in thin plastic, as in the graphic shown next. At the time I am writing this book, compact flash cards lead all of the other media in supplying digital camera memory. They are small and rugged, and they contain a lot of memory. Flash memory combines high read and write speeds with low power consumption. Compact flash cards also have a high tolerance for shock and vibration.

Compact flash cards are smart, too. Controllers are built right into compact flash cards. This allows a compact flash card to tell its host—whether a camera, computer, or any other consumer device—how it operates and how to access its data. Stick a compact flash card into a computer (using an inexpensive adapter), and it looks and acts just like a hard drive. Stick a compact flash card into your camera or MP3 player, and it's ready to store images or music.

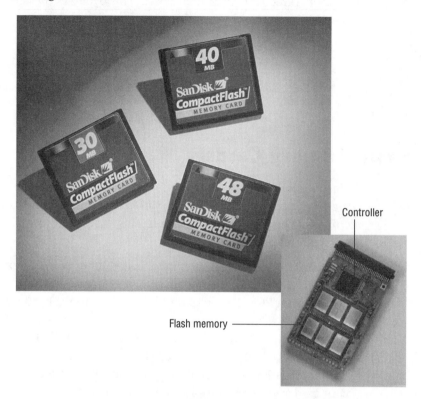

Controller

Flash memory

Compact flash cards are built in many shapes and sizes, although most digital cameras use those about 1-inch square and a quarter-inch thick. In this tiny space, they provide incredibly large memory resources.

Today, you can buy a 64-megabyte (MB) compact flash card for about a $100. Prices for these cards are going down, while their memory size is increasing.

Smart Media

Many cameras makers, most notably Olympus, support a type of electronic memory called *smart media*. The actual name for this type of memory is (get this) Solid-State Floppy Disk Cards, or SSFDC. These cards consist of a flash memory chip embedded in thin plastic, as shown next. Smart media cards are small, usually about one-third the size of a credit card.

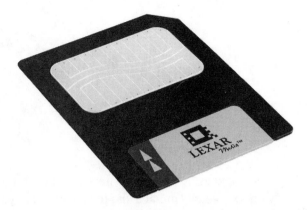

Unlike compact flash cards, smart media do not contain onboard controller chips; they have only storage chips. That means the smartest part of the compact flash cards doesn't appear on smart media cards. Now, if the "smarts" don't actually occur on "smart media," why is "smart media" smart? The world may never know.

Actually, the lack of controller chips is why smart media may be on its way out in the digital camera community. Since cameras that use smart media must provide their own controllers, newer and bigger cards eventually become incompatible with older cameras. In contrast, compact flash and stick memory (discussed next) keep their brains onboard. New cards can always tell older cameras how they work. Recently, Olympus began to ship cameras containing both smart media and compact flash slots.

N O T E You can find smart media support on many cameras. Manufacturers who provide smart media support on their products include Agfa, Ansco, Epson, Fuji, Minolta, Olympus, Phillips, Ricoh, Sanyo, Sega, Toshiba, and Trinus.

Stick Memory

In recent years, Sony developed its own form of flash memory called *stick memory*. You've probably seen this memory in new products. This product shares many of the same features of compact flash cards in a slightly different body shape. Stick memory resembles a half-stick of Wrigley's gum, as shown on the next page.

Stick memory is fast. It can transfer 64MB of information in less than ten seconds and provides a "read-only" toggle to protect data.

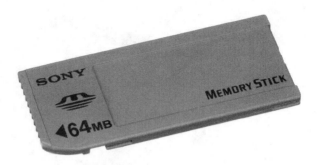

One might ask, "Why do we need another standard when compact flash works so well?" I am at a loss to explain this. Leaving that aside, Sony does have grand plans for stick memory. The manufacturer intends to use stick memory in everything from public information kiosks to music systems in automobiles. Digital cameras provide only one market for this new product.

PC Cards

The term *PC card* refers to any media you can stick in a PCMCIA slot in your computer. PC cards come in four types, designated type I through type IV. Although every PC card shares identical dimensions in width and length (for the curious, those dimensions are just over 3 inches by 2 inches), they vary in thickness (from about one-eighth inch to one-half inch), depending on what sort of memory has been tucked within them. The picture below shows an example of a PC card.

Only type I and type II PC cards use solid-state flash memory. A few digital cameras, including some Ricohs, use PC cards to store photos.

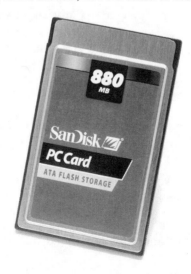

Other Memory Cards

Various other memory cards linger in the digital camera world. These mostly include extinct (or almost-extinct) dinosaurs and yet-to-be-introduced wares.

A good example of a dinosaur is the Intel Miniature Card. Announced in 1996, this card became an also-ran by 1998.

Recently introduced was the SanDisk/Siemens AG offering, shown below. This MultiMedia Card, or MMC, measures about the size of a thick postage stamp and delivers capacities ranging up to 64MB (and soon, up to 128MB). It's still too soon to say how well this card is doing in the ever-more competitive memory card market.

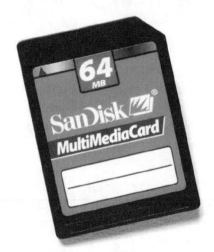

Storing Images on Disks

Some digital cameras also support a variety of conventional disks. The Sony Mavica line used a traditional 3.5-inch floppy disk to store your pictures and newer models actually write to a CD. Iomega and IBM offer miniature hard-disk solutions. Unfortunately, some disks do not provide the stability and trustworthiness you find in flash memory card solutions, leaving them less suited for digital cameras. However, IBM's offerings are quite rugged and provide outstanding storage capabilities.

Clik! Disks

A true disk, the Iomega Clik! (with that irritating exclamation point, which I will now drop) offers 40MB of storage in a small package. The idea works like this: When your compact flash card grows full, you slip it into the compact Clik drive and transfer the data to a Clik disk. Clik disks cost much less than additional compact flash cards, so you don't need to buy extra cards. While they're a nice idea, Clik drives fail in the following ways:

◆ Many compact flash cards now exceed the storage available on Clik disks.

◆ Compact flash card prices are dropping rapidly. With the money you would invest in a Clik drive and Clik disks, you can buy a handful of extra compact flash cards instead.

◆ Clik disks and drives are bulky to carry around, whereas extra compact flash cards fit nicely in your shirt pocket.

◆ Clik disks are vulnerable to thumps and bumps. Compact flash cards are sturdy and less likely to lose data.

Microdrives

IBM's high-capacity, miniature hard drives come packaged in a convenient compact flash type-II shell. These microdrives offer capacities as high as 300MB or more. Microdrives have entered the consumer market and prices continue to drop.

Microdrives have proven surprisingly invulnerable to shocks. They're quite robust. And, because they work in type II slots, they provide easy interchange with traditional compact flash cards.

Floppy Disks and CDs

Some of the most popular cameras on the market, Sony Mavicas, use floppy disks and recordable CDs to store images. You just insert a 3.5-inch floppy or blank CDR into your camera, take your pictures, pop it out, and stick it into your computer.

11 Memory Card Care

Love your memory card and treat it with care. In return, your memory card will reward you with years of faithful and dependable service. Treat your card badly, and you may lose pictures, usually at the worst possible time. It takes so little to keep your digital memories happy. Why not go the extra distance and pamper your cards? They'll appreciate it and, over time, so will you.

Here are some tips for taking care of your memory cards:

Don't launder your memory.   Avoid brain washing. Keep your memory cards dry. Don't put them in the soak cycle. As with any electronics, water can (and usually will) damage memory cards. Their small size makes them a particular laundry hazard—it's easy to put them into a shirt pocket and forget them. Keep them dry and store them away from moisture.

Don't melt or freeze your memory.   Memory cards are sensitive to extremes of temperature. Unlike traditional film, your memory cards will not thrive in your refrigerator or freezer. Instead, keep them at room temperature. Avoid storing your memory in cars that may become over-heated or extremely cold.

Don't fiddle with your memory.   Some memory cards, especially smart media, flex naturally. Take pity on these poor cards. Do not bend or tweak them. Your cards were not designed to function as guitar picks, no matter how perfect the size and feel. And for heaven's sake, don't chew or nibble on them!

Don't scratch the contacts.   You can easily ruin a smart media card by scratching the exposed gold contacts. Hold your card by the other end and avoid handling this area. If needed, gently rub off fingerprints from the contacts with a soft cloth.

Don't drop your memory.   Some memory cards respond badly to rough treatment. Avoid dropping your cards, especially on hard surfaces.

Don't shock your memory.   Do you work in a dry or carpeted area? Discharge any static electricity before handling your memory cards. Touch grounded metal before you touch your cards.

Format your card.   Most digital memory cards work just like hard drives. Occasionally, they need preventative maintenance. Every now and then, say a few times a year, your card needs defragmenting. A fast and easy way to do this is to simply reformat your card. (Make sure you've safely removed any pictures you want to keep from them first.) You can also use a disk-scan/defragmentation utility, but it's much easier just to treat it to a fresh format.

12   Photo-Transfer Hardware

No matter which memory technology your camera employs, eventually you need to transfer your pictures to a computer or another processing device. This section describes the most popular photo-transfer methods.

Cables

These days, almost every camera arrives packaged with one or more cables, either USB or serial. Using the software packaged with the camera, you transfer your images through the cable to your computer. Simply plug one end of the cable into your computer's port and plug the other end into your digital camera. Start the upload process on your computer and wait for the pictures to transfer. If you're using a serial connection, you'll probably wait and wait and wait. Most people find serial transfer unbearably slow (and they're right).

There's only one reason, in my opinion, to use a serial cable to transfer your images: Your camera does not support USB or removable media. Only a few cameras these days truly require you to transfer by serial cable. These include older camera models and what I call "kid-grade" cameras, such as the NickClik and Barbie cameras. With these cameras, you can't access your pictures without a cable. Fortunately, these older or kid-oriented cameras take smaller pictures, which transfer somewhat faster than those from other types of cameras. It may not seem faster while you're sitting and waiting, but small images make it feasible (if not pleasant) to use cable transfer.

USB (Universal Serial Bus) connections have become the new standard. USB, particularly the new USB-2 standard, provides quick and efficient data transfer. Most newer computers provide USB ports, making them an attractive target of opportunity. Most new cameras support USB transfer in place of, or in addition to, the more traditional serial transfers.

Firewire connections, just now arriving, promise even faster connections than USB ones. They provide a huge digital "pipeline" for moving data back and forth between devices. Unfortunately, they still aren't quite ready for the consumer market. Currently, only professionals and "prosumers" are consistently willing to pay for the premium service that Firewire provides.

ATA Adapters

ATA adapters, shown below, allow you to read data using your computer's PCMCIA ports. If you don't have a PCMCIA port, you can probably purchase a SCSI- or USB-compatible PCMCIA drive for under $50.

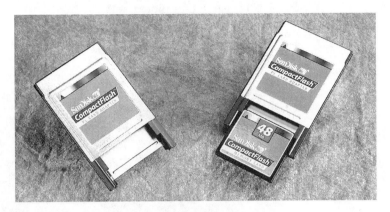

Stick your memory card into the ATA adapter and place the adapter into your port. It appears on your computer just like any other hard drive, ready to be read and provide rapid data transfer. That's all you need to do. How convenient!

JumpShot

Lexar Media offers a compact flash card with USB smarts, which is shown next. This card knows how to talk with the USB port and bypasses the need for an ATA adapter and PCMCIA port.

Just slide your card into the JumpShot adapter (provided free with the USB-enabled memory card) and plug it into your USB port. It appears automatically as an extra drive, ready to use.

The first time you use your JumpShot cable, Windows will ask you to provide a driver. Simply load the CD that comes with the card into your CD-ROM drive and follow the Add New Hardware Wizard instructions:

1. When the Add New Hardware Wizard appears, telling you about the need to find a new device driver, click Next.

2. Choose the Search for the Best Driver for Your Device option and click Next.

3. Tell Windows to search for the driver on your CD-ROM drive and click Next.

4. Windows will find the Lexar Media JumpShot driver. Click Next to install the driver.

5. Click Finish to complete the Wizard.

Now you're ready to go. Use your cable to transfer pictures from your camera to your PC.

N O T E   You only need to install the hardware driver once. After you finish the Add New Hardware Wizard, store your Lexar Media CD in a safe place.

Other Compact Flash Readers

Are you looking for another compact flash reader solution? Consider the following:

◆ Many computers have built-in PCMCIA ports. If yours does, you can purchase an inexpensive ATA adapter. Just slide the compact flash card into the adapter and insert it in your PCMCIA port.

◆ If you don't have an internal PCMCIA port, you can purchase an external PCMCIA reader. These external solutions support a variety of connections, including SCSI, parallel, and serial. As with internal slots, you will need an ATA adapter to read your compact flash card.

◆ Some manufacturers are now shipping dedicated, inexpensive compact flash readers that do not require ATA adapters. These new readers generally work with USB ports.

WARNING Windows NT and Linux do not actively support USB. Users of these systems may need to look for alternative serial, parallel, and SCSI compact flash solutions. Windows 2000 users should carefully examine current technology and proceed with caution. While Windows 2000 provides USB support, many people report spotty performance, particularly with device drivers.

FlashPath

If you're a smart media user, there's an alternative to the slow cable transfer of your smart media pictures to your computer. A FlashPath adapter looks like a 3.5-inch floppy disk and comes with a slot in its side, as shown below. Just insert the smart media and read it from a floppy disk drive. FlashPath systems transfer data from two to fifteen times faster than serial connections.

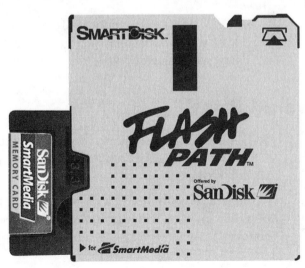

FlashPath adapters work on both Windows and Macintosh systems. A number of vendors, including Toshiba, Olympus, and FujiFilm, produce essentially identical FlashPath devices. Their prices range between $50 and $100. To use the adapter, just place your media into the slot provided on the "disk" and stick it into the floppy drive. You're ready to transfer data.

Here are some things to keep in mind when you're using a FlashPath adapter:

◆ The first time you use your FlashPath adapter, you must install the included batteries. Just open the battery compartment and place the batteries inside. The FlashPath adapter uses two standard CR2016 lithium batteries to provide power. You can pick up replacements at any Radio Shack and many drugstores.

◆ Battery life varies with the type of smart media being used. Some smart media use 3.3 volts; others use 5 volts. Additionally, you can prolong the batteries by removing the FlashPath adapter from the floppy disk drive when it isn't in use.

◆ Always insert the smart media with the electrical contacts down; that is, make sure that the contacts face the bottom of the "floppy." Then place your adapter into your floppy drive.

◆ You may need to download a driver from `www.smartdisk.com`. You can always pick up the latest driver versions at this site. Drivers include those for Windows 95/98/Me, Windows NT/2000, and Macintosh systems.

◆ FlashPath adapters support all smart media. However, they do not work with compact flash cards. Compact flash memory is too thick to fit onto a FlashPath disk.

Infrared Ports

Some cameras provide wireless data transfer through infrared beaming. Although neat, in a Star Trek sort of way, these ports are unlikely to overwhelm the market.

A problem with infrared transfer is that it may not work in warm conditions that interfere with the infrared beam. Also, it's too easy to disturb the connection. When you lose the line of sight, you lose the connection.

N O T E   You can expect your future cameras to support some type of wireless connection. Have you used 900MHz cordless phones? Digital cameras may eventually transfer their data using a similar technology.

13 Memory Management Tips

You can control your camera's memory or let the memory control you. Keeping on top of your memory can make the difference between getting that extra shot and searching for an extra memory card (which you may or may not have on you at the time). It's up to you to make sure that you have enough capacity to take all of the pictures you need to take.

Limit Memory

You can limit memory in three ways:

Take smaller pictures.   By lowering the resolution from 1600 × 1200, to say, 800 × 600, you can take four times as many pictures. Of course, smaller pictures have drawbacks. They may not print well, capture sufficient information, or satisfy your artistic needs.

Use a higher compression scheme.   Most cameras support a number of compression schemes. Usually the best-quality pictures are called Fine, the second best are Normal, and the worst are Compact. The terms vary by camera, but the idea is the same. Changing to more compact pictures means you lose picture quality, but it allows more pictures to fit on each card.

Weed your pictures on the fly.   When you take a bad picture, throw it out. This keeps your memory card full of lean and mean pictures—only your best.

Unfortunately, all three methods not only limit your memory usage, but they restrict your results as well. You should use high resolution and low compression to shoot your images using the best possible settings. This allows you to save and use smaller segments of your images. And you'll never say, "I wish I shot that using better settings."

The problem with using the third method—tossing photos immediately—is that some "bad" pictures may contain hidden gems. Don't throw away borderline images. Err on the side of keeping bad shots rather than weeding them out. You can never recover a shot already thrown away. Consider the picture below. It may not look like a keeper. The composition is poor. The subject's moving arm has blurred. A television set intrudes, making the scene too busy. Now examine the image within the black rectangle. From this poor image, we can extract a great one.

Obviously, if you follow this advice, you will fill your memory cards sooner and more often. In my opinion, rather than try to conserve memory on the fly, most people are better off purchasing more and larger memory cards. Think of the film photographer carrying a lot of extra film. The more memory you bring, the more good pictures you can take.

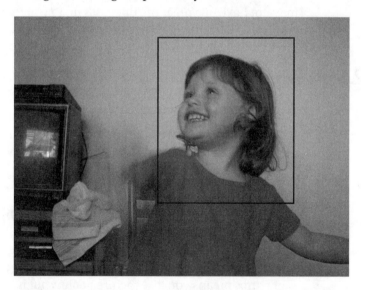

Pick Your Image Format

Your camera may store your images in any of a number of image formats. These formats range from small, compressed images to large, memory-intensive ones. How your camera stores your pictures will greatly affect how many pictures you can store at any time. The larger the images, the fewer that can be stored. The smaller the images, the more you can fit. Know which formats your particular camera supports and choose the format that best meets your needs.

JPEG (pronounced "jay-peg"), which stands for Joint Photographic Experts Group, is the most common image-capture format. It is supported almost universally. You can upload JPEG images to the World Wide Web, edit them in all major photo-editing programs, send them by e-mail, and so on. Storing photos using the JPEG standard means easy retrieval and image sharing. JPEG allows you to store your images with a wide range of compression values. This way, you can trade off size and quality.

Another common format is TIFF (Tagged Image File Format). The TIFF format ensures your pictures are stored at the highest possible resolution. This format produces some of the truest pictures, at the cost of image size. TIFF files are huge.

A couple of dozen manufacturers, including Nikon, Olympus, and Canon, support CIFF (Camera Image File Format) format. Kodak and Fuji use EXIF (Exchangeable Image File Format). Some photo-editing programs can read these formats and convert pictures to TIFF or JPEG.

Along with the more common image formats, you'll find proprietary formats that vary by manufacturer. Fortunately, you can easily find a program that converts these proprietary formats to more widely used and manageable types such as JPEG.

Save Your Negatives

The images you capture on your "digital film" really are your "negatives." Store them carefully and make archives of them. You'll be surprised how well you can retrieve images later when they are stored properly.

Storage Media and Format

If possible, you should store your images on CD-Rs (recordable CDs). These media are cheap. You can create multiple backups for only a few pennies more. CD-Rs are reliable, have a long shelf life, and are almost universally readable.

Store your "negatives" exactly as they come from the camera. Where possible, use the TIFF format setting, available on many camera models. TIFF compression is lossless. This means that when you decompress a TIFF picture, it will produce an image identical to the original. JPEG images, in contrast, are lossy. This means that they may lose information each time they are compressed or go through the open-and-save cycle. When you set your camera to save in TIFF, you'll retain the highest quality image.

Photo Folders

Organizing your images will save you loads of time when you need to retrieve them. Here's the system that works well for me:

◆ Create a directory for each "roll" of digital film. Label this directory with the date the pictures were taken and a description of the event. Use a *YYMMDD* dating scheme. This allows you to use Windows' Sort by Name function and keep the dates in chronological order. For example, pictures taken on July 4, 2001, might be labeled 010704 - Independence Day Party.

◆ In each directory, keep a log of the pictures. Make a list of the photos that you've stored there and a short description of each shot. This allows you to search for key phrases when you want to find a specific shot.

◆ Create four subdirectories for each "roll":

Negatives   Store your original images in the Negatives directory, just as they are, taken directly from your camera. These photos form your basic picture archive.

Low-rez   Create low-resolution, compressed versions of each picture and store them in a Low-rez directory. This allows you to pull up a version of each image that you can easily e-mail or place on the Web. Don't bother with the hassle of converting photos. You don't want to change high-resolution images to low-resolution ones each time you start searching through your archives. Convert them in advance. This way, you can pull up the low-resolution version directly from your CD-R archive.

Flubs   Place any flubbed pictures into the Flubs directory. You can always work on them later.

Processed   Store any enhanced images in the Processed directory. Don't confuse images you've fixed up in a photo-editing program with your negatives. Keep them separate so that you'll be able to easily find and use them later.

◆ Create a master log on the top level of your CD. Make a list of all the logs in each directory, sorted by date. This allows you to search your entire picture disk from a single file.

14 Use Memory Cards outside Your Camera

Memory cards aren't just camera workhorses. You can use them in some novel and interesting ways. Here are a couple of fun things you can do with your digital memory cards.

Stick Your Card into a Photo Printer

Many new photo printers, including the Kodak Personal Picture Maker, allow you to create prints directly from compact flash and smart media memory cards. This means that you don't need to load your pictures into a computer before printing them.

Insert a memory card into the printer itself, as shown below. The printer reads the card and creates an index print showing thumbnails of all the images on the card. You can print all or some of the images. Choose an image by selecting its number off the index print.

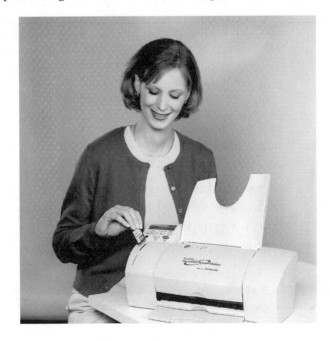

Stick Your Card into a Photo Frame

Sony offers a digital picture frame called the Cyber Frame. This device, which looks just like a normal picture frame, uses stick memory. (See number 10, "Your Camera's Memory" for a description of stick memory.)

Insert your memory into the frame, plug it in, and you're ready to view your images, as shown below. You can set the frame to flip through your pictures as quickly as one picture every 15 seconds or as slowly as one picture a day.

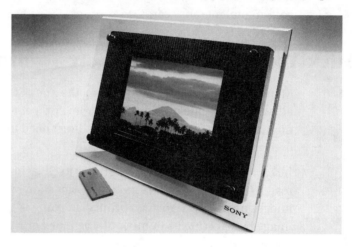

The Sony frame understands the difference between landscape and portrait images and will automatically adjust to display the proper orientation. You can display images as large as 1600 × 1200 on this frame. You can also add sound memos to your stick memory and play them back using the built-in volume-controlled speaker.

As if that were not enough, watch out Martha Stewart. You can accessorize your frame with different shells to coordinate with your decor. Current colors include terra cotta and earthy green.

At this time, you're going to pay through the nose for this toy. The retail price runs about $900. Expect a variety of offerings and competitors to lower prices over the next few years.

N O T E   You can find an alternative, lower-cost solution to the Sony frame in the versatile Ceiva. Read more about Ceiva in the "Share Your Pictures" part of this book.

15 Optimizing Your Camera's Optical Components

Take control of the way that your camera "sees" the world. When you focus, zoom, or filter light, you change the way your digital camera captures images. Digital cameras come with built-in optical components. In addition, you can accessorize your unit in a variety of ways. These features let you play with and direct the way that your camera takes photos.

How to Focus Sharply

The average modern digital camera ships with both manual and automatic focus options. Today's auto-focus systems provide terrific results for almost all your photo needs. They eliminate the need to manually adjust the focus for each picture and generally make life much easier. Auto-focus works by shooting out an infrared beam and measuring how long it takes to bounce back. This lets your camera know the distance to your subject and, therefore, how to set the lenses to create an in-focus photo.

Most digital cameras are built to take slightly wide-angle photos. These wide-angle settings produce larger depths of field. Depth of field can be important. As it increases, your camera can take in-focus pictures over a wider range of distance. In contrast, the more you use magnification—either with a zoom or telephoto lens—the smaller the depth of field, so exact focus becomes more critical.

Even with auto-focus enabled, sometimes you still take blurry photographs. Three culprits account for almost all out-of-focus pictures when using auto-focus: steadiness, low light, and incorrect targeting.

Use a Tripod

Your camera is vulnerable to shaking hands. No matter how superb the auto-focus system, unsteadiness will ruin your shot. This is where a tripod comes to the rescue. Keep your camera steady, and you may avoid inadvertently blurring your pictures.

Match Subject Movement to Light Levels

No matter how steady you keep your camera, a moving subject will blur. To capture a moving subject, you need a very short exposure time. Ambient light levels determine these exposure times. The lower the light, the longer the exposure. The longer the exposure, the more your subject may move and blur. To bypass this problem, avoid taking action shots in low-light conditions.

NOTE "Noise" presents another low-light problem for digital cameras. When you shoot pictures in dim lighting, you're far more likely to produce images with unintentional pixel variation. This noise, which fades to the background in well-illuminated shots, adds graininess to your low-light photos. You can reduce the noise to some degree using a photo-editing program. See number 18, "Basic Photo Fixes: The Get & Fix Photo Menu," for details.

Target Your Subject Correctly

Blurry pictures can also result from incorrect targeting. This focus problem occurs in two instances: off-center subjects and subjects positioned at different distances.

When you shoot pictures of an off-center subject, your camera may not focus correctly. The ultrasound beam bounces off whatever occupies the middle of the picture rather than your subject. Then it reports a meaningless value to the auto-focus mechanism. Fortunately, digital cameras support a quick fix for this problem:

1. Place your subject directly in the center of the frame.

2. Depress the shutter button halfway. The auto-focus system will set the focus correctly.

3. Keeping the shutter button halfway depressed, compose your shot.

4. With the shot composed, finish pressing the shutter button. Your digital camera will take the photo using the correct focus settings.

The problem of dealing with subjects at varying distances proves harder. Unless all of the subjects fall within your camera's depth of field, it's likely one or more of them will end up out of focus. You will not find an elegant solution for this problem. Instead, you must either move your subjects to more uniform distances or use a wider-angle lens with a more robust depth of field.

Optical Zoom Yes, Digital Zoom No

Everyone loves zoom. We like getting up close and personal. When we buy cameras, zoom capability often influences our purchasing decisions. As you probably know, zoom allows you to magnify parts of a scene and photograph it at a larger scale.

Digital cameras support two types of zoom: optical and digital. Let me tell you right off that digital zoom stinks. Digital zoom works in the following way: It takes a normal picture and then blows up a part of the image, just like you would in a photo-editing program. Then it throws away the rest of your image. You don't really get a larger, more-detailed picture; it just seems like a larger picture. Don't get suckered by digital zoom. Make sure your camera supports real zoom, which is optical zoom—the zoom created by lenses that really do create closer, larger, and more-detailed pictures.

That having been said, let's examine the different types of optical zoom you can find on digital cameras.

All optical zoom lenses work in the same way: They change your camera's focal length, magnifying the image passing through the lens to your camera's sensor. If the zoom is built into your camera, it is called a *zoom lens*. If you buy an optional attachment, it is called a *telephoto lens*. You will find two types of zoom lenses:

◆ A *fixed zoom* creates, unsurprisingly, a fixed magnification. Cameras with fixed zoom allow you to swap between normal mode and zoom mode by sliding the zoom lens into place. All telephoto lenses use a fixed zoom.

◆ An *adjustable zoom* allows you to select from a range of zoom values by adjusting the optics in stages. These zooms are motorized and can put an extra burden on your camera's batteries. However, they provide finer control over the zoom.

When you're using a zoom, keep in mind that it decreases your camera's depth of field. While your subject will appear in focus, objects in front of or behind your subject may be blurry. Also realize that using zoom magnifies small motions. You may need to use a tripod to steady your camera when using large zoom.

Customize Light with Filters

Optical filters allow you to customize the light entering your camera. You can accessorize your digital camera with optical filters to create a variety of special effects.

Ultraviolet (Skylight) Filters

Ultraviolet (UV) filters help cut through fog and create clearer pictures in misty conditions. Actually, the reason most people use UV filters on their cameras is to provide a surrogate lens cap. They install the filter and leave it on permanently. Most people figure they would rather damage a $10 UV filter than need to replace their digital camera.

UV filters are made from plain glass. They are easier to clean than your camera's lens, less likely to scratch, and more durable. And you never know when you might run across a misty day, right?

Polarizing Filters

You can use polarizing filters in a number of ways. These filters use circular polarization to allow or deny access to certain types of light. Here are some ways you can polarize:

◆ Use your polarizing filter to shoot dramatic sky scenes. These filters produce a greater contrast between the clouds and the sky.

◆ Polarizing filters help cut through glare and minimize reflection. When you're shooting pictures on a beach or at a museum, use your polarizing filter to reduce these artifacts.

◆ If you don't want to lay out the money for a polarizing filter, you can produce almost all of the same effects by using a pair of polarized sunglasses. Really! Just hold the glasses in front of your lens and rotate them to get the effect needed. I bet you didn't know you could do that!

To use your polarizing filter, point either thumb at the sun and extend your forefinger like a make-believe gun. Take note of the line made by your forefinger and extend it in your imagination in front and behind you. It's this line that you'll use to set up your picture. Maximum polarization occurs 90 degrees off from the direction of sunlight. Use this technique to create a 90-degree reference to set up your shot. Line up yourself, your camera, and your subject.

N O T E Your polarizer works best at midday with the sun directly overhead. As you point your thumb to the sun, you can rotate your finger in almost any direction. At sunset, you'll only be able to shoot along one line.

Next, aim your camera at your subject and manually rotate the polarizing filter. Keep going until you've achieved the maximum effect—you may have to adjust back and forth until you're satisfied with the result. In general, a quarter twist will move between the minimum and maximum effect. Remember that all surfaces, no matter how matte-textured, produce some polarized light through reflection. Position and use your polarizer effectively to reduce glare and add depth and richness to your colors.

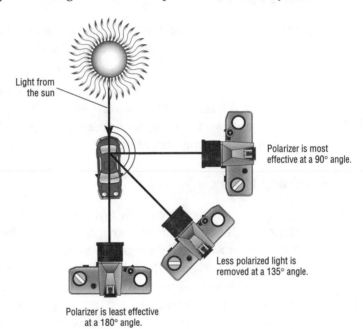

Light from the sun

Polarizer is most effective at a 90° angle.

Less polarized light is removed at a 135° angle.

Polarizer is least effective at a 180° angle.

Eliminating reflections may require a little extra work. When shooting to reduce reflections, position your camera along the 90-degree line, but then shoot your object at an angle of 30 to 45 degrees off that surface. This angle ensures maximum polarization—whether reducing reflections or not—and helps eliminate reflected light. Recall that all reflected light is naturally polarized. It's just the angle that you need to get right for this effect to work.

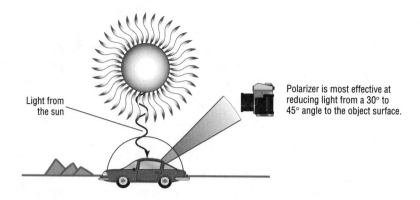

Light from the sun

Polarizer is most effective at reducing light from a 30° to 45° angle to the object surface.

Colored Filters

Did you know you could use your digital camera to take terrific black-and-white pictures? Many recent models support black-and-white photography.

When you're taking black-and-white pictures, you can use colored filters to change the color balance and increase contrast within your pictures. In general, red filters enhance blue objects and blue filters enhance red ones. For example, you can snap some really superb black-and-white pictures of red flowers by using a blue filter to create a dramatic contrast.

Specialty Filters

Specialty filters produce a wide array of effects. These range from star-shaped highlights to multiple images (produced by prism lenses). My advice as far as digital photography goes is to simply skip these filters. You can create these same effects in most photo-editing software with less work and for less money. And if you use photo-editing software, you can preserve better-quality images in their original format—an important consideration just in case you hate the way the special effects turn out.

Infrared (IR) Sensitivity Pros and Cons

Does your camera see into the infrared? Here's how you can find out. Take out your television remote control and push a button (such as the one to increase the volume). Take a picture of the remote control's LED (you can usually find it at the tip of your remote control). If your picture shows a bright, glowing light, your camera is sensitive to infrared (IR) light. This can be a good thing, and this can be a bad thing.

The biggest advantage of IR sensitivity is that your camera provides greater sensitivity in low-light conditions. This allows you to take pictures in a wider range of light conditions. There's another advantage, too: You can easily capture infrared-only images. Just purchase an inexpensive IR-pass filter and use it to shoot your pictures. This filter blocks out all light except the infrared and allows you to capture IR images without special film or processing. Digital photography has really opened up IR photography to the masses. For film cameras, shooting IR images is expensive and complicated.

The IR drawback involves capturing image details that your eye would not normally see. This can saturate your camera's sensors and degrade image quality. Many cameras now ship with internal IR-block filters that reduce some of the IR light entering your camera, while allowing regular visible light to pass through. You can also purchase these filters to use with your digital camera. Some photographers use supplemental IR-block filters to ensure truer color capture. On the other hand, most normal digital camera users completely and happily ignore the IR problem entirely.

Accessorize, Accessorize, Accessorize

As you've seen, you can accessorize your camera with a wide range of filters and lenses. In addition to the accessories described in the previous sections, you can purchase fish-eye lenses, neutral-density filters, and many more items for your camera.

Before you buy any accessories, make sure to determine the ring size for your camera and whether it accepts attachments. You may need to purchase a "step-up" ring to convert between your camera's ring size and that of the attachment. For example, if you own a Nikon 950, your 28mm threads will need a step-up ring to attach to, say, a 39mm telephoto lens. You can find these step-up rings at most camera hobby stores and Web sites.

If your camera does not accept attachments, you can always hold the filter up to your lens and shoot your picture that way. I've snapped photos with a wide variety of filters (although not lenses) and had no trouble. Just make sure to hold the filter tight to the lens and keep your fingers out of the picture.

16 Digicam Resources

Now that you know all about batteries, memory, and lenses, it is time to explore some more resources for making the most of your digital camera.

Print and Web Information

Do you find that good help is hard to find? Here's a solution. You can learn more about your camera with these resources.

Your Camera Manual

Read your manual. No matter how vague or poorly translated, it provides the single best resource for determining exactly how your particular camera operates. And, if your camera's manual fails to help, you can go buy a better one. Dennis Curtin of Short Courses (www.shortcourses.com) offers how-to manuals for a wide range of cameras. These excellent books run for about $20–$30, cover all the most recent camera models and can be purchased online. They're printed on sturdy stock in a handy spiral-bound format.

World Wide Web

Digital cameras seem to breed fan-specific sites. Hop onto your favorite search engine, such as Yahoo! or Infoseek, and hunt down sites that cover your camera model. You might find a few specks of wheat among the great chaff that is the Web.

In addition, you may want to stop by some of my favorite digital camera sites:

The Digital Camera Resource Page (www.dcresource.com) The best page for up-to-the-minute digital camera news and reviews.

Steve's Digicam Page (www.steves-digicams.com) A massive digital camera resource site with a wealth of information.

The Kodak Guide to Better Pictures (www.kodak.com/US/en/consumer/ pictureTaking/index.shtml) This is not really a digital camera page, but the picture-taking advice is so superb, it's worth a visit or two.

Digital Photography (For What It's Worth) (`www.cliffshade.com/dpfwiw`)
Another favorite site with tremendous information and tutorials for the digital camera user.

Usenet

Usenet consists of public forums that allow people to share interests and engage in lively discussions. Several Usenet groups are devoted to the topic of digital photography. If you have a question, or just want to stop by and see what people are talking about, these newsgroups may prove to be just the thing for you:

`Rec.photo.digital`   This newsgroup discusses purchasing and using digital cameras. This group always has a high volume of discussion and a lot of newsgroup traffic. A few highly skilled regulars haunt the premises offering assistance. However, new digital camera users account for most of the postings.

`Alt.comp.periphs.dcameras`   Another newsgroup devoted to digital cameras, with a more technical slant.

`Rec.photo.technique.art,Rec.photo.technique.misc,Rec.photo`
`.technique.nature,Rec.photo.technique.people`   These newsgroups focus on photographic technique and are open to both traditional and digital camera users.

Google Groups

Do you want to search through old Usenet discussions? Stop by `http://groups.google.com`. This easy-to-use search engine allows you to look for old discussions directly related to your camera's model.

A Photo Shoot Packing List

Going out on a photo shoot? Review the following packing list before you go:

◆ Bring a lot of batteries and/or a battery pack. Don't run out of power.

◆ Take along as much memory as you can afford. Don't miss a shot because you're low on digital film.

◆ Pack a tripod or monopod to steady your camera. Many outdoor sporting stores sell miniature tripods that travel well.

◆ Consider bringing a device, homemade or purchased, to shade your LCD from direct sunlight.

◆ Don't forget a lens cap or UV filter to protect your lens from damage.

◆ A soft lens cloth can keep your lens and LCD clean.

◆ Bring any filters that you like to use, such as a polarizing filter or neutral-density filter. Make sure to pack these carefully so they don't scratch.

◆ Gently pack up your extra lenses, such as telephoto and wide-angle attachments. Take good care of these expensive options.

◆ Don't forget your camera's operations manual. Most are sized to fit into a standard camera bag.

◆ And finally, consider investing in a large, padded bag to safely hold all of your equipment.

WARNING   Avoid extreme temperatures. Your digital camera is a sensitive beast. Avoid storing your camera and camera equipment in direct sunlight, hot areas of your car, or outside during cold snaps.

Enhancing Your Images with PhotoDeluxe

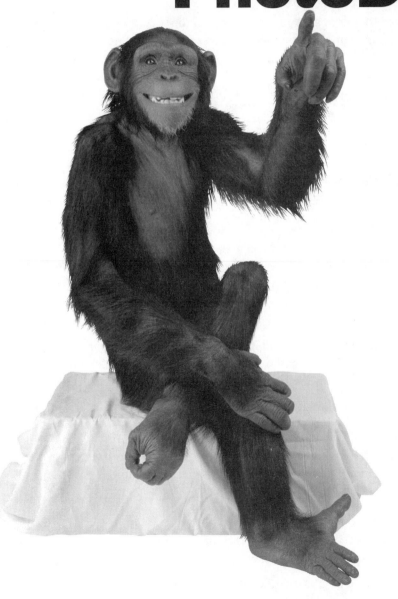

Lucky you! A free copy of Adobe PhotoDeluxe is included on the CD that accompanies this book. This software will help you manipulate, improve, and play with your digital pictures in many ways. Behind its meek and humble interface lies an image-processing tool of surprising power and flexibility. You can learn to unlock the potential that lurks in its shadows and lingers in its wings. With PhotoDeluxe, you can reproduce many of the same effects and techniques that you would expect to find in a full-fledged image-processing program.

But wait, that's not all. You, too, can learn the secrets of a PhotoDeluxe warrior. You can gain skills that let you slice, dice, and julienne-fry your digital images. And, if you read more now, you'll discover the ultra-secret image-processing recipes that grant you PhotoDeluxe superpowers! Just remember to use these powers for the forces of good.

17 PhotoDeluxe: A Quick Tour

Before you attempt to engage your power-mobile's turbo thrusters and rocket drive, make sure that you're comfortable behind the wheel of your friendly, automatic family car. Get acquainted with Adobe PhotoDeluxe's most basic mode. Take it for a spin around the block. Kick the tires and get to know your machine. There's plenty of time for supersonic flight after you've mastered the basics.

Start by tooling around the PhotoDeluxe screen. Locate the main features on your handy-dandy road map (see the following graphic). Look for these features:

- ◆ The activity bar guides you through image-processing activities.

- ◆ The photo window displays your current photo.

- ◆ The photo window toolbar buttons give you instant access to common image-manipulation tools, such as zoom and text tools.

- ◆ The Advanced Menus button opens up the secret world of Photo-Deluxe power.

- ◆ The Open Photos bin stores additional open photos while you work in the main photo window.

- ◆ The basic menus include File, Edit, and Help.

Basic menus (default)

The activity bar   Toolbar buttons associated with the photo window

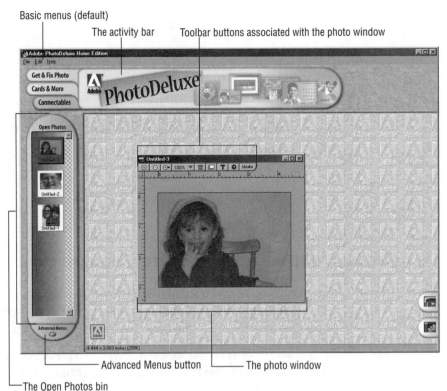

Advanced Menus button   └── The photo window

└── The Open Photos bin

Open Your Photo in PhotoDeluxe

Take the first step in image processing. Open your photo so you can work on it. These instructions guide you through the task:

1. Click the Get & Fix Photo tab of the activity bar at the top of your screen to access the PhotoDeluxe photo-preparation activities.

2. Click Get Photo and select Open File from the list of options presented to you. This tells PhotoDeluxe that you wish to open a file from disk.

3. Use the Windows file browser to select your photo. Then click Open to open the file in PhotoDeluxe.

You are now ready to work on your photo. Notice the toolbar buttons that appear just under the title bar in your photo window (labeled in the following graphic). These buttons offer a variety of image-control options, including zoom, text insertion, and the all-important undo feature.

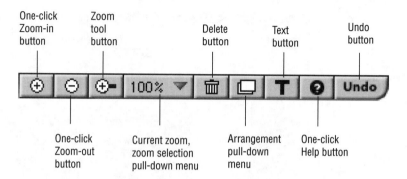

One-click Zoom-in button

Zoom tool button

Delete button

Text button

Undo button

One-click Zoom-out button

Current zoom, zoom selection pull-down menu

Arrangement pull-down menu

One-click Help button

Rotate, Move, and Resize Images

PhotoDeluxe provides a standard interface for rotating, moving, and resizing images. No matter what photo you load or activity you perform, you should know how to manipulate the dots and circles that surround a selection.

By default, when you click anywhere within a photo, you select the entire image (you'll learn about other selection techniques in number 20, "Editing Portions of an Image with Selections"). As you can see on the next page, eight dots line the edge of the image. These dots appear at every corner and in the middle of each side. In addition, a circle with a rounded arrow is next to each corner. These image-adjustment "handles" allow you to fine-tune your picture. Here are the techniques:

Resize Drag a corner handle to resize your selection. Just drag the handle away from the selection to enlarge the image, or drag the handle into the image to shrink it. The image will resize proportionately—if it starts out a square, it will end up as a square; if it starts out a rectangle, it will end up as a rectangle with similar proportions. You can also resize without preserving the proportions by holding down the Shift key while you drag the handle.

Shrink or stretch   The side handles allow you to shrink or stretch your image along one dimension. By dragging a side handle, you can squeeze the image together or stretch it out like Silly Putty. This operation always alters the image proportions.

Rotate   When you move your mouse to one of the rotation handles (the circles with rounded arrows), the cursor changes to a curved-line segment. When you see this change happen, you're ready to rotate. Just click and drag the mouse. A rotating outline will follow your mouse and preview your change. Release the mouse to perform the rotation and update the image.

Move   To move a selection to a new position, click your mouse within the image and drag it. The selection will move with your dragging motion. When you release the mouse, the image updates to reflect its new location.

Drag within the picture to move it to a new location.

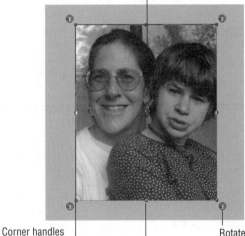

Corner handles resize proportionately.

Side handles shrink or stretch along one dimension.

Rotate handles turn the photo to a new orientation.

18 Basic Photo Fixes: The Get & Fix Photo Menu

You can noticeably improve your pictures just by using PhotoDeluxe's basic tools. You should always prepare your photos before you print or share them. Yes, you can use special printers, buy expensive inks and paper, or order high-end photo finishing. These enhance print quality, but they won't overcome poor contrast, poor lighting, or JPEG artifacts. On the other hand, PhotoDeluxe offers some features that can improve your pictures in a few simple steps.

The activity bar at the top of the PhotoDeluxe window has three tabs: Get & Fix Photo, Cards & More, and Connectables. To prepare your prints, click the Get & Fix Photo tab. A series of labeled icons replaces the PhotoDeluxe logo, as shown below. Each icon leads to a set of guided activities. These activities help you process and improve your pictures.

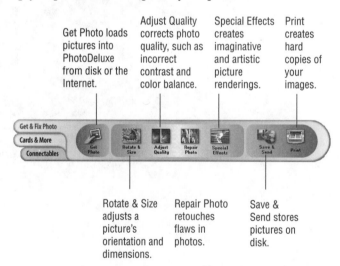

Get Photo loads pictures into PhotoDeluxe from disk or the Internet.

Adjust Quality corrects photo quality, such as incorrect contrast and color balance.

Special Effects creates imaginative and artistic picture renderings.

Print creates hard copies of your images.

Rotate & Size adjusts a picture's orientation and dimensions.

Repair Photo retouches flaws in photos.

Save & Send stores pictures on disk.

NOTE In the instructions for working in PhotoDeluxe, you'll see the ➢ symbol used to indicate chains of selections. For example, "click Get & Fix Photo ➢ Rotate & Size ➢ Rotate Left" means to click the Get & Fix Photo tab, then click the Rotate & Size icon, and then click the Rotate Left option in the menu of options.

Change Your Photo's Orientation

If you turned your camera to take a portrait picture, your picture will display "on its side" in PhotoDeluxe. You should rotate the portrait back to its correct bearings before you do any work on it, for two reasons. First, looking sideways can strain your neck. Second, our brains are wired to see details more effectively straight-on. When photos match our visual orientation, we make better judgment calls about quality.

If your picture is not oriented correctly after you open it in PhotoDeluxe (see number 17, "PhotoDeluxe: A Quick Tour"), use the image-rotation tool to turn it. Just click the Get & Fix Photo tab of the activity bar and select Rotate & Size. To rotate in a counter-clockwise direction, select Rotate Left. For clockwise rotation, select Rotate Right.

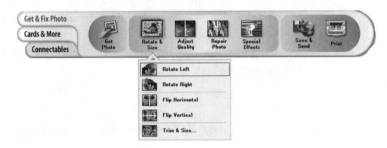

If you make a mistake and rotate in the wrong direction, fear not. Simply rotate a few more times until the picture appears in the proper orientation.

Fast Photo Fixes with Instant Fix Tools

PhotoDeluxe delivers a power-punch with a series of Instant Fix tools provided by Extensis. These tools simplify image enhancement by automating most of the correction tasks for you. With just a few clicks, you can fix your pictures instantly.

Click Get & Fix Photo ➢ Adjust Quality ➢ Extensis Instant Fix Tools. Take a second or two to note the variety of instant tools you can use to improve your picture.

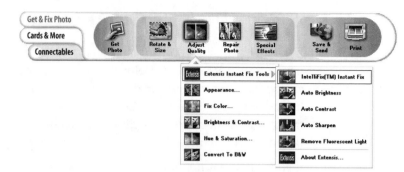

For instant improvement, select IntelliFix Instant Fix from the menu of tools. This option automatically corrects most image flaws for you.

N O T E   We'll explore all of the Extensis Instant Fix Tools in number 30, "Photo-Deluxe's Instant Fix Tools." If you want to spend a little time experimenting with these tools now, just remember the location of the Undo button (in the photo window toolbar).

Remove "Noise" from Your Photos

Sometimes, tiny parts of your photo appear significantly brighter or dimmer than they should. This is called *noise*. Noise is the gremlin of digital photography in that it shows up in all sorts of digital photos. Noise is caused by small current fluctuations in your camera, and it's generally unavoidable.

You might not even notice the noise in your pictures. Sometimes, it can be downright subtle. Still, it affects the quality of your prints. Taking control of noise will produce more attractive prints. Use PhotoDeluxe to remove some of the noise from your pictures:

1. Click Get & Fix Photo ➢ Repair Photo ➢ Remove Noise. You'll see the steps for the Remove Noise guided activity.

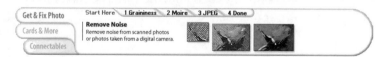

2. Click 1 - Graininess ➤ Reduce Graininess. In the dialog box that appears, you can play with the Smoothness setting, or you can accept the default value of 30. Then click the OK button.

NOTE   At each step, if you're not pleased with the results of the operation, click the Undo button (in the photo window toolbar). Then you can return to the previous step to try again using another setting, or simply proceed to the next step. (The hotkey for Undo is Ctrl+Z. You may find it handy to remember this.)

3. Click 2 - Moire ➤ Remove Moire. The dialog box that appears allows you to remove diagonal distortions from your picture. You can adjust the Angle setting or accept the default value of 45. Then click the OK button.

4. If your image was not saved in JPEG format, skip to step 5. If you do have a JPEG picture, click 3 - JPEG ➤ Clean Up JPEG. The dialog box that appears lets you remove the colored blocks that sometimes appear when you use JPEG compression. Adjust the Smoothness setting or accept the default value of 10. Click OK.

5. Click 4 - Done to finish this task.

Resize Your Photo

Are you planning to print this picture at a particular size? Have you already chosen whether you will make a 4×6, 5×7, or 8×10 print? PhotoDeluxe can help you prepare your photo to fit almost a dozen standard print sizes. Best of all, this step automatically sets a perfect aspect ratio for the print size you choose (see number 64, "Race to the Finish Line," for more on aspect ratios and print sizes). Here's how it works:

1. Click Get & Fix Photo ➤ Rotate & Size ➤ Trim & Size. You'll see the steps for the Trim guided activity.

2. Click 1 - Trim, and then click the down arrow on the right side of the box under Trim Size. From the drop-down list, select a print size and orientation. For example, you might click 5×7 (Portrait) or 2×3 (Wallet-Landscape).

3. Click the Trim icon. A proportionately shaped rectangle will appear on top of your photo. This rectangle provides the correct aspect ratio for the print size and orientation you chose.

4. Drag the corners of this rectangle to resize it and make it fit your picture better. To move the rectangle, drag from inside the corners. Position the rectangle carefully. Everything outside this rectangle will be cropped away in the next step.

5. Click the OK icon. PhotoDeluxe will trim your picture. The graphic below shows the steps for trimming your photo. If you dislike this trimmed image, click Undo. You can return to the previous steps to try another trim size.

6. Click the 2 - Done tab to finish this task.

Click the Trim button to create the trim rectangle.

Select a trim size from the drop-down list.

Click OK to perform the trim.

Drag a corner to resize, or drag within the rectangle to move it around your picture.

Optionally, click the Undo button to revert to the original picture.

Save and Export Your Work

Once you've worked on your picture, save it! Avoid losing your work. Keep a couple of things in mind:

◆ Do not overwrite your original image. Treat your source pictures as your digital "negatives." Save your fixed image to a new file.

◆ Determine what format works best for creating your prints. Most online photo finishers require you to save your photos in the JPEG format. However, when you print directly from PhotoDeluxe, you might choose to save your images using its proprietary .pdd Adobe format. This neatly avoids the image-quality losses that sometimes accompany JPEG storage.

The following instructions assume that you wish to save your image in JPEG format, perhaps as a prelude to ordering prints from an online finisher (see number 64, "Race to the Finish Line," for information about using online photo finishers).

1. Click Get & Fix Photo ➤ Save & Send ➤ Export. The Export guided activity steps will appear.

2. Click 1 - Export ➤ Other Export. This tells PhotoDeluxe that you wish to save your file in a non-Adobe format, such as JPEG. You'll see the Export dialog box.

N O T E   In the Export tab, you can click the appropriate button to save your photo in GIF, Acrobat, Indexed Color, or Grayscale format.

3. Enter a name for the file in the File Name text box.

4. Select JPEG from the Save As drop-down list.

5. Use the Windows browser to select a folder. PhotoDeluxe will store your image in the folder you choose.

6. Click the Save button. The graphic below shows the steps for exporting your photo to a JPEG format.

7. PhotoDeluxe will ask "Continue converting photo to JPEG format?" Click OK.

8. Click the 2 - Done tab to finish.

WARNING When working with JPEG images, avoid the save-load-alter-save cycle. Each time you save a JPEG image and reload it, you can lose image information. JPEG compression is *lossy*, which means that it may not produce identical images after each successive save. Instead, store your photos with another format, such as TIFF or .pdd, until you are ready to save the final image.

Click Other Export to save in formats other than GIF, Acrobat, Indexed Color, or Grayscale.

Click Save to save your image.

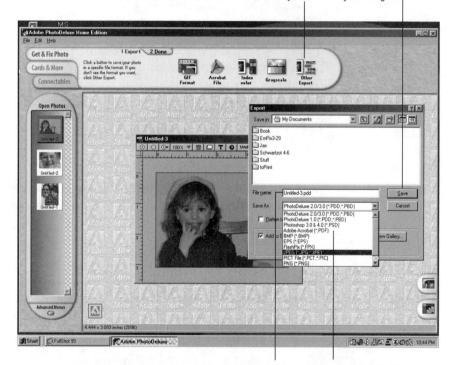

Specify a filename.

Specify the output format.

19 Advanced PhotoDeluxe Skills

Do you think you can handle the full-leaded, high-test, 16-cylinder Photo-Deluxe roadster? If you're ready, you can unlock the power of PhotoDeluxe and put yourself in control!

Introducing Advanced Image Processing

PhotoDeluxe's has many hidden image-processing capabilities. Follow these steps to unleash them:

1. Click the Advanced Menus button in the lower-left corner of your screen. Enabling this feature gives you direct access to PhotoDeluxe's full suite of image-processing features through eight additional menus. Also, this mode allows you to open more than one photo window at once.

2. One of the additional menus is View. Select View ➢ Show Layers. This displays PhotoDeluxe's Layers palette.

3. Select View ➢ Show Selections. This displays PhotoDeluxe's Selections palette.

You now have eight new menus and two palettes on your screen, as shown on the next page. This is PhotoDeluxe's "power mode."

The Layers palette makes it easy to work with layers. Layers allow you to stack photo elements in compartments that float independently. When you change a feature in one layer, it will not affect any features in other layers. For example, in the graphic shown next, the apple, the hand, the clock, and the clamp each resides in a separate layer. So, for example, when you move the clock, it does not disturb the apple, the clamp, or the hand.

The Selections palette lets you choose from a variety of selection tools. Tools include Tracing, Object Selection, Circle, and SmartSelect. Additional tool controls will appear here as needed and appropriate.

You'll get some experience using the Layers and Selections palettes in number 20, "Editing Portions of an Image with Selections." But first, let's check out all of those menus.

The Advanced Menu option adds eight new menus.

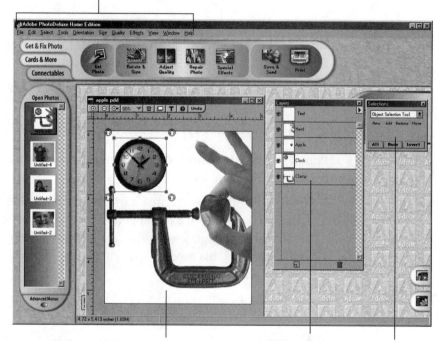

When you use PhotoDeluxe in advanced mode, you can open several photo windows at once.

The Layers palette allows you to add photo elements in free-floating compartments.

The Selections palette includes tools for choosing and controlling your selections.

Meet the Advanced Menus

PhotoDeluxe's advanced menus offer a wide range of options to greatly expand your image-processing capabilities. The menus allow you to fine-tune your images and access features directly without using guided activities. Try to become familiar with which menu hosts which features. This familiarity will help you operate more effectively in your day-to-day photo processing.

File Menu

As you might expect, the File menu offers options for opening, saving, printing, and creating new images. However, the File menu also hosts PhotoDeluxe's preferences. These preferences allow you to control the way PhotoDeluxe looks and operates. For example, you can select different picture background defaults, show or hide the Assistant Drawer, and select cursor sizes.

Edit Menu

The Edit menu offers the same options you will find in most Windows applications. These include Cut, Copy, Paste, Duplicate, and so forth.

Select Menu

The Select menu offers options that allow you to control and manipulate your selections:

- ◆ The Select All and Select None options allow you to select either all of the image layer or none of it. Interestingly, the keyboard shortcut for Select None is Ctrl+D, a carry-over from Adobe Photoshop (the *D* stands for "Drop" the selection).

- ◆ The Invert option allows you to invert your selection. If you've selected a circle in the middle of the picture, inverting it will select everything *but* that circle. Invert it again, and you're back to your original selection.

- ◆ The Selection Tool option opens a submenu that offers nine different selection tools, including shapes, freehand selection, and a special tool called SmartSelect. You can read more about using these tools in number 20, "Editing Portions of an Image with Selections."

- ◆ The Send to Back, Send Back One, Bring Forward One, and Bring to Front options are reordering tools. These allow you to reorder your image layers.

Tools Menu

PhotoDeluxe's Tools menu offers traditional paint tools, such as a brush, a line tool, a text-insertion tool, and an eraser. When you select a tool, a dialog box appears to allow you to choose features associated with the tool. For example, selecting the Text option displays the dialog box shown below. Here, you enter the text that you want to add to the photo and set the text characteristics.

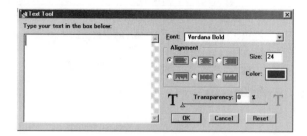

Orientation Menu

The Orientation menu has options for rotating and flipping images. When you rotate an image, the entire image moves around an imaginary axis. When you flip an image, it mirrors itself either vertically or horizontally.

Size Menu

The Size menu offers several resizing options:

◆ The Trim option crops the entire image to the size of the current selection.

◆ The Distort option lets you "distort" an image by arbitrarily stretching or squashing it. When you select Distort, the selection handles appear, as shown next. Drag a corner handle in or out. Each operates independently, so that when you drag one corner, it does not affect the others. You can also drag the side handles to stretch or squeeze your selection. After you specify your distortion, click anywhere but on a handle, and PhotoDeluxe will reshape the picture to your specification.

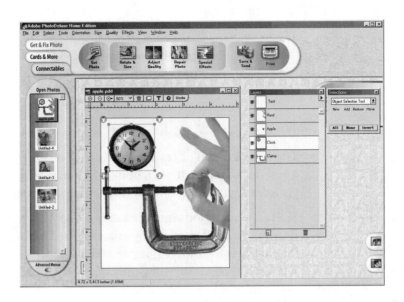

◆ The Perspective option works like a constrained distortion. While you stretch or squeeze, PhotoDeluxe maintains bilateral symmetry. This allows you to create objects that seem to stretch into the distance or explode into the foreground.

◆ The Canvas Size option allows you to adjust the width and height of your picture without affecting your image. If you ever run out of space and need to extend your "canvas," you can add more room to your picture. Note that if you make your canvas smaller, some of your image will be cropped.

◆ The Photo Size option lets you specify your image's resolution. Both the image and the canvas are resized to match this resolution.

The Quality Menu

The Quality menu provides fine control over your image's color balance, brightness, and contrast. Of special note is the Variations option, which allows you to carefully tune your picture's colors. This menu also contains the Instant Fix tool, which automatically improves your photo (it's the same as the tool available when you click Get & Fix Photo ➢ Adjust Quality ➢ Extensis Instant Fix Tools).

NOTE Photographic floodlights sometimes add too much yellow to your lighting. When this occurs, use Quality ➤ Variations to add blue back into your pictures.

Effects

The Effects menu offers a huge range of image-control features. It rightly deserves a chapter, if not a book, of its own. Features fall into three categories: selection operations, color controls, and artistic filters.

Selection operations include filling a selection with a color or gradient, drawing an outline around your selection, and "feathering." Of these, feathering is the most important. This allows you to soften the edges of your selection so you can gently blend it with other picture elements. You'll get some feathering practice in number 20, "Editing Portions of an Image with Selections."

The color controls allow you to transform your colors to black and white. You can also invert your colors to create a "negative" image.

The rest of the Effects menu is a basically a long list of filters associated with PhotoDeluxe. These filters are almost identical to those found in Adobe Photoshop. In addition, you can install your own filters in the PhotoDeluxe Plug-ins directory. Any plug-in that works with Photoshop will generally work with PhotoDeluxe. These filters include everything from turning your pictures into artistic "sketches," to blurring your selections, to adding artificial lighting effects. For example, the following graphic shows some filters applied to the original images shown in the previous graphic. A number of projects in this book will highlight some individual filters.

The Effects ➤ Stylize ➤ Emboss filter was used on the clock.

The Effects ➤ Sketch filter was used on the hand.

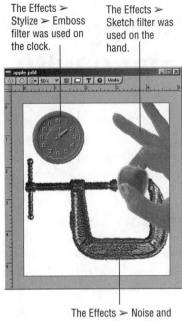

The Effects ➤ Noise and Effects ➤ Texture filters were used on the clamp.

NOTE   You can experiment with each of the filters available from PhotoDeluxe's Effects menu. For more information, you can pick up a book on the subject. Many, many books have been written on how to use the filters available in the Effects menu. Just find a book on Adobe Photoshop.

View Menu

The View menu allows you to see or hide the rulers, the Layers palette, and the Selections palette. It also includes Zoom In and Zoom Out commands.

20 Editing Portions of an Image with Selections

Much of the work involved in editing digital photos requires a skilled use of selections. Selections allow you to isolate part of an image and then move, copy, or otherwise adjust the area you specify. Once you know how to create selections, you can almost magically transform your digital images.

The Selection Tools

You can find the selection tools on both the Selection Tool submenu of the Select menu and on the Selections palette. These tools allow you to select portions of your photo in a variety of ways:

- The Object Selection tool selects the entire image. This is the default tool, and its use is described in the "Rotate, Move, and Resize Images" section of number 17, "PhotoDeluxe: A Quick Tour."

- The Polygon tool allows you to select a section point by point. Use this tool to create your selection in a series of "connect-the-dots" steps. It works particularly well when selecting odd-shaped objects that do not require precise edges. Double-click the last point in your polygon to end the selection process.

- The Trace tool selects an area by precisely tracing its edges. Carefully move the tool around your object's contours. Use this tool to extract fine object detail from your photos.

- The Rectangle, Oval, Square, and Circle tools work exactly as you might think. Pick any one to select an area by shape. When you drag out one of these tools, it will select a rectangle, an oval, or a circle of the size you specify.

- The Color Wand tool automatically selects by color similarity. Use this selection tool to select large areas of continuous color such as walls.

NOTE   If the Color Wand tool seems to select too much, you can lower the tolerance. If it seems to select too little, you can raise it. Select File ➢ Preferences ➢ Cursors and change the value for the Tolerance setting in the Cursors dialog box.

◆ The SmartSelect tool creates a selection that outlines the object you choose. To use it, select the tool, move your mouse to the beginning of your selection, and click. Then trace around the edge of your selection. Do not drag the mouse, but simply move it without pressing either mouse button. You can force the SmartSelect tool to add a point by clicking. When you've reached the end of your selection and you see the text "OK," double-click the mouse.

To practice using the selection tools, work your way through the following examples. They provide a good overview of PhotoDeluxe selection techniques. Master these skills, and you'll find yourself more fully in control of your digital photos.

"Feathering" Edges

When you feather a selection, PhotoDeluxe creates a softened outline. The selection edges blur, creating a gradual transition between the background image and the selection on top of it. This allows your images to blend together without obvious sharp edges.

Follow these steps to create a feathered selection:

1. Open your picture in PhotoDeluxe.

2. Select Oval Tool from the drop-down menu on the Selections palette. Drag out an oval to surround your subject, as shown below.

Oval selection —

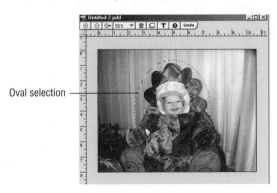

3. Select Effects ➤ Feather. In the Feather dialog box, enter **10** to feather the edge of the selection 10 pixels, and then click the Delete Background button, as shown below. Click the OK button to complete the task.

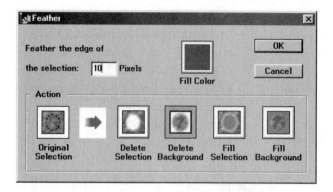

PhotoDeluxe will remove the background, leaving your feathered selection. In the graphic below, notice how this selection blends into the background without any sharp edges.

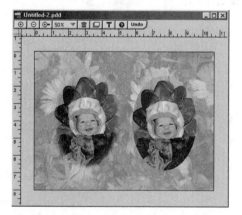

Selecting with SmartSelect

SmartSelect is easily the most powerful selection tool provided by Photo-Deluxe. As you move this tool around your image, PhotoDeluxe automatically looks for edges by comparing color differences. You must move the tool fairly precisely to create a good selection, and this can prove a little difficult for many klutzes (like myself). Still, this selection tool grants you a lot of leeway, and you can always backtrack when you make a mistake. When you take things slowly and smoothly, the SmartSelect tool will save you a lot of time and effort in making your selection.

The basic SmartSelect tool creates a simple selection that outlines the object you choose. Sometimes, however, you will want to create "holes" within your selection. As an example, we'll go through the steps for cutting a costume out of a photo:

1. Open your picture in PhotoDeluxe.

2. Select SmartSelect Tool from the Selections palette. Move the mouse to the beginning of the selection and click.

3. Carefully trace the edge of the selection by moving the mouse (don't press a mouse button).

NOTE   You can back up your mouse if you've traced a section in error. If you need to back up more than a point (the tool automatically creates these as you trace), press the Backspace key and continue your back tracing. At any time, you can click to add a point. In addition to offering extra control over your selection, this allows you to take a break in the middle of tracing.

4. When you've reached the end of your selection and you see the text "OK," double-click the mouse. The result of using the SmartSelect tool to trace around a costume is shown below.

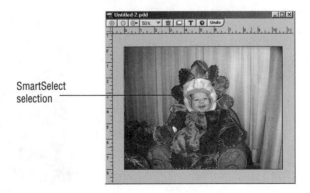

SmartSelect selection

5. Remain in SmartSelect tool mode and click Reduce on the Selections palette.

6. Move the mouse to the start of the selection, click, and carefully trace the outline of the area you want to remove. PhotoDeluxe will remove that area from the current outline. In this example, the selection is the face that we want to remove from the costume, as shown below.

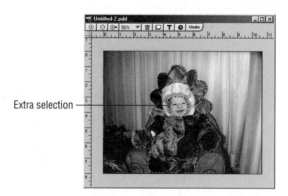

Extra selection

7. Notice that the background remains unselected after both uses of the SmartSelect tool. Now we will remove it. Select Effects ➤ Feather. Enter **5** to feather 5 pixels, click Delete Background, and then click OK. PhotoDeluxe removes all of the image but the costume, as shown below.

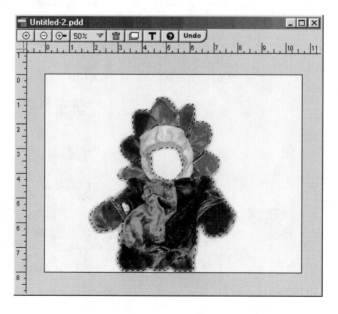

Use this technique to select any sort of object with holes. Here are some ideas:

◆ Select a pair of eyeglasses and exclude the lenses.

◆ Copy a door but not its window.

◆ Cut out a figure of a man with hands on hips and remove the holes between the arms and body.

Once you've created your "holed" selection, you can use it in many different ways. Commonly, such cutouts serve as props. For example, in the graphic below, I've placed the cut-out costume on another person. With a little artistic license, I've planted her next to a fellow flower. PhotoDeluxe provides a nice selection of props created in just this manner. To find them, select File ➢ Open Special ➢ Get Sample Photo ➢ Props.

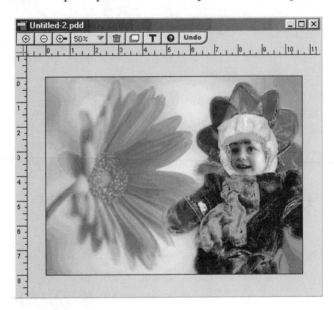

Changing a Selection

Selection errors occur when you include or exclude areas of your image by mistake. As you saw in the previous section, PhotoDeluxe allows you to adjust your selection by adding or removing regions. This provides you with precise selection control. You can edit your selection until it exactly matches your needs. Below the tool-selection drop-down list on the Selections palette are four buttons that provide more selection options, as shown below.

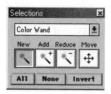

You can change your selection as follows:

◆ Click New to create a fresh selection. When you apply the tool to your image, any previous selection will disappear, and the new selection will take its place.

◆ Click Add to extend your selection. Apply the selection tool, and it will add new areas to the current selection.

◆ Click Reduce to remove areas from your selection. When you apply your tool, you take parts away from the current selection.

◆ Click Move to move your selection around the screen. You can drag to relocate the selected parts of your image.

Let's walk through a selection task so you can see how these operations work. We'll start with the picture of Joanna shown below. To create this initial selection, I applied the Color Wand tool to the blue-green wall behind Joanna's head. The tool properly selected the wall on the top and left, but it missed a section on the right and incorrectly included a good deal of the shirt.

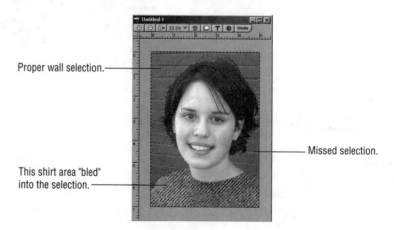

Proper wall selection.

Missed selection.

This shirt area "bled" into the selection.

First, we'll add back the section to the right of Joanna's neck. The tool missed this area because her hair touched the image edge. This blocked the Color Wand from finding this section. Then we'll remove the entire shirt from the selection. Because the shirt's color was too close to that of the wall, quite a lot of it was selected. We'll just shrink the selection by using the Reduce option. Finally, we'll clean up the selection. After you select, you may often notice small selection errors. You will usually want to fix these errors to create as precise a selection as possible.

Here's the procedure:

1. If the Color Wand is not still selected from the initial operation, choose it from the Selections palette and click the Add button. Then click within the new section (in this example, the section to the right of Joanna's neck) to add it to the selection.

2. Choose SmartSelect Tool from the Selections palette, click the Reduce button, and trace the outline of the area that you need to remove from the image (the shirt, in this example).

3. Click the Zoom-in button on the photo window toolbar to enlarge the area you wish to work on.

4. Choose the Trace Tool from the Selections palette. This is a freehand tool, which allows you to freely select areas.

5. Carefully use the Add and Reduce functions on your selection. Just trace the edges of the area you wish change and let PhotoDeluxe do the rest of the work for you. Remember to work a little at a time to prevent mistakes. If you do make a mistake, click Undo to restore your selection to its most recent settings.

Using Layers for Editing Flexibility

Moving your selections to PhotoDeluxe layers allows you to work on parts of your image without disturbing the rest of your picture. You can separate individual picture parts into different layers, and if you like, you can merge two or more layers to make them a single layer.

Instant Layers

To see how layers work, we'll start with the setup shown below, which shows three objects, each in its own layer. I created this picture by dragging three stock PhotoDeluxe images from the Samples window to a new image window.

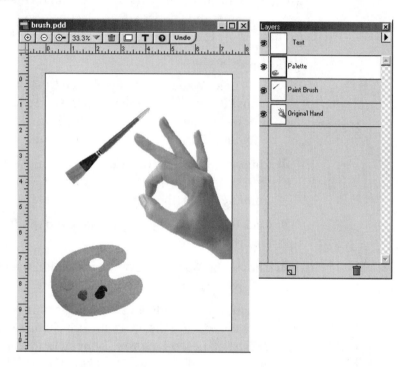

N O T E   PhotoDeluxe offers many other stock photographs. Select File ➢ Open Special ➢ Get Sample Photo and browse through the collection.

Follow these steps to bring the images into separate PhotoDeluxe layers:

1. Select File ➢ New. Create a new image that is 7.5 × 10 inches big.

2. Select File ➢ Open Special ➢ Get Sample Photo to open the Samples window. Then click the Things tab.

3. Drag the hand, the paintbrush, and the palette to your new window. Each time you drag an object to the window, PhotoDeluxe creates a new layer for that object.

4. Resize each object. Click it and use the resizing handles to fit it properly into the window. (See the "Rotate, Move, and Resize Images" section in number 17, "PhotoDeluxe: A Quick Tour," for more information about resizing images.)

To the left of each layer, you'll see a rectangle. An eye in this rectangle indicates that the layer is visible. When the eye does not appear, the layer is hidden. To change a layer's visibility, simply click in the rectangle. It will toggle that layer from hidden to visible and back. To activate a layer, click its name. This automatically selects the layer and whatever object appears in it.

N O T E You can rename a layer by double-clicking its name. Enter a new name into the Layer Options dialog box, and then click OK.

Layer Work: A Hands-on Exercise

Now that you have several layers, you can experiment with manipulating each one. As an example, we will maneuver the paintbrush and the hand to make it appear as if the hand is holding the brush.

We'll start by moving the paintbrush on top of the hand, to a "holding" position. Next, because we need the thumb to hold the brush, we'll make a copy of the hand and then extract the thumb. Finally, we'll remove the part of the finger that obscures the brush.

1. Choose Object Selection Tool from the Selections palette, click Paint Brush on the Layers palette, and drag the paintbrush over the hand, as shown on the next page.

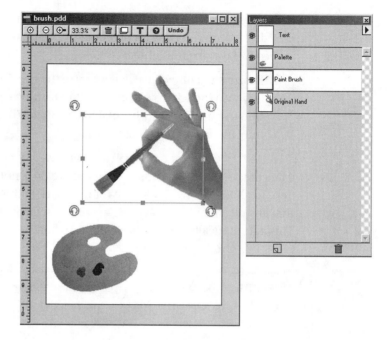

2. Click Original Hand on the Layers palette, select Edit ➢ Copy, and then choose Edit ➢ Paste. This creates a new layer, named Layer 1, containing a copy of the hand.

3. Double-click Layer 1, rename the Layer to **Visible Thumb**, and click OK.

4. Drag the Visible Thumb layer above Paint Brush to reorder it in your layers. The layer order will now read Text, Palette, Visible Thumb, Paint Brush, and Original Hand, as shown on the next page.

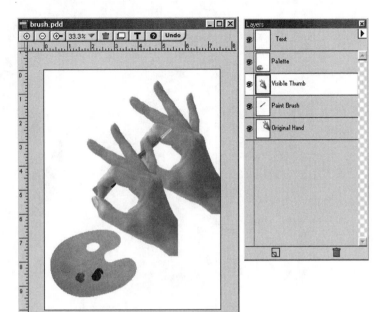

5. Click Visible Thumb on the Layers palette and move the copy of the hand until it precisely overlaps the original.

6. Click the paintbrush (you can click an object as well as the actual layer to select it), choose Color Wand from the Selections palette, and then click in the white space around the paintbrush.

7. Click Invert on the Selections palette to change the selection from everything but the paintbrush to just the paintbrush.

8. Choose SmartSelect Tool from the Selections palette and then click the Reduce button.

9. Use the SmartSelect tool to remove the thumb from the current selection. Make sure to keep the index finger in the selection.

10. Click Visible Thumb on the Layers palette and select Edit ➤ Cut. This cuts away the obscuring index finger while retaining the thumb.

Voila! The hand now appears to hold the brush, as shown next. You may, if you wish, now discard the Original Hand layer by dragging it to the garbage can on the Layers palette.

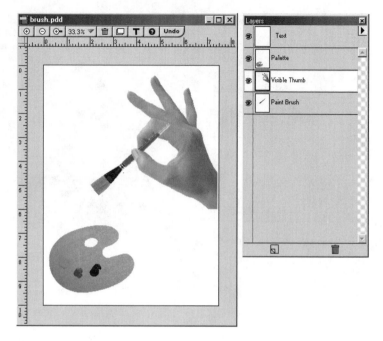

NOTE You can merge multiple layers into one by selecting Merge Layers from the Layers palette drop-down menu. Click the right-pointing arrow that appears to the right of the Text layer to see the drop-down menu. Choosing Merge Layers merges all of the visible layers into a single new layer.

Selection Techniques: A Quick Review

We've covered quite a few important techniques for creating and controlling selections. These techniques are key to working with PhotoDeluxe, and you will use them for many of the neat tricks coming up in this book. Here's a quick review:

Add and Reduce   These buttons on the Selections palette allow you to increase a selection or remove parts from one.

Shape selection   The Oval, Rectangle, Square, and Circle tools (selected from the Selections palette or by choosing Select ➤ Selection Tools) allow you to create a selection using standard geometric shapes.

Color Wand selection   The Color Wand tool (selected from the Selections palette or by choosing Select ➤ Selection Tools) uses color similarity to automatically select picture zones.

SmartSelect selection   When you use the SmartSelect tool (selected from the Selections palette or by choosing Select ➤ Selection Tools), you trace the edges of your selection. PhotoDeluxe intelligently performs the fine-detail work for you.

Trace tool and Zoom selection   The Trace tool (selected from the Selections palette or by choosing Select ➤ Selection Tools) is a freehand tool you can use to expand or reduce your selection. Get in close by zooming in (click the Zoom-in button on the photo window toolbar), so you can use the Trace tool with very fine control.

Feathering   The Feather option on the Effects menu lets you feather your selection. This blends the selection into the picture without sharp edges.

Inverting   You can invert your selection (by choosing Select ➤ Invert) to swap back and forth between the subject and the background.

Layers   Use layers to isolate your picture elements so you can work on each one individually. Each time you paste a new item into a picture, PhotoDeluxe automatically creates a new layer.

Just for the Fun of It: Digital Photo Projects

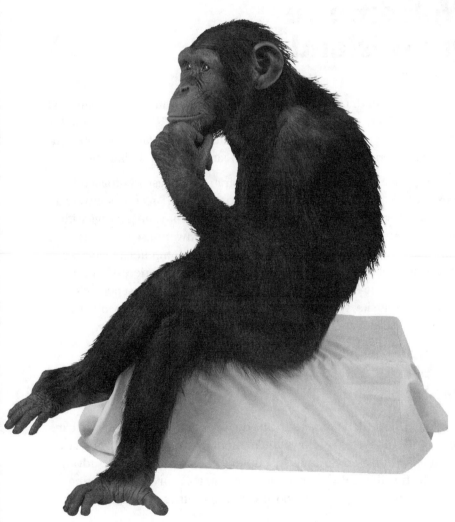

Relax already! Digital photography should be fun. Stop sweating about perfect lighting and exact composition. It's time to kick back and start enjoying your pictures. You've got the power to manipulate, adjust, and enhance your digital images. You can use this power for good, or you can just get silly. Good is important, but so is silly. Let's get silly.

21 Welcome to PhotoIsland.com

Do you remember that old 1970's TV show? The one with the old Spanish guy and the short French one? "Zee plane, Boss, Zee plane"? Well, that's not the only Fantasy Island. Stop by ArcSoft's marvelous PhotoIsland Web site and explore the interactive fantasies you can create with your digital photos.

This free service is based on hope and inspiration. At least, PhotoIsland hopes it will inspire you to purchase a title or two from ArcSoft's software line. For every project on this site, you can buy a similar software package with even more activities and templates. Buying the software also offers a speed advantage. Because the software runs on your own computer, it bypasses variable Internet connection times. Still, the wonderful variety of templates and projects on the PhotoIsland site proves sufficient for most people's needs. From this site, you can turn yourself and your loved ones into astronauts, stretched-out curiosities, freakish animal hybrids, and more.

Go Ape: Merge Your Image with Stock Photography

Have you ever wanted to make an ape out of yourself? Well, now you can. The PhotoIsland Web site allows you to monkey around with your face and turn yourself into a real animal. Just upload your image and take advantage of the free iPhotoFantasy service. You can look forward to pasting your face onto a variety of animals, sports cards, and other novelty fantasies.

The iPhotoFantasy service automatically merges your digital images with elements from stock photography. You can transform your subject into a he-man, an astronaut, a star athlete, or, as you will now see, a monkey. Follow these steps, and you, too, can "go ape":

1. Point your Web browser to `www.photoisland.com`.

2. Click PhotoWorkshop to enter the online interactive photography play center. Then click iFantasy.

3. Click Get a New Template on the left side of the page. As the template selection page loads, you will find various categories listed. These include Animal Kingdom, Sports, Nostalgia, Babes and Hunks, Trading Cards, and so forth. Each of these categories offers a number of fantasy templates.

4. Click Animal Kingdom and wait for the animals to load.

5. Click a dot under an ape picture, and then click Finished. You will return to the iFantasy page.

6. Click Get a New Photo. This allows you to upload your own image to use with the fantasy template.

7. Wait for the photo-selection page to finish loading. Click Browse and select a JPEG image from your computer. Then click Upload and wait for your image to finish uploading.

N O T E Smaller pictures will upload faster (and may work better for this service) than large ones.

8. When your photo appears, click your subject's left eye, as prompted. Wait for the page to reload, and then click the right eye, again as prompted. This information determines the size and orientation of your subject's face. iFantasy will crop the face from your image and merge it with the fantasy template.

9. If you want to experiment, use the tools on the toolbar at the top of your fantasy image. These tools, which include zoom, rotate, and so forth, allow you to tweak the way your image merges with the template. You can play with these or stick with the photo as is.

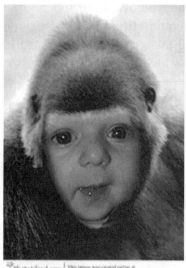

E-Mail Your PhotoIsland Creation

After you create your fantasy, you can choose from a number of Photo-Island services. You can find these on the lower-left side of the results Web page. I like the e-mail option. This allows me to send my fantasy photo to friends and family.

 WARNING Be aware that e-mail can be traced. Some of the more uptight among us might construe as "hostile" a picture of your colleague's face on an ape body.

To use the PhotoIsland e-mail service, follow these simple steps:

1. Click the Send Email button (on the lower-left side of the page where your ape hybrid appears).

2. Fill in the recipient's e-mail address (Email to:), your e-mail address (Email from:), and an optional subject and message.

3. Click Send. Your photo will be on its way. PhotoIsland will notify you that the e-mail has been sent successfully.

22 Stretch, Tweak, and Wiggle with iWarp

Did you ever want to rearrange someone's face? Are you a natural finger-painter? Do you like to stretch, tweak, wiggle, and warp? Well, do I have the place for you!

With iWarp, located at the PhotoIsland Web site, you can distort your digital images to your heart's content. Just follow these instructions, and you'll be on your way to "doing the twist":

1. Point your Web browser to www.photoisland.com.

2. Click PhotoWorkshop to enter the online interactive photography play center. Then click iWarp.

3. Click Get a New Photo. A new page will load, prompting you with the message "Get My Photo from My Computer." Click Browse and select a nice image. Then click Upload. Wait for your browser to complete the upload process. You will automatically return to the iWarp page.

4. Use the iWarp tools to distort the image:

   ◆ Select your brush size at the top of the window. Choose a size between 1 (fine changes) and 4 (big changes). You can change brush sizes at any time.

   ◆ To distort the image, press the left mouse button and drag.

   ◆ To undistort the image, press the right mouse button and drag. As you move over the picture, the original picture will be restored.

   ◆ Click Reset to return the entire image to the original picture.

5. (Optional) You can click Save to save your image to your Photo-Island account, click the Email button to send it to a friend (as per the instructions in the last section), or click Gift to create a custom gift with this picture on it. As you can see, you can have quite a lot of fun with this tool.

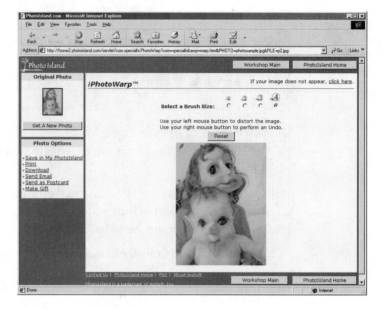

Would you like to increase your photo-warping expertise? The following tips will help you refine your face-squishing skills:

◆ Use a small brush when extending fine facial points like ears and noses. This pulls and extends the desired feature without dragging along and distorting surrounding areas. Use a wide brush to pull out cheeks and foreheads.

◆ Extend features along natural lines to exaggerate them and create a caricature without making the subject look unnatural. For example, pull out a strong chin, extend a dimple, or elongate a nose.

◆ To create the big-eye look, select the biggest brush and then pull down from just under the eye. Don't start on the eye itself. Repeat from just over the eye, pulling up. You can create fairly natural-looking large eyes in this manner.

◆ To create a cone head, use a large brush and start on one side of the head. Move the brush just below the scalp line and push up just a little. Move a little to the side, below the scalp, and push up again. Work your way through an entire layer from one side to another until the whole scalp has been raised just a bit, and then repeat. At each iteration, start your distortion closer to the center.

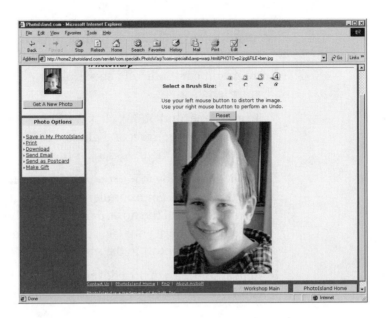

23 Blend Images with iMorph

Did you ever feel psychically linked to a special friend? PhotoIsland has just the solution for those who need to merge with a special someone. It can help you create your own separated-at-birth soul mate and provide the photographic proof that the two of you really share a special relationship.

PhotoIsland Web site's iMorph service will automatically combine facial features for you. Just upload two images and point to common features—like eyes, ears, and noses—and let iMorph do the work. You'll create a blended image that combines the best features from both subjects, merging them through the magic of video.

Follow these steps to create a merged image:

1. Point your Web browser to www.photoisland.com.

2. Click PhotoWorkshop to enter the online interactive photography play center. Then click iMorph.

3. To make this project work, you need to upload two photos. These photos should show faces with fairly similar sizes and shapes. Click Get Photo 1. On the upload page, click Browse. Select your first photo from your computer and click Upload. As prompted, click the left eye and then the right.

4. To get the second photo, click Get Photo 2. On the upload page, click Browse. Select your second photo and click Upload. Once again, click the left eye and then the right as prompted.

5. You are now ready to add points of similarity. Start by clicking a feature on Photo 1. For example, you could click the left corner of the mouth, the tip of the nose, or the base of the right ear. Two red points will appear, one at your click on Photo 1 and one on Photo 2. Drag the red point on Photo 1 to the *same* feature on Photo 2.

6. Repeat step 5 for up to a dozen or so other features, as in the example shown below. When you're finished selecting points, click Morph.

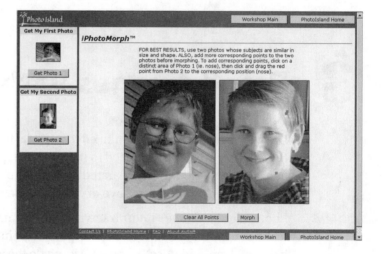

7. On the morph page, you can click a level between 0 and 10 to preview the transformation frames. When you're finished exploring, click the Click Here link to create and download your video.

8. Wait for the video to finish downloading, and then click the Play button. Your morph movie will thrill and astound you. (Okay, it's not a Michael Jackson video, but its pretty good for something you can do on your home computer, right?)

24 Create a Montage with iMontage

A few years ago, I saw the most incredible movie poster. From a few feet away, it just looked like a picture of the main actor. But as I moved closer, I realized the picture was made up of thousands and thousands of smaller pictures. Now you can do the same thing with one of your own digital images. The iMontage service at the PhotoIsland Web site will transform your image into a montage of many, many tiny photos in exactly the same way!

Here are the steps for creating your own photo montage:

1. Point your Web browser to `www.photoisland.com`.

2. Click PhotoWorkshop to enter the online interactive photography play center. Then click iMontage.

3. Click Change Picture to upload your own digital photo.

4. Wait for the upload page to appear, and then click Browse. Select your photo, and then click Upload. Wait for your browser to finish uploading your image.

5. While you sit back and wait, PhotoIsland will attempt to entertain you (whether it succeeds is another story).

6. After the montage is finished, you can click anywhere on your image to zoom in for more detail. You can also click Order a PhotoMontage Poster to purchase a copy for yourself.

25 Bozo-in-a-Can

Are you surrounded by grumps and sourpusses, frowners and grouches, or soreheads and grousers? If it's your job to make them smile, this project is for you. You can bring joy and silliness into their drab and dreary lives. You can amuse, entertain, and enliven with your digital camera and a few special Adobe PhotoDeluxe tricks hidden up your sleeve. Think of the good deeds you will be doing. When you digitally place a clown nose on an ill-tempered friend, you are actually making the world a nicer place to live. Good for you!

NOTE   For instructions on using Adobe PhotoDeluxe, including how to open photos, access the advanced features of power mode, and use the selection tools, see the "Enhancing Your Images with PhotoDeluxe" section of this book.

Clown noses are easy to create and can prove enormously amusing when done with a good heart and righteous intentions. Here's how to add a bit of merriment to your digital photos:

1. Fire up PhotoDeluxe and set up power mode (click the Advanced Menus button if the advanced menus are not already displayed and show the Layers and Selection palettes). Then open your picture and pick a photo with a good head shot, facing forward. Try to select a picture with a large, clear head (or two, as shown below) that a big, red nose won't obscure.

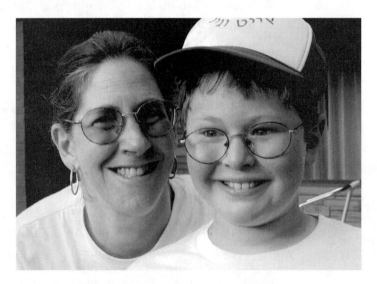

2. Choose Circle Tool from the Selections palette and select a circle around your subject's nose. Keep the circle fairly small—less is better in this case. Do not overwhelm your subject's face.

3. Select Effects ➢ Selection Fill. Click Color, and then click the button just beneath it. This opens the color swatch selection dialog box. Choose a red swatch and click OK to return to the Selection Fill dialog box. Click Selection and then click OK. A large, red circle will appear.

4. Select Effects ➢ Render ➢ Lighting Effects. In the Lighting Effects dialog box, move the light bulb (where the line crosses the circle) to roughly approximate the natural source of light in your picture, as shown below. You can increase light intensity by widening the circle or by moving the light bulb closer to the red circle. When you've created a three-dimensional-looking sphere, click OK.

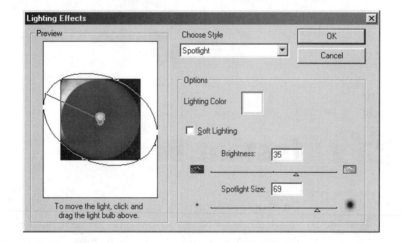

5. Choose Tools ➢ Brush. Click the Color square, select a white swatch from the color swatch selection dialog box, and click OK. Then click a nice, fuzzy brush. I like the one on the second row, third from the left.

6. Paint a small, white highlight at about one-third of the way in from the top left of your red circle. This creates the illusion of shininess on your clown nose.

7. Select Tools ➢ Smudge. Choose a large smudge brush, such as the 45 brush. Now nudge up the ends of your subject's face to create a more clown-worthy smile. Turn the least-amused subject into a true smiling clown. This feature proves especially important when altering pictures of your boss.

Enjoy your newly clowned friend.

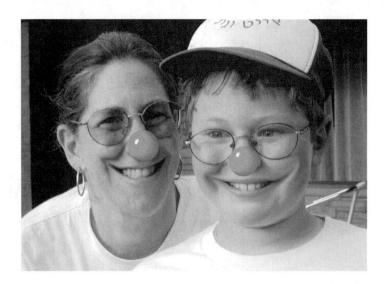

26 Instant Brainiac

 Do people say you have a swelled head? Do you say that other people have swelled heads? Now you can have actual photographic proof! If you're in the mood for a mind-blowing experience, this project is for you.

With just a digital photo of your subject and Adobe PhotoDeluxe, you can transform anyone into an instant brainiac. Here's how:

1. Launch PhotoDeluxe, set up power mode, and open your picture (see the "Enhancing Your Imags with PhotoDeluxe" section of this book).

2. Create a copy of your subject's head. Choose Select ➢ All, then Edit ➢ Copy, and then Edit ➢ Paste. This creates a new layer on top of your original photo. You will edit this copy.

3. Choose Polygon Tool from the Selections palette and select your subject's forehead and hair, as shown on the next page. (For polygon selection, click at each point and double-click the final point.) Avoid selecting your subject's eyes, eyebrows, and ears.

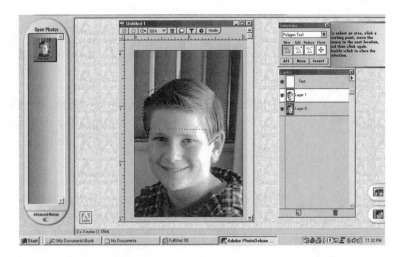

4. It's time to blow your mind. Select Size ➤ Perspective. Pull the upper-right handle first to the right and, only then, up to distort and magnify the head.

5. Now clean up your image. Select Tools ➤ Smudge and smudge away any awkward transitions. Wow, instant smarty-pants!

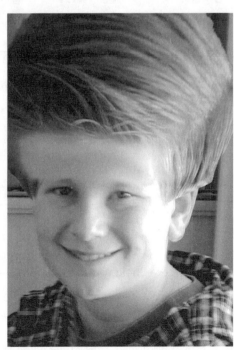

27 Whose Head Is It Anyway?

With Adobe PhotoDeluxe, you can enter the demanding and challenging world of cerebral translocation. Don't play second fiddle to Alice's Red Queen. Let yourself learn to be the one shouting, "Off with her head!"

N O T E   For the projects in this section, you'll be using the SmartSelect selection, layers, and other neat PhotoDeluxe tools. See number 20, "Editing Portions of an Image with Selections," for more information about these features.

Silly Head Tricks

Have you ever dreamed of creating Frankenstein's monster? Have you wondered how you, too, might become a head-relocation specialist? Now you can.

Select a photo with two good head shots. Both subjects should face fully forward, but it's okay if they have different head orientations and sizes. Then just follow these simple instructions:

1. Fire up PhotoDeluxe, set up power mode, and open your picture.

2. Make two copies of the original picture. Choose Select ➢ All, then Edit ➢ Copy, and then Edit ➢ Paste. Then repeat the process to create another copy.

3. Select your first copy by clicking Layer 1 on the Layers palette.

4. Choose SmartSelect Tool on the Selections palette and outline the first head.

5. Remove the entire picture except for the head. Select Effects ➢ Feather. Specify to feather the edge of the selection to 4 pixels, click Delete Background, and then click OK.

6. You're now ready to work on the second head. Click Layer 2 and repeat steps 4 and 5 for the second head. At this point, your picture should contain three layers: Layer 0 will hold the original picture, and Layers 1 and 2 should each contain one head.

7. Hide Layer 2 by clicking the rectangle (the one with the eye icon) to the left of its name.

8. Choose Object Selection Tool from the Selections palette, click Layer 1, and then click the first head.

9. Now you'll transplant the first head onto the second body. Use PhotoDeluxe's move, resize, and rotate features to move the first head into the second one's position. In general, you will need to resize the head to slightly larger than life in order to fully cover both the head area and any small artifacts around it.

10. You're ready to work on the second head. To hide Layer 1 and redisplay Layer 2, click the square to the left of Layer 1. The eye icon should disappear from Layer 1 and reappear next to Layer 2. Now click Layer 2.

11. Ready for another head transplant? Click the second head and move it into place on the first body. Once again, use PhotoDeluxe's move, resize, and rotate features to place the new head.

12. Click the square next to Layer 1 to bring back the first head.

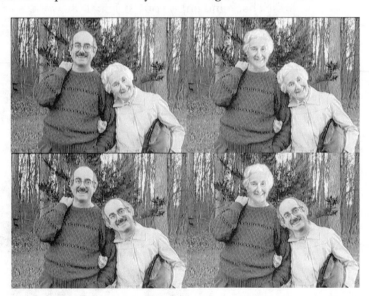

Congratulations, Dr. Frankenstein. Your next patient is waiting.

The Mona You

Has anyone ever called you a classic beauty? Do poets write odes to your eyes? Now you can emphasize your timeless splendor with just a few image-processing steps. Here's how to celebrate yourself with a fine portrait:

1. Launch PhotoDeluxe, set up power mode, and open your picture.

2. Find an archetypal picture and load it into PhotoDeluxe. In this example, we'll use Da Vinci's *La Gioconda*, better known as the Mona Lisa.

3. Follow the instructions for the previous head-swapping project to extract your subject's face and paste it into a layer over the Mona Lisa background. Replace her face by moving, rotating, and resizing your selection.

4. To adjust the new face to match the tones and colors of the underlying picture, select Quality ➢ Variations. For the Mona Lisa, progressively add more yellow and red to your subject's face. Just click More Yellow and More Red until you're satisfied that your picture matches the original's tones. Then click OK.

Kick back and enjoy your "original" artwork.

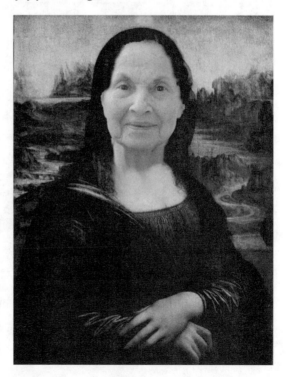

Do you like "using your head"? Here are a few more ideas:

◆ Replace the faces in your favorite cartoon with heads extracted from photos of your friends and family. If you can get a few pictures of your colleagues, Dilbert cartoons work particularly well. (Just remember about fair use and copyright issues.)

◆ Place a favorite pet's head on a supermodel's body. Better yet, stick your *own* head on the body of the aerobics instructor whose picture can be found in the PhotoDeluxe sample photos.

◆ Stick your head in unlikely places. Let your head peek out of a coffee mug, from behind a door, or in a famous news photo. You, too, can be a "Forrest Gump," appearing in famous historical scenes.

28 Make "Funny Money" with Your Photos

 Adobe PhotoDeluxe comes packed with a whole bunch of special goodies. These include stock photography, clip art, and other props to play with.

Here's how you can create some illegal tender starring your digital photo:

1. Launch PhotoDeluxe and open your picture.

2. Click the Get & Fix Photo tab of the activity bar at the top of the screen.

3. Click Special Effects ➢ Collage ➢ Funny Money.

4. Click 1 - Trim. Leave the Trim Size at Any Size. Click Trim, select your subject's face, and click OK.

5. Click 2 - Money ➢ Get Sample Photos. When the Samples window appears, click the Things tab. Scroll down and choose one of the money templates. Double-click your choice to continue. Close the Samples window.

6. Click 3 - Resize. Resize your subject's face to roughly match the face oval.

7. Click 4 - Move ➣ Move. Move your picture on top of the oval.

8. Click 5 - Done. Enjoy your "money," but do not attempt to spend it!

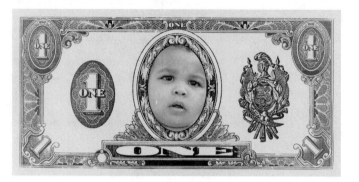

29 Create Travel Photos without Leaving Home!

Have you ever wanted to visit the Eiffel Tower? Now you can make it happen. Not only can you visit places you've never been, you'll bring back pictures as evidence!

When you're stuck with a limited travel budget, Adobe PhotoDeluxe will leap to the rescue. Follow these steps to be on your virtual way to exotic locales:

1. Start PhotoDeluxe and open your picture.

2. Click the Get & Fix Photo tab of the activity bar.

3. Select Special Effects ➣ Collage ➣ Change Background.

4. Click 1 - Select ➣ SmartSelect. Use the SmartSelect tool to extract your subject (in this case, Joanna) from the picture. When you're finished, click Delete Background. Use the Eraser tool as necessary to clean up any spare bits and pieces.

5. Click 2 - Add Background ≻ Sample Photos. In the Samples window, click the Scenes tab and double-click the Eiffel Tower. Close the Samples window.

6. Click 3 - Resize. Adjust the size of your subject.

7. Click 4 - Done.

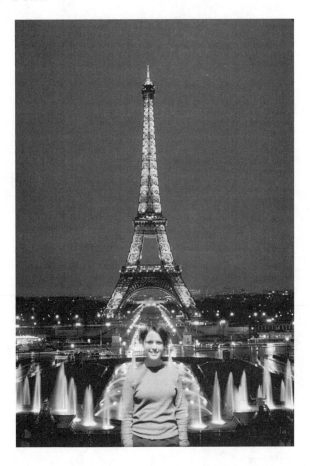

In these few steps, you've created travel memories to last a lifetime. If only you could remember having been there in the first place.

N O T E   Just before the second edition of this book went to press, Joanna and family travelled to Paris. They report that it was fun to finally visit the Eiffel tower in real life. Of course, I will now have to "send" her someplace else: maybe Japan!

Fix Your Digital Photo Problems

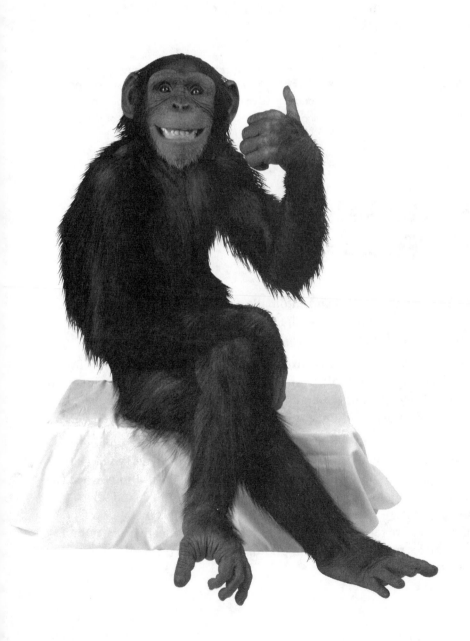

Even the best photographers make mistakes. Don't let a little problem ruin your picture. Fix up your picture and make the best of it. You'll be surprised how well and how much you can tweak, twiddle, and nudge your pictures into their best possible shape.

Using the handy tools in Adobe PhotoDeluxe's toolbox, you can perform some major and minor miracles, ranging from adding a bit of contrast to hiding an ugly background.

NOTE We'll be using Adobe PhotoDeluxe, included on the CD that accompanies this book, to perform the photo fixes covered in this part. For details on using PhotoDeluxe, see the "Enhancing Your Images with PhotoDeluxe" part of this book.

30 PhotoDeluxe's Instant Fix Tools

Wouldn't you like instant and automatic digital photo enhancement? Could you ask for a better friend? Sure, a dog is great, but a quick fix is another matter entirely.

Fortunately for you, PhotoDeluxe arrives with not just one, but with five (count 'em!) quick-fix tools, courtesy of Extensis. You can use these tools to automagically evaluate your photo, decide what levels and options to use, and perform the fix without any human intervention. How convenient!

Because the Instant Fix tool is such a boon to digital photographers, I suggested that you use it as part of your basic routine when you first bring a picture into PhotoDeluxe (see number 18, "Basic Photo Fixes: The Get & Fix Photo Menu"). Just click the Get & Fix Photo tab and select Adjust Quality ➤ Extensis Instant Fix Tools ➤ IntelliFix Instant Fix for miracle picture repair. When you want to be more selective about the instant fixes performed on your photo, you can use one of the other quick-fix tools.

N O T E   The photos in this section show "before" and "after" effects in the same picture. In each photo, the left half appears unretouched, and the right half demonstrates the quick-fix tool results. Look carefully to recognize each enhancement. They can be quite subtle.

Snap into Focus: Auto Sharpen

Use the Extensis Auto Sharpen tool to automatically "unblur" your photos. Here's how it works:

1. Fire up PhotoDeluxe and open your picture.

2. Select the area you wish to fix. To fix the entire photo, choose Select ➤ All. Otherwise, pick a selection tool from the Selections palette and mark the area you want to change.

3. Click the Get & Fix Photo tab of the activity bar and select Adjust Quality ➤ Extensis Instant Fix Tools ➤ Auto Sharpen.

The graphic below shows what happens after auto-sharpening. You'll notice that there isn't much difference between the original and auto-sharpened areas.

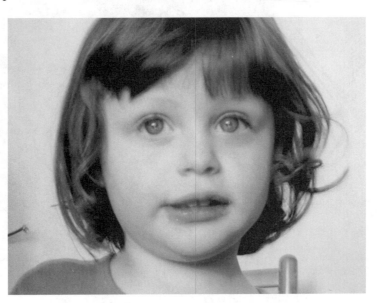

NOTE Of all the Extensis tools provided by PhotoDeluxe, Auto Sharpen ranks as my least favorite. I do not believe it creates particularly good results. Instead, let me recommend the sharpening technique covered in number 35, "Improve Focus with a Sharpening Filter."

Correct Poor Contrast: Auto Contrast

In contrast (sorry!) to the Extensis Auto Sharpen tool, the Auto Contrast tool works very well indeed. This tool automatically corrects poor contrast caused by any number of lighting problems. Follow these steps to automatically add contrast:

1. Launch PhotoDeluxe and open your picture.

2. Select the area you wish to fix. You can choose Select ➤ All to select the entire photo or use a selection tool to mark an area of the photo.

3. Click the Get & Fix Photo tab and select Adjust Quality ➤ Extensis Instant Fix Tools ➤ Auto Contrast.

In the graphic below, you can see that Auto Contrast can improve a photo.

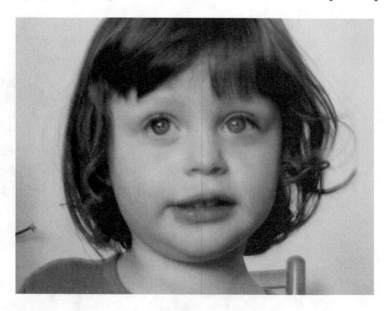

Enhance Light Levels: Auto Brightness

The Extensis Auto Brightness tool enhances ambient light values, although the results are often subtle. It expands your photo's dynamic range so you can see a wide variety of light levels, where, originally, there may have been few. Here are the steps for auto-brightening:

1. Launch PhotoDeluxe and open your picture.

2. Select the area you wish to fix with a selection tool or choose Select ➤ All to select the whole photo.

3. Click the Get & Fix Photo tab and select Adjust Quality ➤ Extensis Instant Fix Tools ➤ Auto Brightness.

You'll need to look very closely at the picture below to see the effect of using the Auto Brightness tool.

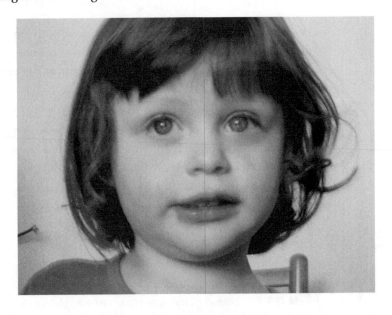

Remove Fluorescent Light Effects

Fluorescent lights can add unnatural green and yellowish tones to your photos. This makes your subjects look sickly and vampiric. Of course, it's best to turn off fluorescent lights and use natural daylight, photo floodlights, or even your camera's flash where possible. When opportunity does not permit these solutions, you can repair your pictures back at the computer.

PhotoDeluxe provides an Extensis tool designed to automatically readjust your image's flesh tones and restore missing health and vitality. Just apply this "fix" to improve your photos:

1. Launch PhotoDeluxe and open your picture.

2. Use a selection tool to select the area you wish to fix or choose Select ➤ All to select the entire photo.

3. Click the Get & Fix Photo tab and select Adjust Quality ➤ Extensis Instant Fix Tools ➤ Remove Fluorescent Light.

31 Repair Red-Eye

Do you have red-eye—that demon-look, with those glowing red eyes? How embarrassing—it's almost as bad as halitosis (well, maybe not quite as bad). Whatever can you do? What would Emily Post say?

Red-eye occurs when your subject's eyes dilate too much. Light reflects off the retinas and bounces back to the camera. This creates the signature red glow we hate so much. Sometimes we don't even know that we've caught red-eye. With small LCD screens and obscured visibility, we often do not discover red eyes until we're back at our computer. How frustrating!

Put away those "red-eye marking pens" (otherwise known as expensive magic markers). Shun the black-tipped paintbrush tool. Let PhotoDeluxe leap to your rescue. With just a few quick steps, you can relieve that red-eye condition.

N O T E   Instead of trying to repair red-eye, you can sometimes avoid it in the first place. See number 2, "Use Light Effectively," for tips on reducing red-eye when you're shooting pictures.

PhotoDeluxe will walk you through a guided activity that instantly repairs red-eye in your photos. Here are the steps:

1. Open your picture in PhotoDeluxe.

2. Click the Get & Fix Photo tab and select Repair Photo ➢ Remove Red Eye.

WARNING   Keep your box small and do not attempt to correct both eyes at once. PhotoDeluxe sometimes creates weird side effects when you attempt to remove red-eye with a large selection.

3. Click 1- Select ➢ Select Rectangle. Drag a box around the first eye, as shown below.

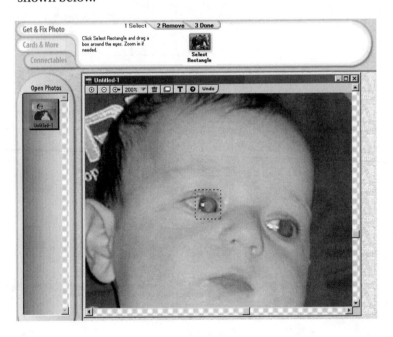

4. Click 2 - Remove ➢ Remove Red Eye. PhotoDeluxe automatically corrects the eye for you, as shown on the next page.

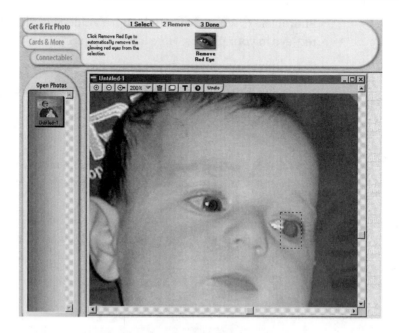

5. Repeat steps 3 and 4 to correct the second eye.

6. You can repeat this process for each eye in your photo. (No, I'm not suggesting your subject has more than two eyes—I'm suggesting that your picture may have more than one subject!)

7. Click 3 - Done to finish.

32 Remove and Replace Unwanted Elements

At times, unwanted but subtle details seem to creep into our pictures. We never even notice them until long after we've shot our photo. Often, we're back at the computer, sorting through the "rolls," and up crops a marvelous picture with one or two minor flaws.

Take charge of your pictures. Don't "learn to live with it." You can fix these flaws and bring your photos to their full potential. The secret is *cloning*. When you clone a part of a picture, you replace the flaws you don't want with other, more desirable, features. The big advantage is that these features share the same general lighting and texture as the rest of the picture. You hide flaws with authentic picture parts.

PhotoDeluxe's Clone Tool

PhotoDeluxe provides an easy-to-use Clone tool. With this tool, you set a bulls-eye at your replacement source. Then you brush this texture over the area you want to hide. The tool replaces the flaw with the copied texture and blends it into your picture.

Suppose that you took the picture below. It would be a great shot, if only you could get rid of the hand and the book it's holding in the background behind the subject's back. This is where the Clone tool saves the day (or more precisely, the photo). Using it, you can replace the hand and book with additional fiberboard. This works because it will paint over the intrusion with a nice, mottled texture that should blend into the rest of the background.

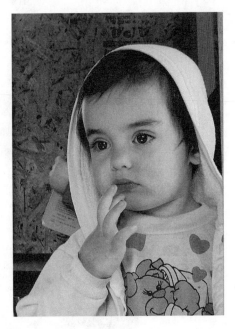

"Clone-away" your picture problem areas with just a few steps. Follow these instructions to clean up your photos:

1. Fire up PhotoDeluxe, set up power mode (click the Advanced Menus button if the advanced menus are not already displayed and show the Layers and Selection palettes), and open your picture.

2. Choose SmartSelect Tool from the Selections palette. Draw an outline around the features you wish to remove.

3. Select Tools ➤ Clone. Drag the bulls-eye to an area that has the texture you want to use to replace the features you're removing, as shown below.

The bulls-eye sets the center of the area to be cloned.

Select the area you wish to replace.

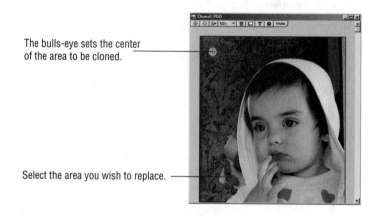

4. Paint your selection with this texture. Your picture is now rid of its flaws, as shown below.

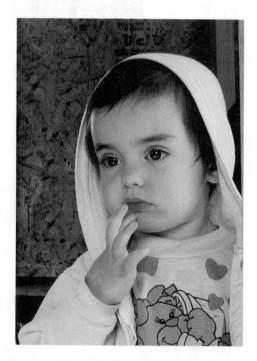

Photo Cloning Tips and Tricks

Here are a few tips to help you make the most of your cloning:

◆ Select precisely when a flaw rests next to your subject, but select loosely when it's adjacent to a common texture. You're trying to balance two issues here. First, you don't want to remove any part of your subject. A careful selection ensures that your subject will remain entirely intact. On the other hand, you want to avoid "ghost" edges. These may form at the edges of your selections when you select too closely. When you need to replace a feature with a texture, you'll want to make sure you completely cover it.

◆ Set your bulls-eye in the middle of a texture rather than at an edge. This affords you the greatest latitude in sweeping your brush back and forth. After all, you don't want to go beyond the edge of your texture and start cloning actual features like hands, houses, and trees.

◆ When your texture area is small, make many small brush strokes. The clone "resets" after each repetition. By keeping your strokes small, you ensure that you do not stray from your desired texture.

◆ Stick to backgrounds. Do not attempt to hide a flaw by cloning a "feature." The whole point of this repair exercise is that the noise and randomness inherent in your texture will blend in well. When you attempt to cover a wall-socket with a chair, you'll invariably produce a lot of edge effects (artificial transitions between the original and the added image elements) that will not blend well.

N O T E According to my husband, you may no longer refer to this process as "doctoring your pictures" because that's too politically incorrect. After discussing "picture nursing," "picture surgery," and "clinical picture overhauls," we finally came up with a less discriminatory and more PC phrase. When you apply this process to your images, you will become a "picture healthcare worker."

33 Alter Photo Backgrounds with PhotoDeluxe Tools

Sometimes a lovely picture happens against an ugly background. The picture below shows a typical nice foreground/awful background image. In this picture, the subject poses in front of construction site. Behind her, you can see plywood, protective plastic sheeting, and part of a warning sign. Fortunately, this problem is easy to fix. When you de-emphasize the background, the focus switches to your subject. The key is to camouflage any feature that might draw away the viewer's eye. We do this through filters.

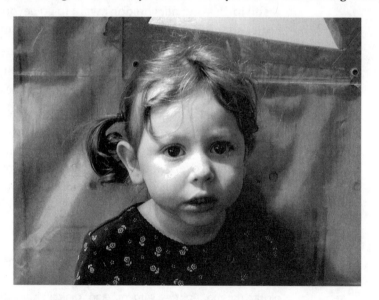

PhotoDeluxe filters allow you to alter image quality in a variety of ways. Many filters produce blurred and distorted versions of an image. When you apply these effects exclusively to the background of your image, you bring your subject into sharp relief.

N O T E   To fix an ugly background, you'll need to use PhotoDeluxe layers and selection tools. See number 20, "Editing Portions of an Image with Selections," for more information about these features.

You can use any of a number of filters to produce the effect you need. However, no matter which filter you choose, the method you follow to create the distorted background remains the same. These instructions will show you how to isolate the foreground of your image and apply a filter to the rest:

1. Fire up PhotoDeluxe, set up power mode (click the Advanced Menus button if the advanced menus are not already displayed and show the Layers and Selection palettes), and open your picture.

2. On the Layers palette, pull Layer 0 (your picture) down to the paper icon and let go. This will create Layer 0 copy, a copy of your original image.

3. Click Layer 0 copy. Choose SmartSelect Tool from the Selections palette and outline your subject.

4. Select Effects ➤ Feather. Specify a nice, wide feathering, such as 6. Click Delete Background, and then click OK. This will remove the background from Layer 0 copy, but create a smooth transition between your subject and the background.

5. On the Layers palette, click Layer 0. Select Select ➤ All.

6. Apply your filter of choice by selecting it from the Effects menu.

Now that you know the general method for applying a filter to a background, let's take a look at what each of these filters can do.

Create a Mosaic of Dots with the Pointillize Filter

The Pointillize filter transforms your background into a mosaic of tiny dots. In an attempt to emulate French Pointillism, it produces dreamy, unrealistic pastels that contrast sharply with the vibrant colors of your subject.

To apply the Pointillize filter, select Effects ➤ Pixelate ➤ Pointillize. This filter obscures many of the background details to the point that they cannot be identified by those unfamiliar with the original, as you can see in the picture below. This, too, helps move the image focal point to your subject.

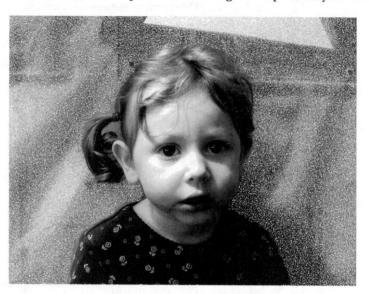

Remove Background Color

By removing all color from your background, you create an eerie blend of reality and fantasy. Your subject becomes a splash of color in an otherwise colorless world. When you remove background color, it seems to also remove emotional contact at some level. We relate more fully and emotionally to full-color images than to black-and-white ones.

The Black/White effect draws the eye, particularly because many people do not realize for a few seconds what is "wrong" with the background. This effect can produce some truly eye-catching results. To apply this effect, select Effects ➤ Color to Black/White.

Distort with the Ripple Filter

When you apply the Ripple filter, your background appears as if you're looking at it through a pane of rippled glass, as shown in the picture on the next page. This filter produces a blurry, not-quite-real overlay, while leaving major background features undisturbed.

To apply the Ripple filter, select Effects ➤ Distort ➤ Ripple, choose a very high ripple amount, such as 999, and click OK. After you apply the filter, click the Undo button a few times. Look closely as you move back and forth between the original image and the filtered one. You'll be surprised at how little the actual features change. And yet, they distort just enough to push away the eye and force attention on your subject.

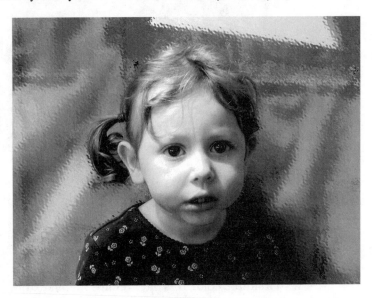

Roughen with the Crackle Filter

The Crackle filter makes the background appear as if it were painted on stucco. Small cracks and crevices appear in the image, and the shadows that fill these add noise and texture to the photo.

Because of the added shadows, the Crackle filter will also tend to darken the background somewhat. As the background grain and roughness increase, the subject is left to provide a smooth refuge for your eye, as shown next. To apply the Crackle filter, select Effects ➤ Texture ➤ Crackle.

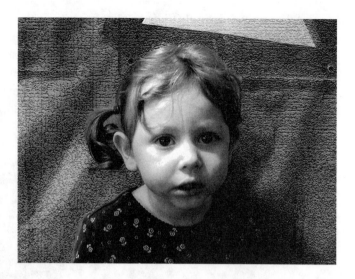

Add Texture with the Emboss Filter

Embossing your background turns it into a gray, textured backdrop, reminiscent of a fabric. Details remain, but at a very subdued level, as shown below. Although you could create a similar effect by filling the background with a simple color, this filter retains many textural details that provide lingering visual interest without strong detail. To apply this filter, select Effects ➢ Stylize ➢ Emboss.

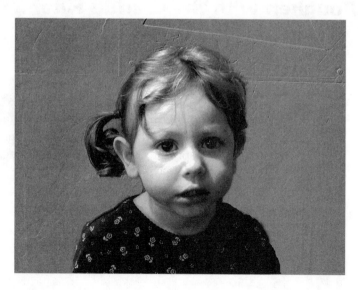

34 Fix Facial Blemishes

Facial blemishes happen to the best of us. When you set out to create precious heirlooms, why not take the time to digitally clean up your loved one's face and create a more flattering portrait. As you can see in the "before" image below, even the sweetest baby occasionally suffers imperfections. With just a little work, as in the "after" image, you can eradicate some obvious flaws and produce a more timeless keepsake.

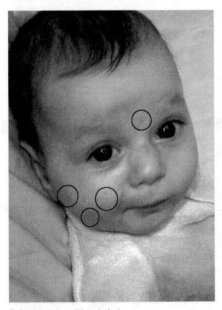 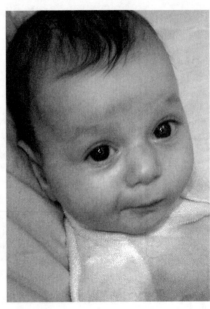

Before touchup (the circled areas are the "problem spots")

After touchup

Use PhotoDeluxe's Smudge tool (Tools ➤ Smudge) to nudge away any blemishes. Select a medium to small brush and pull color in from just above, below, or to the side of a flaw. Here are some tips for a smooth cover-up:

◆ Use small strokes. These will give you more control over the smudging effect.

◆ Avoid pulling in color from too far away. This will just magnify the existing problems. Our eyes are very sensitive to sudden changes in color. Bypass this neurological quirk by using nearby colors instead.

◆ After you've smudged away your flaw, you may want to blend it a little. Use a selection tool, like the Trace tool or the Circle tool, to select a small area around the former blemish. Then choose Effects ➢ Blur ➢ Blur More to even out the changes you've made.

WARNING Do not give in to the temptation to use the Clone tool to clean up blemishes. Although it might seem like an ideal solution (copy smooth skin areas to the problem spot), you'll create more problems than you solve. The skin patch you copy will not naturally blend into the new spot. Human skin of every flavor, color, and gender is not highly textured. It displays smooth gradations from one point to another. You just cannot expect to match this gradual color change with a relocated patch.

35 Improve Focus with a Sharpening Filter

Fuzzy happens. You snap a picture, and the focus is off. Your image turns out soft and a bit blurry. Whatever can you do?

I offer you three alternatives to dealing with those fuzzy pictures. Ponder them carefully and choose the option that best suits your needs.

First, you can throw up your hands, indulge in a well-deserved hissy fit, and throw away the picture (and, optionally, the camera). Scream out loud. "These pictures are an insult to me as an artist! I refuse to acknowledge them. They are the spawn of evil technology. I shall now return to painting outlines of my hands on cave walls. That will show them!" (Whoever "they" are.) In technical jargon, this is known as "walking away from the problem."

Second, you can adjust your way of thinking. Or, as they say in biz-speak, "create a paradigm shift." Instead of bemoaning your lost photo opportunity, learn to "celebrate" your mistakes. Point out how soft focus enhances the beauty and romance of your image. After all, they used soft focus in the Star Trek classics all the time. Every time the camera angle changed from Captain Kirk to the pretty girl, the focus would go out of whack. Explain to others that you are paying homage to the 1960's retro-tradition of soft-focus photography. Rather than admit that you (or the camera) messed up the focus, state firmly that you were aiming for the "indeterminate transition effect expressed as a rejection of overstructured object independence." That'll show 'em.

Finally, you can fire up PhotoDeluxe and attempt to sharpen your picture with an image filter. The results won't be great, I assure you, but you can often add a little optical clarity to a fuzzy situation. This may not offer the emotional release of the prior two methods, but it does allow you to create pictures with some small visual improvement. To apply a sharpening filter, open your picture in PhotoDeluxe and choose Edit ➢ Select All. Then select Effects ➢ Sharpen ➢ Sharpen *or* Effects ➢ Sharpen ➢ Sharpen More. Repeat as desired.

Applying a sharpening filter is more an art than a science. You must control each iteration and decide when the picture has reached its peak. These tips should help you when sharpening:

◆ Copy the image to a new layer and experiment with the copy. This allows you to test different approaches without altering your original picture. To copy a layer, drag it to the paper icon on the bottom left of the Layers palette. (Don't forget to turn off the display of the original image by clicking the "eye" icon.)

◆ Use the Undo function liberally. After you test a sharpening effect, revert it with Undo to swap between the new and the old. This allows you to compare the results and decide whether you like the new effect or not.

◆ Zoom in. View your picture with at least a 100% zoom. A picture will naturally look better when shrunk down. A larger view allows you to see image flaws more clearly.

◆ Balance too much and too little. You must decide how much sharpening your image requires. Sharpen too little, and you won't see much difference between your original and the new. Sharpen too much, and you'll introduce noise, darkness, and unflattering edge effects.

◆ Blur a little. If the results between one sharpening and the next introduce too much noise, you can add a light blur or "unsharp" effect. This reduces the high-frequency edge effects. Select Effects ➢ Blur ➢ Soften and adjust the radius until the noise just barely disappears.

◆ Watch an eye. Although you can pick any feature to compare before and after, eyes offer a great combination of lines and texture. Watch the eye as you sharpen your image and see how image quality improves.

As I noted earlier, a sharpening filter can't turn a blurry picture into an in-focus one. However, using the techniques described here, you can usually improve your photo to some degree.

The black-and-white digital photographs reproduced throughout this book cannot do justice to the full range of color and tone that you can capture with your digital camera. The images presented here illustrate some of the visual and emotional impact that color photographs can convey.

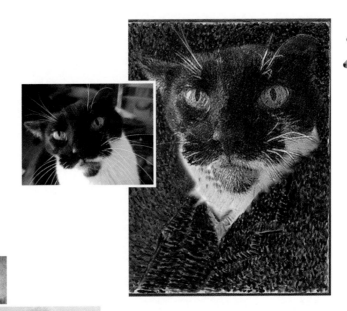

Have Fun!

Never forget that your digital camera is supposed to be fun. Use your camera and PhotoDeluxe to add spice, interest, and above all, enjoyment to your life. These images use feathering, color variations, and filters to match the original artwork. (See number 27, "Whose Head Is It Anyway?")

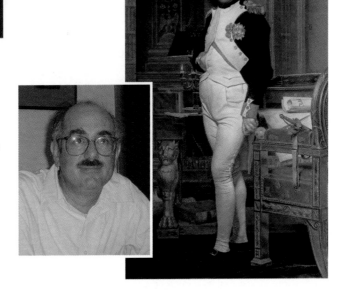

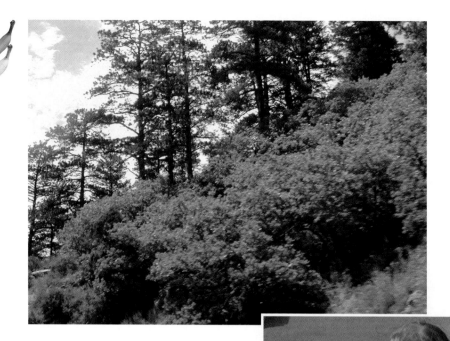

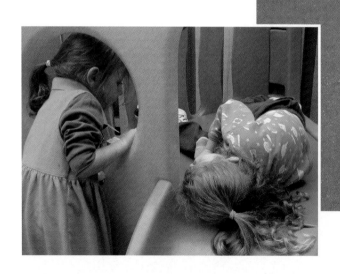

Good Composition Adds Interest

Simple shapes, like triangles, resonate with your viewer's eye. You might be surprised where you'll find natural patterns: ripples across the sand, the bend in the road, a row of glass doors in an office building…. Don't feel you must always photograph your subjects face-on. A simple image of unconscious grace makes a lovely picture.

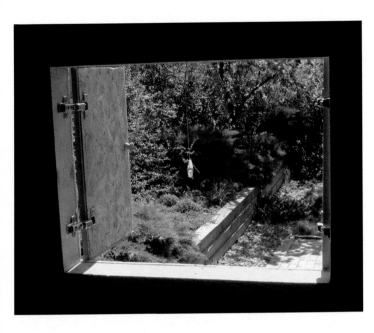

Use Natural Compositional Elements

Use natural frames wherever you find them. They add important artistry to your pictures. Look for doors, windows, overhanging branches, sculptures, planters, and trellises. Keep your depth of field in mind. Both your "frame" and your image should remain in focus at the same time.

A splash of natural color lends particular beauty to your digital photographs. Zoos, aquariums, and botanical gardens provide fruitful sources for rich and varied color.

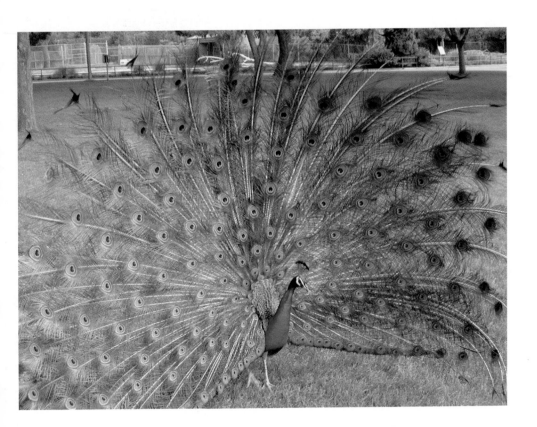

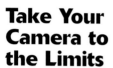

Take Your Camera to the Limits

Use your macro lens to get in close to a flower, butterfly, or stone. Then step back and allow your camera to take in the entire vast splendor of nature in the grander scheme of things.

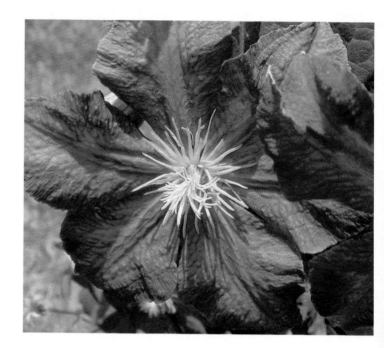

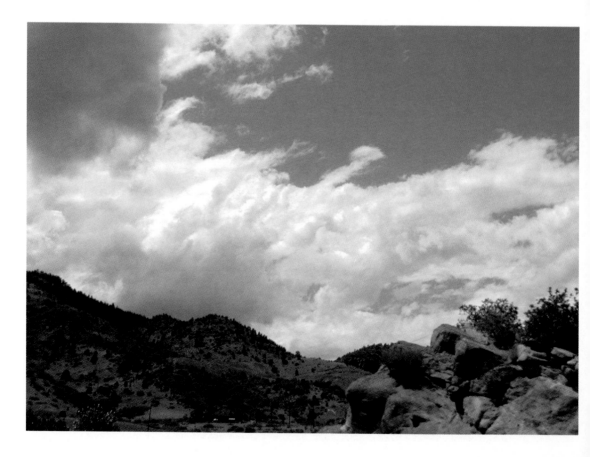

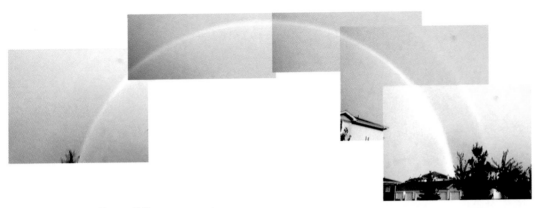

Capture the Moment

This image of a double rainbow was created by snapping a series of exposures. Then the exposures were assembled by hand in an image-processing program. By overlapping the images, an image "quilt" was created. (See number 41, "What a Vista! Create Panoramas.")

Experiment with Focal Effects

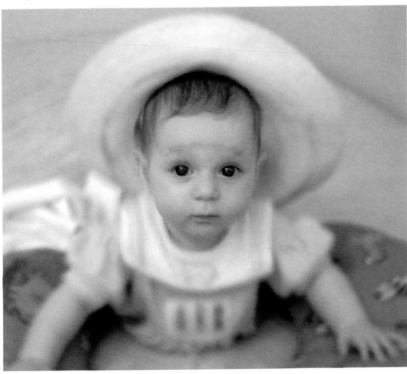

A subject in focus surrounded by a fuzzy background produces a particularly artistic image. You can achieve this effect by adjusting your camera settings when you take the shot or by editing the photo in an image-editing program. This image was captured using maximum zoom and produced a very shallow depth of field. (See number 3, "Understand Depth of Field.")

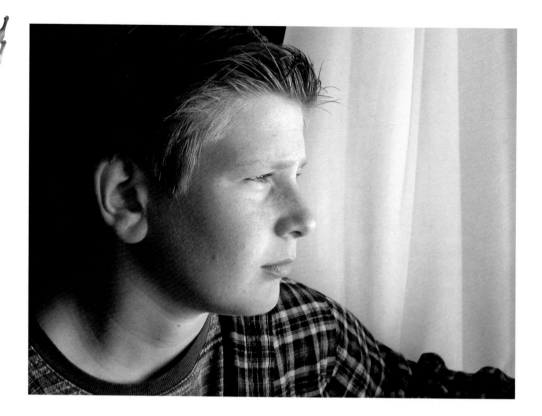

Encourage Freedom of Expression

Let your subjects guide you, but open yourself to experimentation. Sometimes a subdued pose best flatters an outgoing personality or vice versa. Take risks, and you will often find rewards in your portraits.

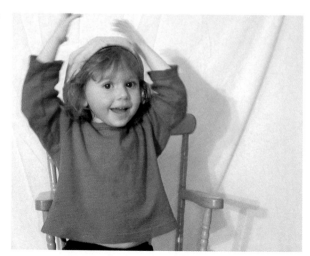

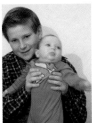 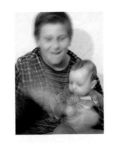 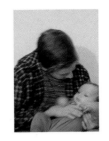

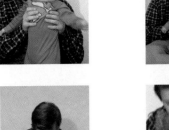

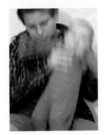 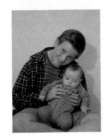 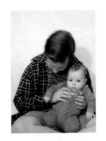

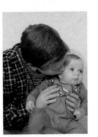

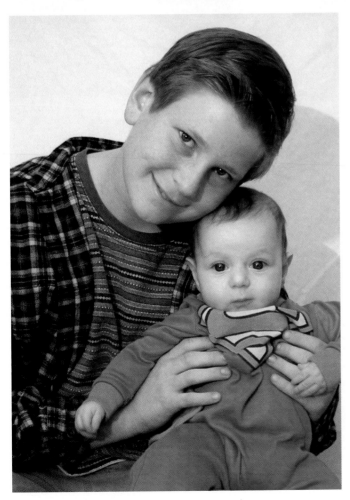

Take Lots of Pictures!

You never know when the right pose will come along. The more pictures you take, the more likely you'll capture the perfect shot when it arrives. This proves especially important when shooting pictures with multiple subjects. Keep snapping and don't lose that perfect shot!

Try Long Exposures

Long exposures taken at night can produce eerily beautiful images. With proper timing, you just might capture a ghost! Make sure to use a tripod to steady your camera and start your shot early. This exposes your subject for the longest time possible and produces the best results. (See number 2, "Use Light Effectively.")

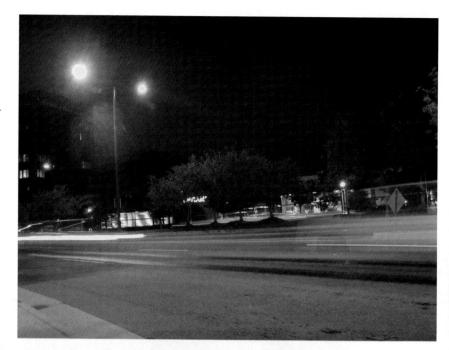

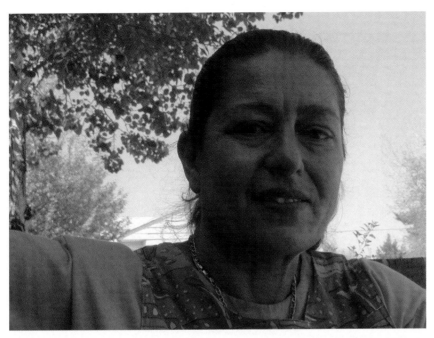

Watch Your Backlighting

Backlighting can destroy a beautiful moment. Always turn on your flash to fill in a backlit picture and reveal your subject. Of course, the best way to avoid backlight is to turn your subjects around. Have them face the light. Move yourself and the camera to make the most of natural illumination. When this is simply not possible, activate your camera's flash-fill feature and shoot.

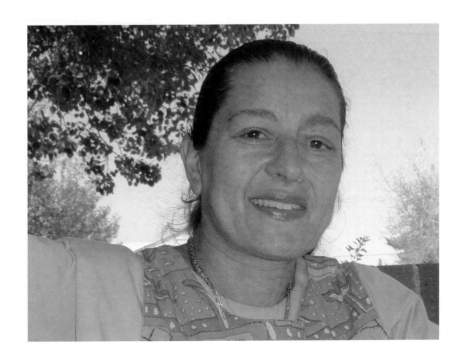

Use Polarizing Filters

A polarizing filter on your camera cuts glare and enriches color. The cloud-filled sky in this photo was given a more dramatic contrast with a polarizing filter.

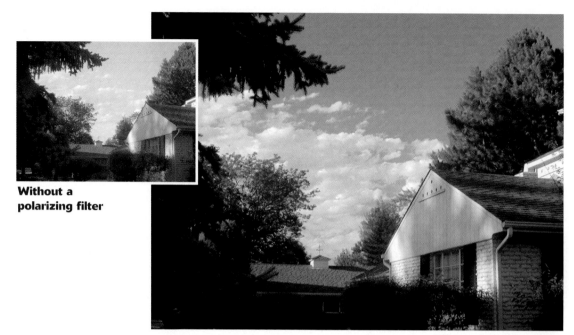

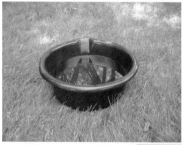

Without a polarizing filter

With a polarizing filter

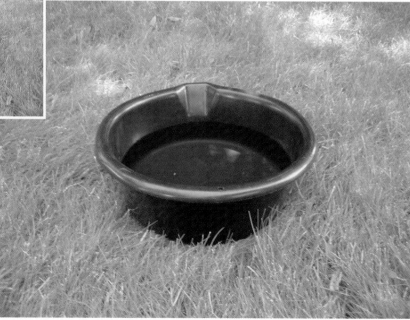

Without a polarizing filter

All reflected light—from a mirror, picture frame, pond, etc—produces polarized light. Use a polarizing filter to remove some of these reflections. Learn to use the rule-of-thumb (see number 15, "Optimizing Your Camera's Optical Components") to place your camera at the ideal angle to sunlight.

With a polarizing filter

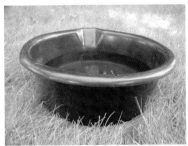

About 15 degrees

You'll find the most polarized light between thirty and forty-five degrees from any surface. Shoot within these angles to remove reflections and glare.

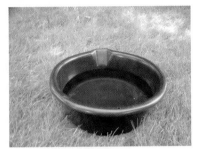

About 40 degrees (the reflections are nearly gone)

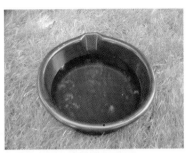

About 60 degrees

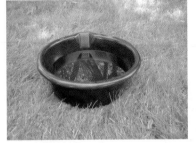

No polarizing effect

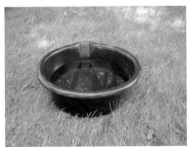

Some polarizing effect (⅛ twist)

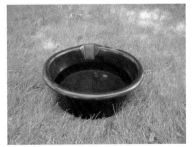

Complete polarizing effect (¼ twist)

Twist your polarizing filter until the reflections are nearly gone. A quarter-twist is usually all you need.

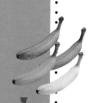

Improving Images with the Instant Fix Tool

Adobe PhotoDeluxe and Extensis's Instant Fix tool will automatically improve your image's brightness, contrast, color balance, and sharpness in one step. Use this tool to produce better pictures instantly. (See number 30, "PhotoDeluxe's Instant Fix Tools.")

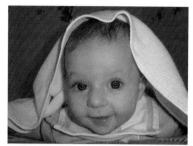

Original picture

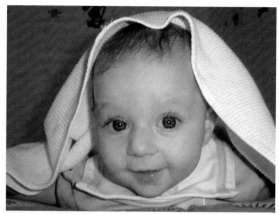

After Instant Fix

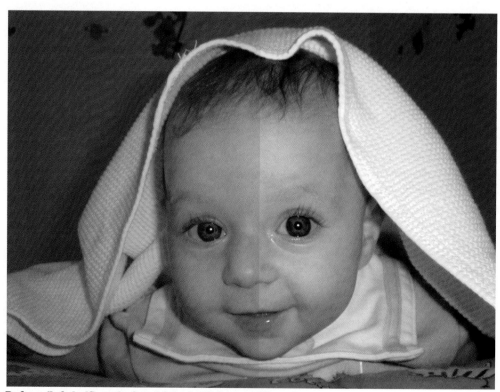

Before (left half) and after (right half) Instant Fix

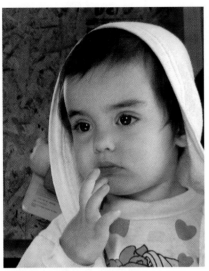

Original image, with hand holding book in background

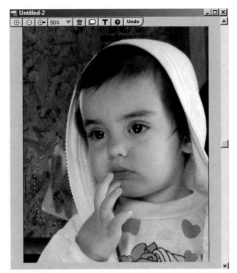

Using the Clone tool

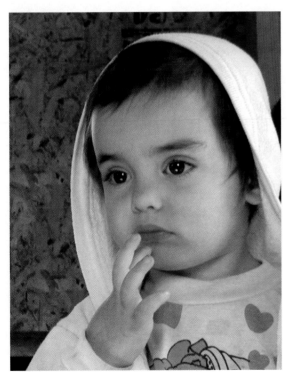

The fixed image

Make a Good Photo Even Better

Don't let a small flaw ruin a great picture. Use Adobe PhotoDeluxe's Clone tool to remove an unwanted feature from your photograph. In this example, the intruding hand was removed from behind the subject's back. Then the hand was selected and the particleboard was cloned from the upper-left portion of the photograph. This covers the hand and repairs the image. (See number 32, "Remove and Replace Unwanted Elements.")

PhotoDeluxe Effects Sampler

PhotoDeluxe offers many built-in filters and special effects. They can produce artistic and dramatic results. Select one from the Effects menu and try it on your picture. This sampler displays only a fraction of the available effects.

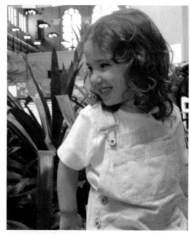

Original Image

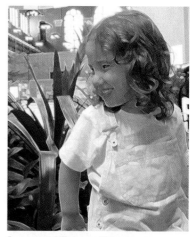

Accented Edges Filter

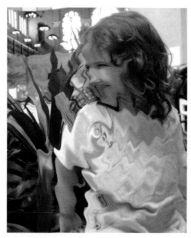

Pond Ripple Filter

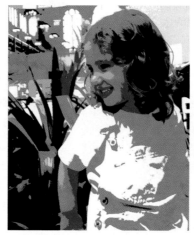

Posterize Filter

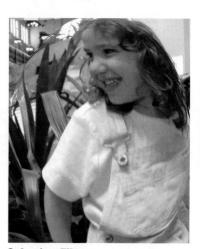

Spherize Filter

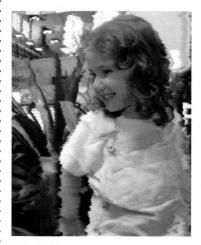

Wind Filter

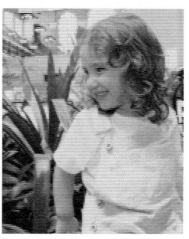

Patchwork Filter

Emboss Filter

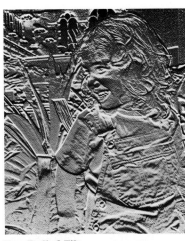

Bas Relief Filter

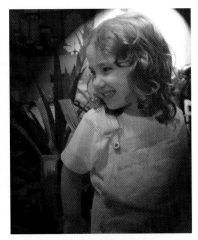

Lighting Effects Filter

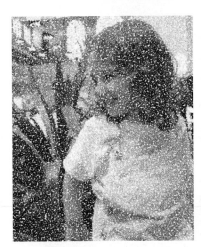

Pointillize Filter

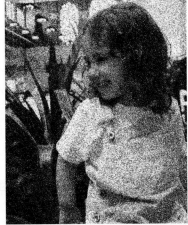

Mezzotint Filter

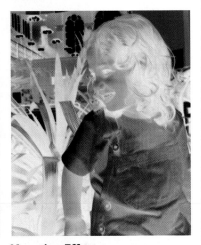

Negative Effect

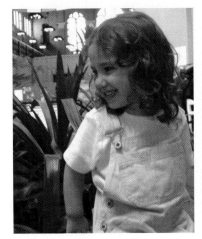

Black and White Effect

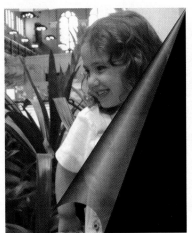

Page Curl Filter

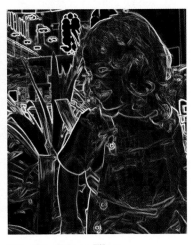

Glowing Edges Filter

Digital Photo Sampler

Enjoy Your Photos

Adobe PhotoDeluxe provides the tools you need to create fun and exciting picture projects including detailed poster work.

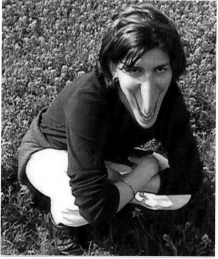

PhotoMorph project

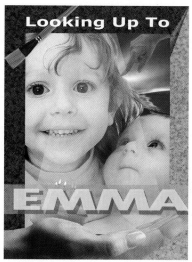

Poster project

ArcSoft's PhotoIsland Web site offers unusual photo manipulation projects. PhotoMorph allows you to stretch and bend any photograph.

Indulge yourself in a little freehand fun. Play with your photos and see where they will take you.

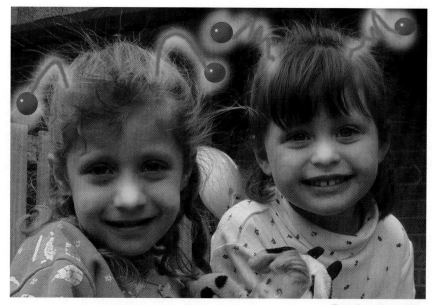

Freehand project

Cool Picture Projects

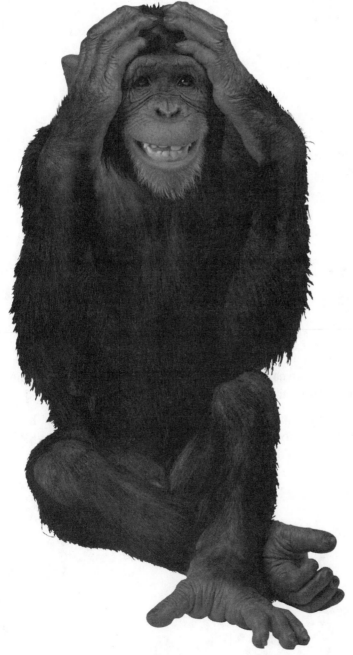

You might be surprised at what amazing things you can do with your digital pictures. I bet you didn't know that you can do all this:

◆ Launch someone into the clouds

◆ Create a slide show parade

◆ Make coloring book pages

◆ Produce calendars

◆ Animate your photos

....

NOTE For many of these projects, we'll be using Adobe PhotoDeluxe, included on the CD that accompanies this book. For instructions on using PhotoDeluxe, see the "Enhancing Your Images with PhotoDeluxe" part of this book.

36 Launch Someone into the Clouds

Do you want to liven up your images? Ask your subject to jump up and down. Perhaps you can capture that moment when both feet are off the ground and the head is tossed back in laughter. You'll be glad you did.

Once you've shot your jumping picture, you can have some fun with it using Adobe PhotoDeluxe. As an example, we'll transform a jumping subject, like the one shown on the next page, into a super-cloud-jumper.

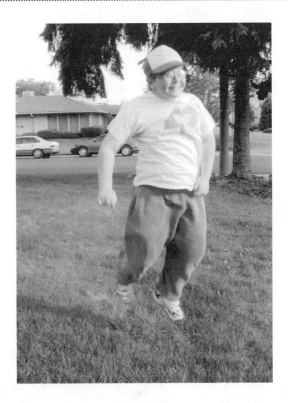

Here are the steps for launching a jumper:

1. Start PhotoDeluxe, set up power mode (click the Advanced Menus button if the advanced menus are not already displayed and show the Layers and Selection palettes), and open your jumper photo.

2. Choose SmartSelect Tool from the Selections palette and outline your subject.

3. Click the Invert button on the Selections palette to invert your selection. It should now outline every photo element except your subject.

4. Select Effects ➢ Feather and choose a high feathering value, such as 10. Click Delete Selection, and then click OK. This invert-and-feather process creates a feathered selection that eliminates any unwanted background intrusions. In this example, it ensures that no grass, trees, cars, or houses will intrude into your selection.

5. On the Layers palette, double-click this layer, label it **Base Image**, and click OK.

6. Drag this layer to the paper icon at the bottom of the Layers palette to create a copy. Rename this copied layer **Blurred Image**.

7. Click the Blurred Image layer to select and display it. Then click the All button on the Selections palette.

8. Select Effects ➤ Blur ➤ Motion Blur. Rotate the blur angle to produce a blur angled along the same general lines as your jumper. Select a large distance, such as 300 to 600, to blur widely, as shown below.

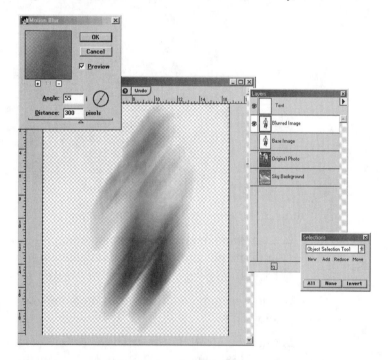

9. Make sure that both your Base Image and Blurred Image layers are displayed. Click the rectangle to the left of each layer on the Layers palette until the small eye appears. Then click Blurred Image to make it your active layer.

10. Select Trace Tool from the Selections palette. Use this tool to select the blur in front and above your jumping subject, as shown next.

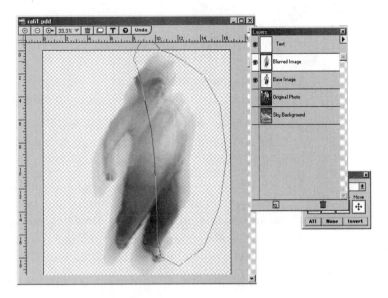

11. Press the Delete key to remove the excess blur.

12. Drag the Blurred Image layer below the Base Image layer. The blur should now trail behind your subject, as shown below.

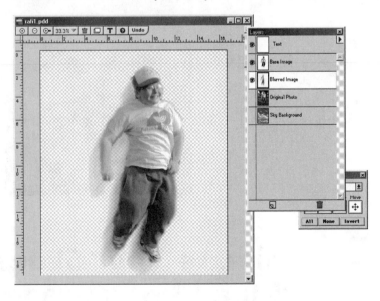

13. Optionally, you can intensify the blurred image by copying it. Just drag it to the paper icon on the lower left of the Layers palette.

14. Select File ≻ Open Special ≻ Get Sample Photo. Choose a scene or background for your subject. In this example, we use the Clouds photo as a background.

15. Drag the background to your picture, resize it to cover the image, and move its layer behind your subject and the motion blur.

16. Click the arrow to the right of the Text layer on the Layers palette and choose Merge Layers to merge the background and jumper into a single layer.

17. Select Effects ≻ Render ≻ Lighting Effects and add some dramatic lighting from the direction of movement. The light source derives from where the line crosses the oval. Drag this intersection to set your light. Drag the oval wider for more light; drag the oval thinner for less light. When you're satisfied with the effect, click OK.

You have now lifted your jumping subject into the clouds.

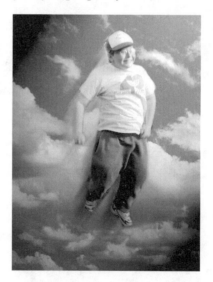

37 Animate Your Slideshow with a PhotoParade

If you want to create slideshows with your digital images, you don't need to settle for the dull and usual. Photo parades add a whole new twist to your slideshows.

With a photo parade, your digital photos appear as part of a high-quality animated cartoon, as shown below. I'm not talking clunky just-cute-enough cartoons, but slick, professional stuff. It's really too cool to describe, so I'll have to recommend that you try it yourself. Fortunately, you can. PhotoParade is a commercial product that comes bundled with Adobe PhotoDeluxe and is yours for free! Just install PhotoDeluxe from the CD that accompanies this book.

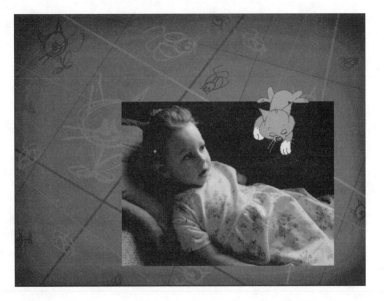

Create Your Own PhotoParade

After you've decided which pictures you want in your photo parade, you're ready to get them marching. Here's how:

1. Start PhotoDeluxe and click the Cards & More tab on the activity bar. Then select PhotoParade ➢ Create a PhotoParade.

2. Click Gallery ➢ Open Gallery. The My Photos gallery will appear, automatically switching you to the PhotoParade section.

3. Click Photos ➢ Add Photo. The standard Windows open file dialog box appears. You're now ready to add images to your parade. You can add and arrange pictures as follows:

◆ You don't need to select and open your images one at a time. Instead, just drag each image to the gallery. You can do this while the open file dialog box is open.

◆ To remove a photo from the gallery, click it and press the Delete key. You don't need to use the Remove Photo button or any special interactive procedure. Again, you can do this while the open file dialog box is open.

◆ To reorder an image in the gallery, just drag it to its new location. As with adding and removing images, you can do this while the open file dialog box is active.

◆ If you wish, you can drag files from any Windows directory directly to the gallery and bypass the open file dialog box entirely.

4. When you're finished adding pictures, close the open file dialog box. Click Cancel or the Close button (in the upper-right corner of the dialog box).

5. Click Captions. If you like, you may rename and caption each image in your photo parade. To do this, select an image and click Add Caption.

NOTE Captions and titles do not appear in most photo parades, but they do appear in Carousel mode (which presents a simple slideshow). If you plan to present a plain slideshow without animation, make sure to properly annotate your images.

6. Click Theme. The PhotoParade software bundled with PhotoDeluxe arrives with four themes: Birthday Magic Show, Cubism, Kitty Playtime, and Underwater World. For this example, select Kitty Playtime (my favorite) from the Choose Theme drop-down list.

7. Click Build ➤ Build PhotoParade. You can safely ignore the whole Segment Size drop-down list. Save your parade in your favorite folder as **MyParade.PhP** and click OK.

8. Wait for your parade to build. This may take several minutes. As with other PhotoDeluxe operations, a progress bar appears at the bottom of the screen during the process.

9. When the parade has been built, a confirmation message will appear. Click OK.

10. To see the results, click Play ➤ Play PhotoParade. Sit back and enjoy the music, pictures, animation, and sound effects.

N O T E   You can switch from your animated photo parade to a simple slideshow at any time. Tap the Escape key, and then click Carousel ➢ Play.

You can accessorize your photo parades by stopping by the PhotoParade Web site at www.photoparade.com. Browse the catalog and download software updates. At this site, you can purchase additional parades and parade packages for a small fee. Parade themes range from special occasions like birthdays or Mother's Day, to humor, to an "out-of-this-world" space adventure.

Share Your PhotoParade Project

Sharing your photo parades with friends is easy. Just place your PhotoParade (.PhP) file on a disk along with the player. You will find the player installer file, PhPSetup.exe, on the CD in PhotoDeluxe's Extras\PhotoPrd folder. Your friends can then install and run the player and view your parade. You may want to use a Zip disk or a CD-R, because these files can run to the multiple megabytes.

N O T E   For those of you with access to an NTSC scan converter or a video card that produces NTSC output, you can hook up your computer to a VCR and save your parade to video! Make sure to hook up the audio track, too. If you're not sure if your video card supports NTSC output, check to see if it has SVHS or RCA connectors. You can generally buy a video card with RCA output for about $50 at most office supply stores.

38 Create a Coloring Book from Digital Photos

Do you have a special child in your life? Here's a cute project that you can share: Convert your digital photos into a coloring book. Let your child, or the child in yourself, express his or her artistic side.

For this project, pick a few simple images, The best images will contain strong, clear subjects with few textures and patterns, like the nature shot shown below. Then use Adobe PhotoDeluxe to transform the images into black-and-white pictures, ready for coloring.

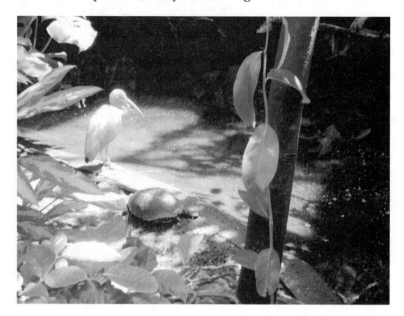

After you've selected your coloring book candidates, follow these steps:

1. Fire up PhotoDeluxe, set up power mode, and open your photo.

2. Select Quality ➢ Instant Fix to automatically enhance the brightness and contrast.

3. Click the All button on the Selections palette.

4. To transform this image into a black-and-white picture, select Effects ➢ Color to Black/White.

5. Select Effects ➢ Blur ➢ Blur More. Then select it again to repeat the blurring operation. This will smooth all the fine, noisy textures in your image, while leaving the strong edges untouched.

6. Select Quality ➢ Brightness/Contrast. Move the contrast up by about 50 and click OK. This will emphasize the image contrast.

7. To transform the image into a line drawing, select Effects ➢ Stylize ➢ Find Edges.

8. Print your coloring book page.

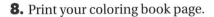

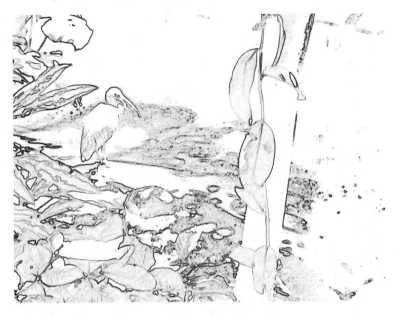

You can follow these directions for each page. When you're finished, staple the pages together to make a special gift for your little one.

39 Feature Your Photo on a Calendar

If your cutie is a real pinup, why not make a calendar to show him or her off? Let PhotoDeluxe transform your photo into a calendar. It takes only a few steps and produces some great-looking results. You can use these calendars for the home, for the office, or even for gifts.

Here's how you can create a (dated) cheesecake of your own:

1. Open your snapshot in PhotoDeluxe.

2. Click the Cards & More activity bar tab and select Calendars ➢ Monthly Calendars.

3. Click 1 - Month and select a month, such as February. Click OK.

4. Click 2 - Year and select your year, such as 2002.

5. Click 3 - Layout ≻ Choose Layout. Select a nice layout (I like the Tall/Above layout). Double-click the layout and wait for it to load.

6. Click 4 - Style ≻ Choose Style. Pick your style, such as Style 2, and double-click.

7. Click 5 - Add. Double-click your original snapshot. It should be minimized and stored in the Open Photos bin. When you double-click it, PhotoDeluxe automatically adds it to the calendar template.

8. Click 6 - Edit and adjust your picture as needed. Move, resize, and rotate it until everything looks just right.

9. Click 7 - Done.

10. Print and enjoy your calendar page.

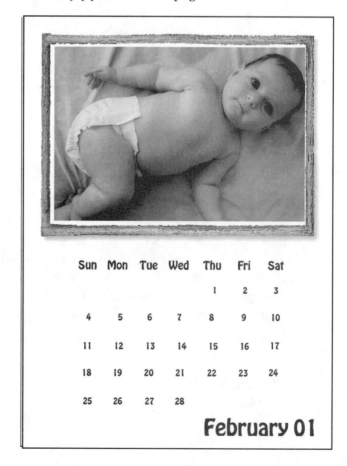

40 Add Animation to Your Photos with GIF Animator

Way, way long ago (in the late 1980s), there once was a fairly brilliant person, or to be more accurate, a fairly brilliant committee. This person/committee, almost as an afterthought, decided to include animation in a new graphic file format. This standard came to be known as GIF89a. For a long time, no one could figure out what to do with this ability, so everyone more or less ignored it. Then along came the World Wide Web. Someone remembered that GIF images supported animation. People started building animation support into their Web browsers, and presto—GIF animation took off like wildfire. Everybody wanted Web pages that moved, and GIF gave it to them.

 Fast-forward to 2002, and we're still using GIF89a animation to add motion and interest to our Web pages. Don't feel left out. You, too, can easily create animations. Between PhotoDeluxe and Ulead's GIF Animator, you have all of the tools that you need (and both are on the CD that accompanies this book).

The GIF Animator Roadmap

After you've installed GIF Animator, you can start up the program. Don't be put off by the confusing GIF Animator main window, shown below. Although the design is a little confusing, the program is powerful, and it's much easier to use than it first appears.

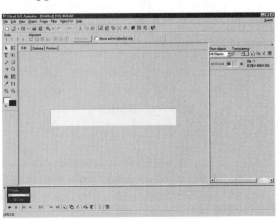

Look for these key features in the main GIF Animator window:

◆ The main workspace contains your GIF image. By default, a white rectangle appears in this space. When you load your image, it replaces the rectangle.

◆ The three control tabs located directly above the main workspace allow you to select a task. Click the appropriate tab to edit your image, optimize for output, or preview the animation in an uncluttered "full-screen" mode

◆ Animations are composed of a series of frames. The frames timeline appears at the bottom of the window. You can play these frames to view your animation. Simple controls (Play and Stop, First Frame, Previous Frame, Next Frame and Final Frame) appear just below the timeline.

◆ Each frame is composed of one or more images, called "objects." Object information is stored to the right of the main workspace and includes all loaded images. The small "eye" icon indicates which objects are visible for each frame. (If you wish, you can simplify this display by selecting Visible Only from the Show objects pull-down menu.) This window updates as you step through the animation, reflecting all visible images for each frame.

◆ The tool panel appears to the left of the main workspace. This palette provides basic image editing functions for GIF animator. You will, for the most part, not need to use this as this book uses PhotoDeluxe for all image editing tasks.

◆ The Attribute toolbar, which rests just above the main workspace, allows you to control layout and alignment for frames with multiple objects.

◆ The Standard toolbar rests just under the menu. This toolbar includes a series of incomprehensible icons that allow you to perform most of the more common animation functions without going through the menus. To determine what each button does, move the mouse over the icon and wait a second. A helpful pop-up message will appear with a clarifying note.

N O T E   If you need more space to work in GIF Animator, feel free to hide the Standard and Palette toolbars. You can turn these off from the View menu.

Animating a Photo: A Step-by-Step Guide

GIF Animator provides all of the tools you need to create animations. You simply load a single image into GIF Animator and allow the program to add special effects. Save the results, and you're finished—instant animation!

Here's a simple example of how you can animate a photo:

1. Fire up GIF Animator. Select File ➢ Open Image and load your picture. GIF Animator will import a wide variety of formats, including BMP and JPEG, among others. To see the full list, select the Files of Type pull-down menu from the Open Image File dialog box.

2. Now we'll add a basic video effect. Select Video F/X ➢ 3D ➢ Gate-3D to bring up the Add Effects dialog box, as shown below. Click OK. This will add a series of 15 transitions to your image that make it appear as if the photo is rotating away from the viewer.

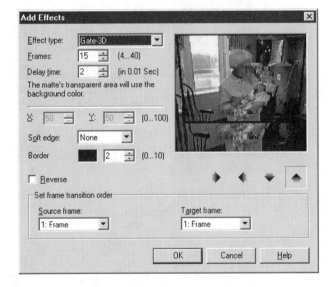

3. Now we'll add a delay to the first image. This will insert a pause at original image between animation cycles. Select the first frame and click on it with the right mouse button Choose Frame Properties from the pop-up menu. Enter **300** for a 3-second delay and click OK.

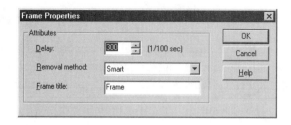

4. You can now preview your animation. Press the Play button, at the bottom left of the timeline. (It looks like a right-facing triangle.) After viewing, press the Stop button (small square).

5. Now we'll reverse the animation to make it appear as if the picture is arriving rather than departing. Right-click any frame. Select Reverse Frame Order from the pop-up menu. A small dialog box will appear. Confirm that you've selected Reverse the Order of the Entire Animation and click OK.

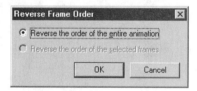

6. Again, click the Play button to view the animation and make sure it works as expected. Then click the Stop button to leave the preview mode.

7. Now click the Optimize tab. GIF Animator will automatically optimize your animation for output.

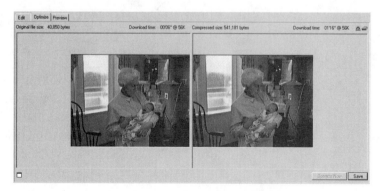

8. (Optional) If you like, click the Play button to view the original and optimized versions playback side-by-side in the main window. Click Stop to end the preview.

9. Click the Save button in the lower-right corner of the Optimize window. Navigate to where you wish to save your animation, enter a name and click Save.

10. To view your image, fire up your Web browser and open the location `file:///C:/`. This corresponds to the top level of your C: disk. Navigate your way down to where you've saved your animation and double-click it.

Add Text Effects with GIF Animator

In addition to cool 3-D effects, GIF Animator also offers a suite of text tools. You can add animated banner text to your photos. Use these banners for all sorts of effects. You can wish someone a happy birthday, identify the image subject, caption the image, and so on. Here's how:

1. Fire up GIF Animator. Select File , Open Image and load your image.

2. Select Frame ➤ Add Banner Text.

3. Enter the text you want to appear with the animation in the text field. Use the controls provided to change the font, size, alignment and so forth associated with your banner text.

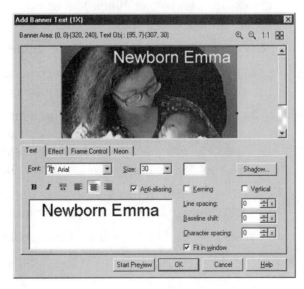

4. Click the Effect Tab and choose a pair of effects from the two scrolling lists. These options add the way the text enters and leaves the scene. I'm partial to the Fade effect. You may click the Start Preview button at any time to preview your selections. Click again to stop the preview.

5. Click OK and choose "Create as Banner Text (Recommended)" from the pop-up list. GIF Animator will add the new banner to your image.

6. Click the Optimize tab, and then click the Save button in the lower-corner of the main window. Navigate to where you wish to save your animation and click Save.

7. To view your image, fire up your Web browser and open the location `file:///C:/`. Navigate your way down to your animation and double-click it.

"The Active Hat": An Animation Using PhotoDeluxe and GIF Animator

For our next project, we'll use PhotoDeluxe's Changeables feature to add an active hat to your subject. Then we'll move the image into GIF Animator to animate the images. When you flip through these images, the droopy "changeable" hat will appear to stand up on its own.

A forward-facing shot with plenty of headroom will work best for this animation. Also, you should select a small image. Aim for a photo no larger than 360 pixels in either dimension. One of the keys to GIF animation is to create a simple image with a few changing elements.

Here are the steps for creating the animation in PhotoDeluxe:

1. Fire up PhotoDeluxe, set up power mode (display the advanced menus, Layers palette, and Selections palette), and load your image.

2. Start by extracting your subject from the background. Choose Smart-Select Tool from the Selections palette and outline the figure. Then select Effects ➢ Feather, feather your selection a few pixels out (say, 5), click Delete Background, and click OK.

3. If you need more headroom, select Object Selection Tool from the Selections palette and drag your figure downwards.

4. Select File ➢ Open Special ➢ Changeables. Double-click the cap.

5. Start with a very "asleep" hat. (In each successive step, you'll add a hat that's more alert.) In the Changeable dialog box, move the Style slider about two-thirds of the way to the right, and the Awake – Asleep slider all the way to the right, as shown below. Then click OK.

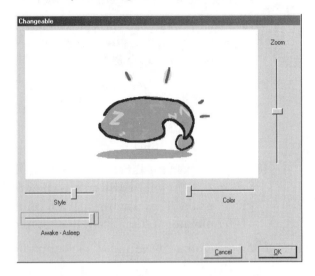

6. Drag the cap onto your image to create your first hat layer.

7. Repeat steps 4 through 6 for a series of three or four additional caps. Make each cap more alert than the one before it. Below is an example of the third hat in the series.

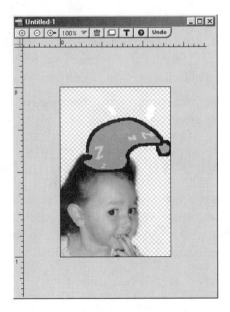

8. On the Layers palette, click the eye icon to the left of each layer except the one that contains your picture with the first cap to hide all of the layers except that one.

9. Select File ➤ Export ➤ GIF89a Export and save your image.

10. For each remaining cap, repeat steps 8 and 9 to create an image and save it. You're now ready to create your animation using the "cells" you just produced in PhotoDeluxe.

11. Minimize PhotoDeluxe and fire up GIF Animator.

12. Select File ➤ Open Image and navigate to your first image. Select it and click Open. Your image will appear in the main workspace and as a frame in the timeline.

13. Right-click in the timeline and select Add Frame from the pop-up menu. GIF Animator will create a new frame and automatically select it. Press the Insert key, navigate to your next image and click Open. GIF Animator automatically loads it into the selected frame.

14. Repeat until you've added all your photos (in order, please!) to your animation.

15. Click the Play button to see your animation in action. Click Stop to finish the playback.

16. Click the Optimize button and press the Save button in the lower-right corner of the Optimize window.

17. Navigate to where you wish to save your animation and click Save.

18. To view your image, start your Web browser and open the location `file:///C:/`. Navigate your way down to your animation and double-click it.

Keep your current setup, because we're going to try another animation in the next project.

Add a Wink to Your Animation

Are you feeling a little mischievous? Why not add a little animated wink to your picture? Winks are easy to simulate. Just smudge shut an eye and add the "wink" to your animation for the briefest time possible.

To see how this works, we'll add a wink to one of the hatted images we created in the previous section. Here are the steps:

1. Maximize PhotoDeluxe. Copy one of your original figures by pulling the layer down to the paper icon on the bottom-left of the Layers palette.

2. Select Tools ➤ Smudge. Choose a brush that approximately matches the size of your subject's iris.

3. From *above* the eye, smudge down the skin onto the eye until you've created a wink, as shown in the example below. You need not create a perfect artistic rendering. Just the suggestion of a wink is all that you need. The animation will display this image very briefly. Do not fret over a slightly sloppy result.

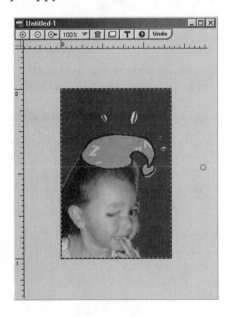

4. Select File ➤ Export ➤ GIF89a Export and save your image.

5. Import both the original and the wink image into GIF Animator, as you did in the previous section.

6. Right-click your original image and choose Frame Properties from the pop-up menu. Enter **300** for the Delay option in the Attribute toolbar. At the end of each 3-second interval, your image will wink—briefly!

7. Click the Play button to see your animation in action. Click Stop to finish the playback.

8. Click the Optimize button and press the Save button in the lower-right corner of the Optimize window.

9. Navigate to where you wish to save your animation and click Save.

Share Your Animations via E-Mail

You've created some great animations. Why not share them by e-mail? Here's how:

1. With your animation open in GIF Animator, select File ➤ Export ➤ As Animation Package (EXE). This brings up the Export Animation Package dialog box.

2. Choose how many times your image will loop, or select Loop Infinitely.

3. Select a message box, such as Memo.emf, from the Message Box Styles list and add a message, as shown below.

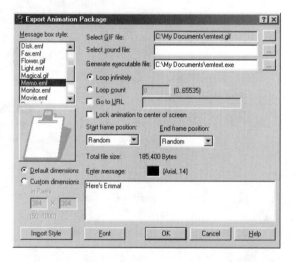

4. Click OK to save your animation.

5. Attach the .exe file you've created to an e-mail message and send it to your friends.

When your friends receive your animation package, they can run it and enjoy your creativity. They do not need any special browser or program. The file you created is a self-contained executable, which means you can just double-click its icon to run it.

New Viewpoints: Postprocessing Your Images

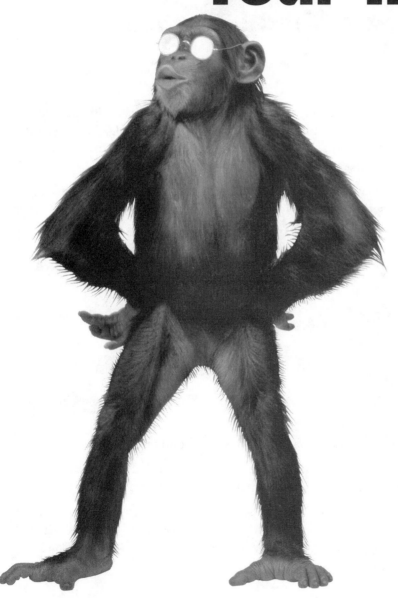

With your computer, you can postprocess your digital images to look at them in novel ways. By using special software, you can create panoramic views, murals, 3-D models, and entire 3-D scenes. You can even blow up your digital images to poster size or larger. Let your computer's processing power calculate new viewpoints for your digital snapshots.

41 What a Vista! Create Panoramas

Does your vision exceed your viewfinder? Does your resolution fall short of your landscape? Sometimes, we come across scenes so big, detailed, or geometrically complex, we cannot hope to photograph them in their entirety—or at least with just one picture.

Panoramas can capture a greater whole. With panoramas, you can stitch together a series of images to produce a composite image of arbitrary size. Panoramas create a wider reality than any single image can hope to show. For example, a panorama can present the entire arc of a rainbow, as shown below.

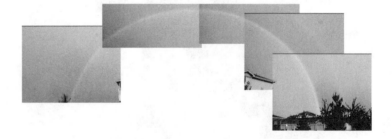

You may run across two basic varieties of panoramas:

◆ The more common row-type is generally referred to as a *vista*. To produce a simple vista, you stitch together a linear series of pictures.

◆ A two-dimensional version is called a *quilt*. Quilts are made up of photos snapped in two dimensions, both rows and columns. Stitched together, side by side and up and down, these form a full mosaic.

When you create a panorama, you can either work by hand or with a special-purpose program that stitches your image for you. Each has its advantages. Working by hand is essentially free. It can be done quickly in almost any image-processing program. It also allows you to stitch quilts, a capability that many stitching programs lack.

In contrast, a stitching program creates much better results without the obvious edges you'll find in homemade panoramas. It automatically handles image rotation and warping caused by camera angle, unsteady hands, and varying lens properties. Stitching programs range from freeware to quite costly commercial products. They generally produce superb results, but you may need to wait a while for your panorama to process.

Panoramas with PhotoDeluxe

You can create your own panorama using Adobe PhotoDeluxe. Take out your digital camera and snap a few pictures along some natural line.

After you've taken your panoramic shots, follow these steps:

1. Fire up PhotoDeluxe and set up PhotoDeluxe in power mode (display the advanced menus, Layers palette, and Selections palette).

N O T E   See the "Enhancing Your Images with PhotoDeluxe" section of this book for information about setting up PhotoDeluxe power mode and using other PhotoDeluxe features.

2. Create a new, large, blank image in PhotoDeluxe. Select an image size larger than you think you'll ever need space for. You can always crop it down later.

3. One by one, copy your images into separate layers. Open each image, copy it, and paste it into the panorama image. PhotoDeluxe will create a layer for each pasted copy.

4. Use PhotoDeluxe's move and rotate features to arrange your images. Make sure that common features align correctly. If you need to see both layers at once, double-click the upper layer and reduce the layer transparency to 50%. Align the layer and then make it opaque again.

5. Merge the image layers. Click the right-pointing arrow below the Close button on the Layers palette (to the right of the Text layer) and select Merge Layers. This will collapse your image into a single layer.

6. Click the Get & Fix Photo tab of the activity bar and select Rotate & Size ➢ Trim & Size.

7. Click 1 - Trim ➢ Trim. Outline the final image, omitting the uneven edges. Then click OK.

8. Click 2 - Done to complete the task.

This method provides a simple way to create a panorama. However, it almost always produces natural flaws. Take a look at the image shown below. The rectangles highlight the obvious stitching errors: the clouds that moved between the shots, slight rotation errors where the tree does not line up with itself, and the lighting gradient between the right and left edges of each image.

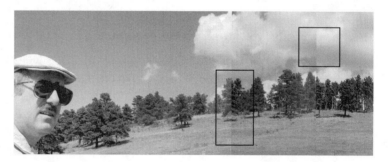

Panoramas with PhotoVista

Compare the results of creating a panorama in PhotoDeluxe (the rainbow photo) with the panorama shown on the next page, which was created with MGI® 's PhotoVista software. This software produces an almost flawless image, displaying none of the imaging errors inherent in a hand-stitching attempt.

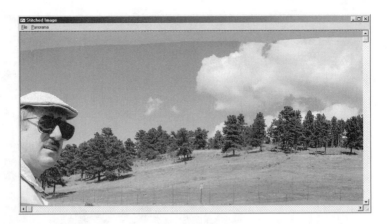

 MGI PhotoVista Virtual Tour (`www.mgisoft.com`) provides excellent panoramic vista creation and interaction software. A copy is included on the CD that accompanies this book. This software allows you to stitch panoramas into immersible views. If you like, you can then upload a special interactive version to your favorite Internet hosting site. On-site, you and your online friends can dive into your vistas. A special-purpose Java applet lets you zoom around your panorama. With just a few steps, you can create a "virtual reality" of your own.

PhotoVista stitches your photos together automatically. To create and then upload your panorama, install the PhotoVista software from the CD (see the CD's readme instructions for more information), and then follow these instructions:

1. Select File ➤ Open Source Images.

2. Select the images you wish to add and drag them to the Source Files box on the right side of the window. Then click OK.

3. If you snapped your pictures in portrait mode, click the rotation icon (the bent arrow) until your photos return to their upright and locked position.

4. If needed, drag each image into its correct position.

5. Click the camera icon, select your camera, and click OK. Your pictures are ready to stitch, as in the example shown next.

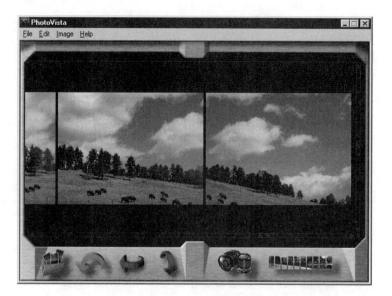

6. Click the stitch panorama icon, found at the bottom right of the screen. This icon looks like a series of upright rectangles. Doing so brings up the Stitch Options dialogue box. If you're stitching a circular panorama, make sure to check the Full 360 Degree Panorama option. You can either preview the stitch or simply click Full Stitch to create your vista.

NOTE   Other stitching options allow you to disable the warping and blending functions and to crop non-image areas from your results.

7. Wait for the stitching to finish. In the case of a full stitch, this may take several minutes.

8. Enjoy and explore your new panorama. You can move between the stitched image and the panoramic viewer by selecting from the Panorama menu. You can also print your panorama by choosing File ➤ Print View.

9. When you're satisfied with your creation, you can save it as a picture file. Choose File ➤ Save As…, choose JPEG or Bitmap, navigate to any location on the disk, name the file and click Save.

10. Having saved your picture as a flat image, you may now want to explore PhotoVista's 3-D fly-around capabilities. To continue, you must keep the Stitched_Result window open. Select Panorama ➤ Save As… and choose the Flashpix file type. Select "For Java" for Export to HTML, navigate to where you wish to save your file, name it and click Save.

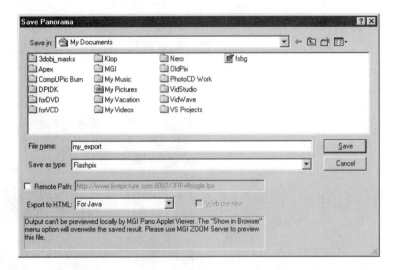

11. Choose an image quality level and click OK. The better the quality, the bigger the file size.

12. In the directory you specified, you will find four files. In the example I used in the above picture, PhotoVista created `my_export.jpg`, `my_export.ivr`, `my_export.htm`, and `panoapplet.jar`. The first three depend on the filename you specified. The last is always named "`panoapplet.jar`".

13. Upload these four files to your favorite Web hosting site or open the `my_export.htm file` locally in your Web browser. The interactive applet will appear. You can explore the panoramic view by panning through it and zooming in and out, as follows:

◆ Drag your mouse along the image, and the panorama will move in that direction. (It's a little counterintuitive, but it works.)

◆ Keep the mouse button depressed to continue panning. You don't need to move the mouse once the pan starts.

◆ As you move the mouse farther from the image center, the pan speed increases.

◆ Tap the A key to zoom in and the Z key to zoom out.

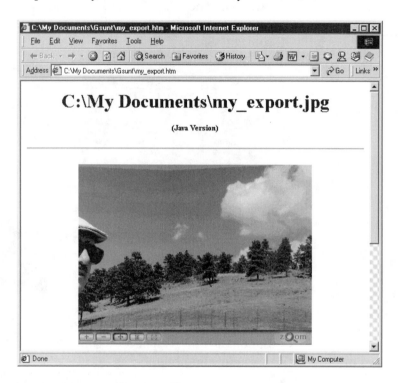

Comparing Panorama Software

MGI PhotoVista's fly-around applet does not provide the only draw for the program. Output, 3-D object creation, and virtual tours all add to its value.

PhotoVista's excellent rendering and superior output offer the most important reason to use this software. Compare the following image output, from PhotoVista, Ulead Cool 360, and Adobe Photoshop Elements. Notice the difference in quality along the blends and, particularly, among the buffalo towards the right of the picture. Only PhotoVista gets each buffalo right, without a tell-tale stitching shadow.

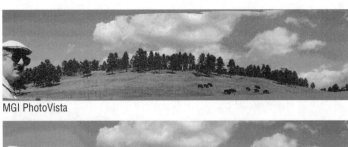

MGI PhotoVista

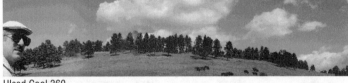

Ulead Cool 360

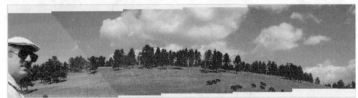

Adobe Photoshop Elements

In addition, the MGI package offers 3-D object creation and virtual tours. By photographing an object from multiple angles, you can create a "fly-around" that allows people to see the object from all sides. This can prove especially useful for those who want to buy or sell on an auction site, such as eBay. Potential buyers can see an object from many angles. The virtual tours add hotspots to your interactive panoramas so your viewers can "click through" to associated Web pages. For example, clicking on a restaurant in an image of a city street might link you to its menu. This feature takes panoramas into a whole new dimension, adding meaning and function to mere fly-around capabilities.

Low-Tech Panoramas

Are you looking for the truly low-tech approach to creating a composite image? Try this one: Snap a whole bunch of overlapping pictures that cover a small area, print them, and tape them together by hand. You can't get any more primitive than that. This method allows you to create life-size or near-life-size collages. Tons of detail result with minimal computer work.

Take a look at the baby (Sofia) next to her mural in the photo below. Of course, the fine details in this image might have worked better had she stayed asleep during the photo session. (Sometimes, it's hard to combine good lighting and no flash with a sleeping baby.) To assure uniform image distance, I laid a yardstick over the rails of her crib and used it to steady my digital camera. It's important that you don't vary the distance. When elements scale differently, they cannot be matched between photos.

I printed each image on large-sized, stiff paper, and then reassembled her on the wall. With some scotch tape, a little scissors work, and patience, I was able to create a special and unique montage.

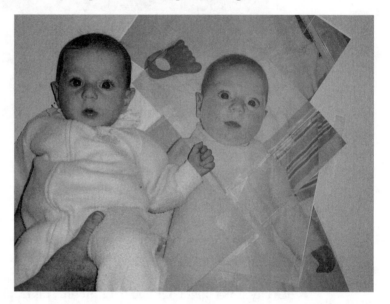

Panorama Tips

Digital cameras easily capture panoramas. Just fit pictures together with your favorite image program or stitch them in a special-purpose application. Shoot as many images as you can—the more, the better—and overlap, overlap, overlap! Here are some tips for creating panoramas:

◆ With digital cameras, you never know which picture will turn out to be the best. Image quality varies, as does color, contrast, and focus. Take many pictures to maximize your keepers.

◆ Don't try to be efficient when snapping your pictures. Trying to match image edges is a surefire way to lose important pieces of your picture. Instead, overlap and take extra shots where possible. You'll be surprised as many unimportant details become fascinating or merely helpful when you compile the collage. Remember that there's no film to waste in digital cameras.

◆ Tripods hold your digital camera steady. Admittedly, they are cumbersome and cannot be carried in your pocket the way you carry a digital camera. If you don't have a traditional tripod with you, use a makeshift object to level your camera—a flat fence-top, a friend's shoulder, or even an upright stick.

◆ Scaling occurs when pictures are taken at different distances from a relatively close object (a building, say, rather than distant mountains). Try to maintain a uniform distance from your subject when you get close up.

◆ For far-away panoramas, rotate your camera to take pictures of rainbows, mountains, or city skylines. Because they are far away, the scenery does not change significantly when you move left and right. Instead, swing your camera around a fixed point to capture a distant panorama.

◆ For nearby panoramas of murals, houses, family groups, and so forth, be careful how you move your camera. Odd angles may distort nearby objects, so you should set up your tripod parallel to the desired scene and move your camera strictly left and right, up and down, to shoot your pictures.

Cool Panorama Ideas

Panoramic vistas give us a view of the world that we normally wouldn't see. Panoramas can take place outside or inside, with multiple subjects or just a few, and very close in or very far away.

You'll be surprised at the varying ways you can use panoramas in your everyday life. Here are some ideas:

◆ If you're selling your house, use a panorama to let people "walk" around your rooms and get a better feel for the property. Create a 360-degree panorama to allow people to visualize space from any angle. Since, panoramas work both inside and outside, you can just as easily create a panorama of your living room as your backyard.

◆ When you're visiting a garden, panoramas let you get very close to a bed of flowers or a vine-laced trellis. Stitch together the small "detail" pictures, and you'll get to see all the little facets and textures that make up the planting. Detail panoramas also allow you to photograph a favorite painting or tapestry.

◆ Perhaps you need to take a picture of a large group of people, such as a graduating class or the crowd at a football game. Stitch together your images, and you've created a complete picture that offers greater image detail and a wider scope than you could possibly capture in a single snapshot.

◆ Head up to the mountains to create a panorama. Panoramas easily capture the magnificence of nature. Photograph the wide vistas as they completely surround you. Nothing works better for feeling immersed in a scene than a photo that extends beyond your natural limits of view. Whether you're on a plateau or in a valley, a panorama can capture that special feeling of "being there."

◆ If you're decorating a room, you can use a your panoramas to create a wall border or a special art piece. Let your imagination go wild!

42 Create 3-D Images

Let's put aside the camera and the software for a moment and work with our hands. Hold your thumb out at arm's length and look at it first with one eye and then the other. Notice how it seems to move a little? Now move your thumb about 6 inches away from your eye and repeat. Your thumb will seem to jump even more as you switch eyes. Put down your arm and look at some object far across the room. When you switch between your left and right eyes, it will hardly appear to move at all. This magical property is called *parallax* or *stereopsis*, and it's how we humans see three dimensions. When our eyes record slightly different positions for objects in our view, our brains go to work and figure out how far away each object lies.

"How quaint," you might be thinking as you glance surreptitiously at your watch. Don't be so blasé! This wonderful expression of optical science allows you to create your own 3-D photos. With just your digital camera and a little careful alignment, you can tame parallax.

The 3-D Key

The key to creating 3-D photos is to begin with two photos that approximate the location of our eyes. You need a left image and a right image taken at exactly the same height and orientation, but offset horizontally by about 2.5 inches. You can do this the easy way or the precise way.

Here's the easy way: Hold your camera's viewfinder up to your left eye and snap, and then transfer the viewfinder to your right eye and snap again. You need to stay very still between the two images, and you must keep the camera absolutely level. This cheap and fast method gives decent results for very little effort. It's the one that I use most of the time, particularly when I'm on vacation. For reasons that I don't even begin to understand, this technique is called the "Cha Cha" or "Rock and Roll" method.

N O T E   By changing the spacing between the images, you will change the way we see 3-D. Use a larger spacing, such as 6 or 8 inches, to make your subjects appear smaller, as if seen from a "giant's eye" viewpoint. A smaller spacing enlarges your subjects, as viewed from an "ant's eye" viewpoint.

The precise way for creating 3-D pictures requires only a tripod and a yardstick. Tape the yardstick to the ground perpendicular to your subject. Set up your tripod with two legs facing forward, each touching the yardstick. After snapping your first image, slide your tripod along the yardstick to ensure that you maintain absolute horizontal integrity. The yardstick will also help you measure the absolute change of 2.5 inches.

Whichever way you decide to snap your pictures, make sure to remember which image is right and which image is left. You'll need this information when you return to your computer and prepare your 3-D stereo pair.

N O T E   If you have the time, the money, and the will, you can purchase a special-purpose dual-CCD digital camera that takes stereo images with a single click. These cameras tend to be bought by 3-D hobbyists with a lot of money. You can see one at http://www.stereoscopy.com/3d-images/camera.html.

Side by Side

 It's easy to create a stereo pair, like the sample shown here. You just print the left image next to the right one. However, getting them both on the same page, aligned, and the right sizes may take a few steps. You can use PhotoDeluxe's sizing tools to match up your images.

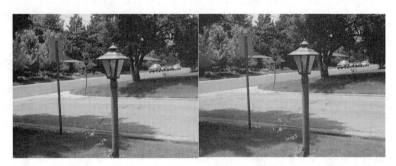

You'll want to end up with a small, sharp print. The following steps set a final print width of 6 inches, a stereo-image standard. You can choose other widths as desired. You may also opt for resolutions other than 300 pixels per inch, although this resolution provides high pixel density while shrinking the print size.

1. Start PhotoDeluxe and open your "right" image. Select Size ➤ Photo Size. Change the resolution to 300 pixels per inch and the width to 3 inches. Notice that the height resizes automatically. Click OK. Minimize the window.

2. Repeat Step 1 for the "left" image. This time, leave the window open and displayed.

3. Select Size ➤ Canvas Size. Change the width to 6 inches and click OK.

4. Drag the left image all the way to the left of the canvas.

5. Open the right image and drag a copy of it onto the right side of the canvas. Adjust the alignment as needed.

6. Save your image and print it.

Congratulations! You've just created your first stereo image pair.

Stereo Viewing

When I was in school, we learned to cross our eyes to see stereo pairs. The cross-eye method works by teaching you to focus your eyes at infinity rather than on a particular object. Do you see the two circles below? If you can relax your eyes until you see three circles rather than two, you can learn to view stereograms without a special viewer.

On the other hand, if this headache-inducing method is not for you, I offer two alternatives: You can use a commercial viewing product, or you can create your own stereo-viewing box.

Use a Lorgnette

Lorgnettes are a type of glasses with a short handle. You hold the handle and look through the lenses.

Berezin Stereo Photography Products offers a 3-D viewing lorgnette for just a few dollars. The Berezin lorgnette, shown below, allows you to view stereo pairs without effort. The special optics do all of the work for you. Just hold the lorgnette in front of your eyes (or eyeglasses) and move your stereo picture until it "pops" into 3-D. The effect is spectacular.

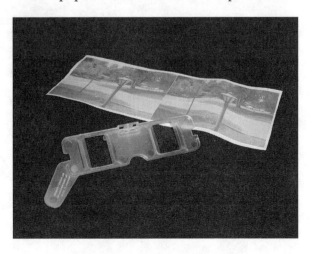

N O T E To order or get more information about the Berezin lorgnette, visit the Berezin Web site at www.berezin.com/3d.

The lorgnette arrives flat in a standard envelope. Remove it and fold down the spacer bar at the top of the unit. Hold the lorgnette by the handle and place the spacer bar at the top of your nose. With your other hand, hold the stereo image pair at arm's distance. Slowly move it back and forth until the two pictures merge into a single 3-D view. And that's all there is to it. With a lorgnette, viewing stereo pairs is a snap!

Build Your Own Viewer

Are you ready to build your own stereo viewer? All you need is a shoebox, a manila file folder, tape, and scissors. This box approximates the stereo-optiscopes that were all the rage in the nineteenth century. You can still find 3-D stereo pictures at most antique stores and auctions. In fact, there are entire books devoted to stereo images from the U.S. Civil War.

Here are step-by-step instructions for this project:

1. Cut two holes on one of the short sides of the shoe box, as illustrated below. You will look through these holes to see the pictures. Make them about three-quarters of an inch across and spaced comfortably to look through. You may also add a space to accommodate your nose so it will not press against the box.

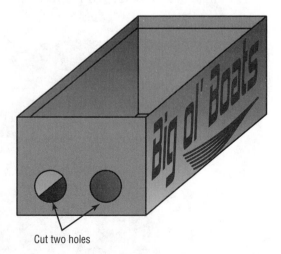

Cut two holes

2. Place the folder, with the bent side down, along the side of the box. Fold the folder top over the side, as shown next.

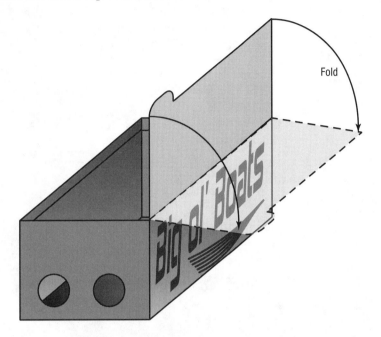

3. Staple or tape the bottom of the folder to keep it together. Open the top to make a T-shape along the crease you just made, as in the following illustration.

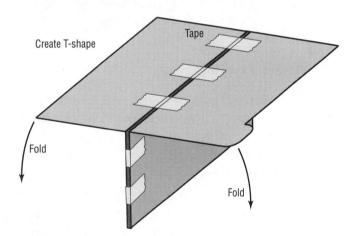

4. Tape the folder to the exact center of the box with the top of the T-shape resting on the top of the shoebox. When you look through the holes, you should now only see either one side or the other of the folder. Make sure to leave some space at the end of the box to insert your pictures and to allow light in, as shown below.

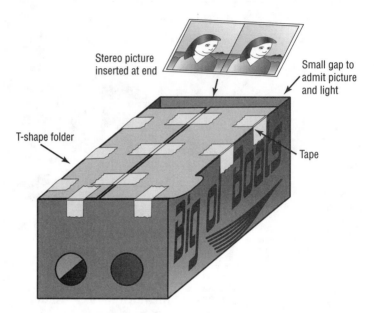

Stereo picture inserted at end

Small gap to admit picture and light

T-shape folder

Tape

5. Place your picture opposite and facing the eyeholes. Look through the eyeholes—you should be seeing in 3-D. It's not exactly a View-Master, but it works.

Stereo Prints

When you read the instructions for sizing your image pairs, you may have wondered why you needed 3 inches per stereo view. There are two reasons for this sizing. First, many historical 3-D viewers used 3-inch prints. Second, 6 inches just happens to be the width of the most common photo print, the 4 × 6–inch print.

If you've created two 3 × 3–inch stereo pictures, you can easily order prints. Just use one of the many online photo-finishing services. Combine your prints with a pair of viewing lorgnettes, and you're ready to roll out an entire stereo world of your own.

WARNING Make sure to avoid the Zoom to Fit or Zoom and Crop options when ordering your prints. You may want to fit your pictures in a black-filled 4 × 6–inch frame before uploading them.

Are you looking for a larger solution? Several online finishing sites, most notably Wolf Camera (www.wolfcamera.com), provide "panorama-sized" finishes, which are approximately 4 × 10 inches. These prints cost under a dollar and allow you to print larger-format stereo pairs.

You can read more about using online photo-finishing services in the "Some Day My Prints Will Come" part of this book. Also, see the "Field Guide to Online Photo Finishing and Album Sites" at the back of this book.

43 Blow Up Your Images

You can always recognize 35mm snobs. They pin you to a wall at parties, talk about how wonderful traditional optics are, and lecture on how digital photography will never catch up. In particular, they mention how they can enlarge their photos "to the limits of the silver-halide molecules," a feat that you can never hope to accomplish with your new-fangled (and doomed-to-obscurity) digital camera. This may have been true once, but it isn't any more.

With Genuine Fractals, an Altamira PrintPro product, your digital images can decorate the side of a barn. You can snicker at the poor 35mm camera snobs holding tight to their miserable and costly poster-sized enlargements. With Genuine Fractals, the power is digital, and it is only going to get better.

Here's how it works: The Genuine Fractals PrintPro product converts your image into a mathematical representation. The best part is that this representation is resolution-independent. With fractals, you don't deal with pixels; you deal with scalable textures. And you can scale these textures arbitrarily. The mathematical model allows you to open your pictures at any virtual resolution. You can create images ten times as large as the original or bigger.

> **N O T E** Genuine Fractals uses a special technology called *wavelets* to encode your image. Unlike other wavelet products, Genuine Fractals places emphasis on image scaling rather than file compression, although a certain degree of image compression occurs as a side effect.

Fractalize It

A demo version of Genuine Fractals PrintPro is included on the CD that accompanies this book. You'll need to install the demo so that you can try it out. Do not use the Search for the Plug-in Folder Automatically option. Instead, open your PhotoDeluxe folder. The PhotoDeluxe plug-ins folder can usually be found at C:\Program Files\PhotoDeluxe HE 3.1\PlugIns\. Select the PlugIns folder and click OK. This step creates a Genuine Fractals folder in your PlugIns directory. Drag the Genuine Fractals plug-in from the Altamira folder into the main PhotoDeluxe\PlugIns folder to complete the installation.

Once you've installed the Genuine Fractals demo, you can try it out. First, fire up PhotoDeluxe, load a picture, and save it in the Genuine Fractals format. Then you can reopen your picture and scale it.

Here are the steps for putting a picture in Genuine Fractals format:

1. Open your image in PhotoDeluxe and select File ➢ Export ➢ File Format.

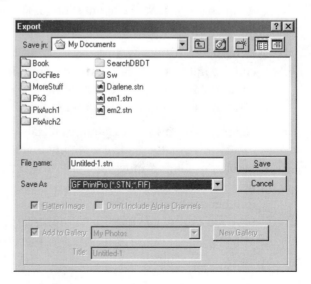

2. Choose GF PrintPro from the Save As drop-down list.

3. Name your image with the `.stn` extension and click Save to save it to disk.

4. The Altamira demo screen appears, as shown below. This screen tells you how many demo uses you have left before your demo license expires. In all, the demo allows you to open or save files 20 times. Click this screen to continue.

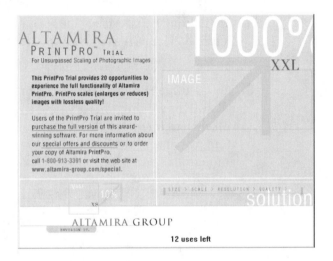

5. Choose an encoding scheme. As shown below, your choices are Lossless or Visually Lossless. Lossless takes more space but preserves image quality exactly. Visually Lossless provides more disk-efficient encoding at the price of small changes in your image. Click Save to save your file in Genuine Fractals format.

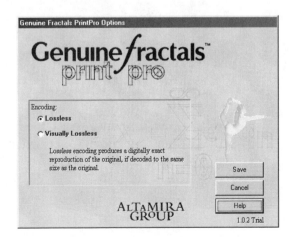

Big Is Beautiful

When you save your image using Genuine Fractals PrintPro, it converts your photos into a fractal representation and writes it out to disk. To enlarge your photo, you need to read the image back from disk. Because Genuine Fractal images are saved without pixels, each time you open a fractal file, you must re-create an image.

Here's how you can open and resize your Genuine Fractal file:

1. From PhotoDeluxe, select File ➢ Open File and double-click the Genuine Fractals file (with an .stn extension) that you wish to open.

2. The Altamira demo screen appears. Click this screen to continue.

3. The Genuine Fractals PrintPro Options window opens, as shown below. This window allows you to specify the size of the window you wish to open. For this example, in the Scale To section of the window, set the Width option to 400 percent. The Height scale will automatically update.

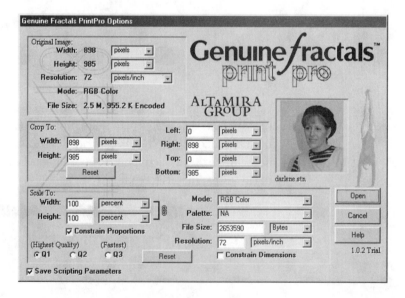

4. Click Open. Your image will open in PhotoDeluxe. The new photo will be 16 times larger than your original (both the height and width scale by a factor of four).

5. As with other PhotoDeluxe operations, a progress bar will appear at the bottom of the window. Watch this bar to estimate the amount of time left to reconstruct your photo. The larger the original photo and the larger the magnification, the more time it will take your computer to create the new image.

6. Save, print, and enjoy your enlarged image.

As an example of the results, the graphic below shows an original photo superimposed on the enlargement. Compare the sizes of the images and the excellent quality of the blown-up image. Keep in mind that the original is 1600×1200 pixels.

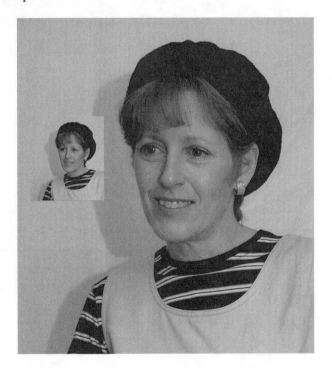

WARNING Enlarging images to excess can adversely affect your computer. Always keep your PC's memory limitations in mind. Ideally, when working with digital images, you should have as much RAM, speed, and hard disk space as you can afford. What makes up the ideal computer darkroom? It's hard to say. However, working with the image shown above regularly crashed my 96-megabyte, 366-megahertz PC.

The graphic below shows detail from the left eyes of both images above. The original image, zoomed, is on the left. The Genuine Fractal version sits to its right. I've used PhotoDeluxe's built-in resizing to expand the original to the same dimensions as the Genuine Fractals image.

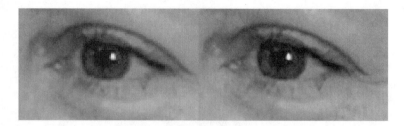

NOTE PhotoDeluxe, like many other image-editing programs, uses bicubic interpolation to guess intermediate values between pixels. The fractal results don't need to guess. They build texture from underlying patterns and lack that blocky, zoomed-in look you usually get when enlarging photos.

When using Genuine Fractals, keep in mind that it needs a fairly large picture to start with. When it creates fractals, more data means better enlargements. I've gotten terrific results with my Nikon CoolPix 800, a 1200 × 1600 pixel camera. However, I've also gotten decent enlargements from my Ricoh-2e, with only 768 × 512 pixels. Most people use Genuine Fractals with scanned pictures and negatives, but it works extremely well with digital camera shots, too.

Digital Camera Crafts

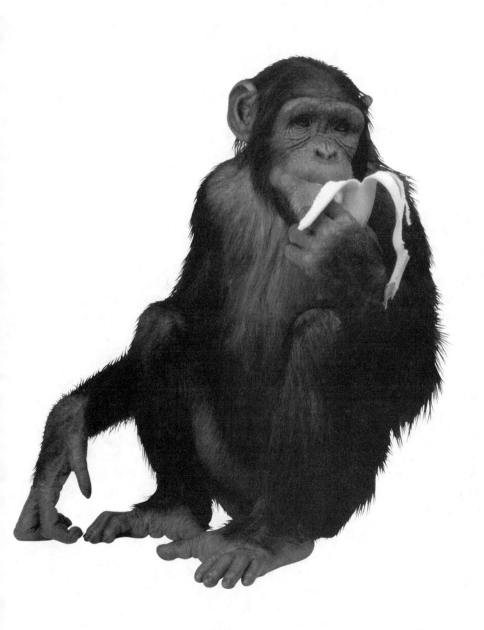

A digital camera makes the perfect companion for crafts. New and exciting materials, techniques, and equipment offer many ways to combine digital photography with your favorite hobby. Whatever your crafting area, a digital camera can probably add a personal touch to your projects.

With the supplies for your particular project, your digital camera, and, in some cases, some help from Adobe PhotoDeluxe, you can create truly personalized items. Craft projects range from iron-on appliqués to charm bracelets to tattoos.

N O T E   Adobe PhotoDeluxe is included on the CD that accompanies this book. See the "Enhancing Your Images with PhotoDeluxe" part of this book for instructions on using this photo-editing software.

44   Photo Fashions

Whether you're making presents or a fashion statement, personalized accessories are *in*! Now you can plaster the faces of your loved ones on everything from T-shirts to sneakers to handbags. Pick up a pack of photo transfers and see where your imagination can lead you.

Photo transfers transform your digital photos into iron-on appliqués. You print on the transfer, as you would print on paper, and then iron the transfer to put your photo onto fabric.

You'll find photo-transfer kits at any office supply store or major family store chain, like Wal-Mart and Target. They're usually called T-Shirt Maker kits, T-Shirt Transfers, or simply Photo Transfers. Each set usually contains between five and ten transfers and normally costs about a dollar per sheet. You can often find great bargains on these sheets by watching the Sunday newspaper ads.

Material Matters

You will find that a wide variety of materials and fashion-wear will work with your appliqués. On a recent visit to a hobby store, I made a quick list of some of the items there that accept iron-on transfers: T-shirts, baseball caps, cooks' aprons and hats, painting smocks, white denim shoes, baby bibs, totes, purses, backpacks, nightgowns, and vests. This list represents just a fraction of the items that that particular store carries. The possibilities really are nearly endless. And because the transfers are washable, you can include these items in your everyday wardrobe. Just choose, personalize, and wear.

To select an item, just keep two things in mind: the ironable area and the color. First, examine the size and location of a flat, ironable area. Remember that you must achieve good contact between the area and your iron. Small, flat portions interspersed among textured fabric may not allow your iron to reach the area fully without damaging the surrounding textures. Then you need to choose between bonding the transfer securely and harming the rest of the item. Try to avoid this situation. Look for materials that contain a large area that easily accepts ironing.

Second, select light-colored items. Do not attempt to iron a transfer onto a dark-colored background. It will subdue your image and may hide it entirely. Avoid using patterned materials. Unlike traditional iron-on transfers that can be applied to any color surface, ink-jet transfers provide tint without much substance. The hues are very thin and allow a lot of light and color to pass through. If you iron over a bright red T-shirt, you probably won't be able to see your transfer at all. Pick white, beige, or other light colors. And remember that any fabric color, however light, will bleed through your images.

Create Transfers

Making transfers is simplicity itself. It takes only a few steps:

1. Design your transfer, both text and images.

2. Prepare the transfer using Adobe PhotoDeluxe.

3. Create the transfer on your ink-jet printer. Let PhotoDeluxe's transfer-specific printing routine help you.

Although the process is easy, there are some things you can do to ensure that you're happy with the results.

Design It

Transfer material is expensive. Before you print on a transfer, take some time to think about your project and plan. Here are some suggestions:

◆ Measure your target areas and decide how big your images need to be. Be sure to leave a little extra space around the transfers to allow for complete and effective ironing.

◆ Think about text. PhotoDeluxe makes it easy to add captions. Are you giving a gift to the "Best Grandma in the World"? Plan for caption space as well as image space.

◆ Choose clip art. Small artistic flourishes can enhance your photographic images. You don't need to simply plaster a face on a T-shirt. You can surround it with borders, leaves, angels, and hearts. Survey whatever artistic clip art you have on hand and see how it might soften harsh picture borders and balance your presentation.

◆ Choose photos carefully. Pictures with a lot of background detail may not work well as transfers. Try to select good head shots taken against fairly plain backdrops. Determine in advance how you might want to crop or edit your pictures for your layout.

◆ Be big. Fashion items make their statement at a distance. Don't plan on people coming up very close and putting on their reading glasses. Select big, simple designs—both text and pictures—that can be seen and recognized easily from at least 6 feet away. For this reason, avoid using group shots for photo transfers. Individual or paired subjects work far better.

◆ Be compact. Avoid space in your transfer layouts. Extra space wastes precious transfer material. Instead, plan on cutting elements apart with scissors and applying them to different parts of your project as needed. Any un-inked transfer is effectively wasted.

Prepare It

Once you've planned your transfer, let PhotoDeluxe help you prepare it. PhotoDeluxe offers many layout and adjustment features you might otherwise overlook.

Use the following PhotoDeluxe features to prepare your photo for the transfer:

◆ Create a new canvas by selecting File ➤ New. Make the canvas the exact size you'll be printing, typically 7.5 × 10 inches. (You need to leave room for margins.) Make sure to select a good resolution that matches the power of your printer. If you skimp on resolution, your transfers may look cheesy.

◆ Turn on your rulers by selecting View ➤ Show Rulers. The rulers will help you to lay out features more precisely. Use these rulers to determine and plan the size of each iron-on element.

◆ Use Quality ➤ Instant Fix to enhance your images before adding them to your canvas.

◆ Add captions with Tools ➤ Text. Make sure to print large, bold letters using the thickest fonts you can find. The thicker the letters, the better they will look and the easier they will be to read. Arial Black makes a good caption font.

◆ Avoid the "block." Rectangular pictures with sharply defined edges generally look awful when transferred to fabric. Instead, soften the edges with feathering (select Effects ➤ Feather) for a smooth transition to the underlying fabric. Also consider using ovals rather than rectangles as your primary shape. Use the Oval tool (from the Selections palette or the Select ➤ Selection Tools submenu) to choose part of your photo, and then feather the selection to create a softer, more interesting photo.

◆ Remove backgrounds. Consider using the selection tools to entirely remove the backgrounds from your pictures. Floating heads work much better than full pictures with transfers.

◆ Add test items. If you have a little leftover space, add a few hearts or flowers that you can use later for testing. These small test features allow you to check for proper iron temperature and give you a way to perfect your transfer technique.

Print It

Printing your transfers involves little more than loading your blank sheets and letting PhotoDeluxe handle the rest. Still, there are a few things you must keep in mind:

◆ Print in reverse. When you print on a photo transfer, you're actually printing on the transfer's back. This side will touch the fabric, and a protective coating will cover it. That means you need to print your image in reverse in order for it to look right after ironing. Fortunately, PhotoDeluxe makes this a breeze. Select the Get & Fix Photo tab, choose Print ➢ Print T-Shirt Transfer ➢ 1 - T-Shirt, and then click the T-shirt icon. PhotoDeluxe will automatically print a reversed image.

◆ Test first; commit later. Paper is a lot cheaper than a photo transfer is. Print a test run on paper first. This lets you catch mistakes without wasting expensive transfer blanks.

◆ Make sure to print on the "fabric" side. When you load your transfers, take note. One side is textured; the other is smooth. The textured side accepts the ink, and the backing side will peel away after ironing. Make sure the textured size faces the ink-jet heads.

◆ Print several on a page. Consider printing several images at once. Because transfer material is expensive, consider loading up your "page" with multiple images and captions. After printing, you can cut the transfers apart and apply them to separate projects or parts of projects.

Ironing Tips

After preparing your transfers, it's time to iron them onto your fabric. Here's the most important thing you should keep in mind: *Follow the manufacturer's instructions*! Transfer material and technology vary by manufacturer. Make sure to read the instructions completely and follow them to the letter. You will achieve the best results when you work with the needs of each individual transfer type.

Here are a few other tips to keep in mind:

◆ Trim away excess transfer material. Use a pair of scissors to clip out areas that do not contain print. Transfer material is stiff. The less you apply, the better your garments will feel and look.

- Give your iron extra time to reach and settle on the right temperature. A few extra minutes will give you consistent and appropriate heat for the transfer process.

- Cut apart individual items and lay them out before committing any item to ironing.

- Test! Test! Test! If you've added a few test features to your transfer, now is the time to pull out some scrap material and test your ironing technique. The more you practice, the more likely your transfer will work correctly with your real project. Nothing is more frustrating than a bad transfer using expensive materials. Practice really does make perfect. You may need to adjust the iron's temperature or your timing to get the best result possible.

More Transfer Ideas

Don't think that the digital photo/iron-on transfer story stops at wearables. You can use transfers for all sorts of fabric-based projects. Here are just a few ideas:

- Create a friendship quilt for a pal who is about to move away, go to college, get married, or join the Army. Take a picture of each member of your circle of friends. Sew the photo panels into a quilt, and you'll have made a special treasure that will last for years. And if your friends have access to a computer, they can personalize their panels with their thoughts, memories, and best wishes.

- Make a family book. Iron pictures of each family member onto a long strip of cloth. Fold it into a book and run a seam along the binding. It makes a wonderful gift for a toddler!

- Personalize sheets and pillowcases. Are you sending little Susie to summer camp? Keep your family as close as her cheek. Iron a picture of the whole clan onto your child's pillowcase. Who needs power heroes when you've got mom, dad, and the dog on your pillowcase?

N O T E   The textile fun doesn't end with iron-ons. Many computer-controlled sewing projects (such as knitting machines and embroidery attachments for sewing machines) now allow you to import digital photos into their setup programs. You can embroider your face on Junior's polo shirt—what an idea!

45 Lamination Creations

With a laminating machine, you can make some very creative gifts. Laminated items are durable, waterproof, and make excellent craft projects. If you don't happen to own a laminating machine, don't despair. Many office supply stores will do the lamination work for you.

Sports Legends

A popular lamination project is sports cards. You can use PhotoDeluxe to create a sports card that turns heads, and then laminate it to create a keepsake.

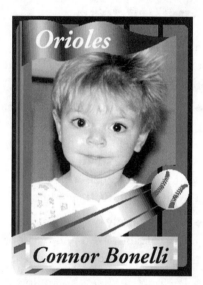

Follow these directions to create a sports card of your own:

1. Fire up PhotoDeluxe and click the Cards & More tab of the activity bar. Then click Cards ➤ Sports Cards.

2. Click 1 - Choose Sports Card ➤ Choose Card and select a card (for example, the baseball template) by double-clicking it.

3. Click 2 - Add ➤ Open File. Select an image file from your computer and open it. PhotoDeluxe will automatically add it to your template.

4. Click 3 - Edit and adjust your picture to better fit the sports card.

5. Double-click the default name on the card (for example, Bill Howard on the baseball card) and change it to your subject's name.

6. Double-click the team name and change it to your subject's favorite team.

7. Click 4 - Done.

8. Save and print your picture.

9. Create and print a patterned sheet for the back of the card. Any regular pattern will do. It just looks better than a plain, white back. You may want to print the sports card backing onto standard card stock. This will create a thicker and sturdier lamination.

10. Lay the photo on top of the backing. Make sure the back sheet is face down while the front is face up. Cut out the card, leaving a small border.

11. Take the finished card to your favorite office supply store and have it laminated.

More Laminated Projects

Here's an idea: Laminate photos of your entire family and cut them into circles to use as coasters. Make sure to cut out the photo circles first, before lamination. This prevents the lamination from falling apart. Afterwards you can trim the laminate material into another circle.

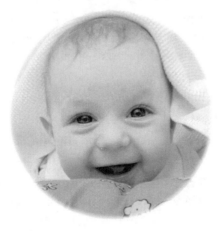

Here's another idea: Make an ID badge for your mom, your teacher, your scout troop leader, or some other favorite person in your life. This makes a terrific "thank you" for those who have touched your heart in a special way.

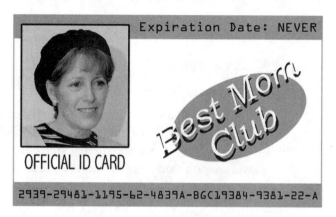

46 You're Such a Card!

PhotoDeluxe makes it easy for you to create memorable, personalized greeting cards with your digital photos. There's probably already a card designed for any occasion you might think of. And if there isn't, you can easily adapt a card template to your needs.

You can pick up good-quality, inexpensive card stock at a major family store such as Wal-Mart or Target. (Georgia-Pacific also makes very affordable offerings.) You can use plain card stock or prefolded stock, with matte or glossy quality.

Here's how you can make your own greeting card. For this example, we'll create a card for Father's Day:

1. Start PhotoDeluxe and click the Cards & More tab of the activity bar. Then select Cards ➤ Greeting Cards.

2. Click 1 - Layout. For this example, select Single Fold Side-Fold. This style allows you to print on both sides of the paper, making a card with a single fold along the left-hand side.

NOTE Double-fold cards allow you to print on a single side and fold your card into front, back, in, and out sides. However, I feel that result doesn't looks quite as nice as a single-fold card.

3. Click 2 - Style ➢ Choose Style. Select a style with a double-click. We'll use the Father2 pattern here.

4. Wait for the card to open. Click 3 - View. The Views list will appear on the right side of the card window, as shown at the top of the next page. This allows you to see and edit the front, back, and inside of your card.

5. Click Inside in the Views list to edit the inner section of your card.

6. Click 4 - Add ➢ Open File. Select a photo and open it. PhotoDeluxe will automatically add it to the inside of your card.

7. Click 5 - Edit and adjust your photo to fit the card insert.

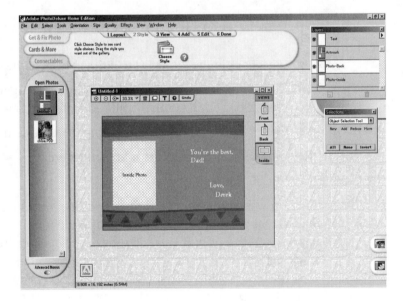

8. Double-click the default sender's name (Derek, in the case of the Father's Day card style) and change it to your own name, as in the example below.

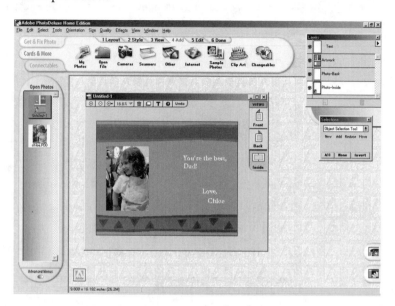

9. Click Back in the Views list to edit the back of the card.

10. Click 4 - Add ➤ Open File. Select a photo and open it. PhotoDeluxe will automatically add it to the back of your card.

11. Click 5 - Edit and adjust your photo to fit the card insert.

12. Double-click the sender's address and edit it.

13. Click 6 - Done.

You're now ready to print your card. Because you chose a single-fold card in this example, you'll need to print both sides of the card. Remove all paper from your printer and add only one sheet, preferably of good card stock. Select File ➤ Print and print your picture at the highest resolution. After the first side has printed, allow it to dry for a few minutes, and then reinsert it to print the second side. Always make sure that you've oriented the card so the second side prints correctly.

47 Get Organized with Photo Labeling

Whether you have an attic, a storeroom, a pantry, or just the natural disorder of kids, finding things you've stored can prove a real headache. Fortunately, digital cameras provide a near-perfect solution for figuring out what's inside boxes, canisters, cartons, and crates with just a glance. Snap a shot of the contents, print it, and tape it on the outside of the container. You'll be able to sort through your things with a quick visual inspection.

Labeling Tips

Picture labels are simple to make and use. Don't try to achieve artistic greatness. Focus on utility instead. Here are some tips to get you started:

◆ Picture quality matters little. You can get by with economy-mode shots and low-resolution prints. Consider printing on a laser printer (if you have one around) to save ink.

◆ Keep things simple. Use plain backgrounds when you shoot pictures. Don't lose information in the confusion of a complicated backdrop. Solid-colored sheets and blankets make excellent backdrops.

◆ Use the flash. You don't need perfect illumination when photographing a can of soup or some Legos. Your camera's flash provides excellent lighting for general-purpose needs.

Label-Mania

You can label just about anything around your home or office. Here are some examples of items that could use a photo label:

Toy boxes   Everyone knows that storing toys in individual crates helps organize a playroom. But there's one problem: Kids won't play with toys if they don't remember what's in the box. So take a picture of a representative toy and paste it on the end of the box. Now when your children look up and down the toy shelves, they'll be able to tell which box has the Legos, which one contains the Matchbox cars, and which one has the Barbies.

Boxes of clothes If you're like me, you'll have stored a half-dozen boxes, all labeled "Winter Clothes," in the attic. Consider taking a picture of some of the clothes you use the most to help identify the box. Just lay them out on your bed and take a photo. It's easy, and it sure saves time when you're in a hurry to find that one special coat.

Drawers When dealing with the preliterate or foreign-language speakers, it helps to label things with pictures rather than words. Putting a picture of a shirt on a drawer instantly communicates what-goes-where for your toddler.

Refrigerator magnets Do you want to know what's in the fridge and what needs to be bought? Take pictures of your most common staples and attach magnets to the back (also see the "Magnetic Sheets" section in number 50, "New Materials for More Photo Projects"). When you run out, move the picture from the front of the refrigerator to the side. Not only do you end up with an instant shopping list, but you also save energy by avoiding opening and closing your refrigerator repeatedly. (And you can always take a digital snapshot of the "things to buy" section and take it with you to the store!)

Folders Do you keep project and art folders for each of your kids? Why not attach a photo of each child to his or her folder. In fact, photos make great "name tags" for many things in a child-friendly household.

From Inspiration to Real-Life Expression

Lisa Kmetz read the first edition of this book and became inspired. "I took everything out of my kid's bins, grouped the contents and took pictures to make labels for the bins," she told me. "It made a huge difference in keeping that toy room clean!" It didn't stop there. She went into her son's preschool coop and evangelized there. "Cleanup time was a nightmare because none of the bins were labeled. One afternoon, we just did it. It's a simple thing, but it makes such a big difference." It turns out that a local shop was going out of business. Lisa had picked up a box of whole-sheet sticker paper for free (similar to Avery 5165, approximately $15 for a box of a hundred sheets). She printed the pictures directly to each sheet. Then she peeled the sticker off and applied it directly to the container. "It couldn't be easier," she reported.

Lisa's creativity didn't stop there. She asked her students, special-needs autistic kids, to show her different facial expressions and snapped pictures as they did. She turned these into individual "expression books," one for each kid, and has successfully used these nonverbal reminders for behavior modification. She also plans to create flashcards and labels around the house, at work and the preschool. She believes that the concrete nature of photos will help connect words with objects for better word recognition skills.

48 Capture Digital Photos from Old Prints

A few years ago, I surprised my husband and his brothers by returning home from a trip abroad with pictures of their late father—pictures they had never seen before. Finding these sorts of pictures is always providential. When an opportunity arises, you must seize it. You'll find that a digital camera can help you instantly recapture precious memories.

In this case, I had visited an elderly aunt. During our time together, she took out a large album of photos collected over the years and began to tell me stories about them. Immediately, I took out my digital camera, and as we talked, I began snapping pictures of pictures, like the one shown below.

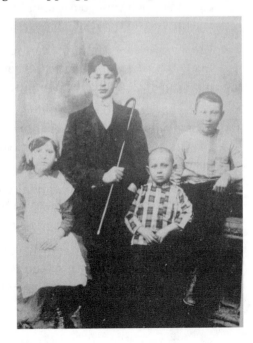

NOTE Unlike a scanner, the camera will not stress the album itself. Unfortunately, the quality of these reproductions cannot match the quality possible with even a halfway decent scanner.

Keys to Capture

Digital cameras are terrific at capturing pictures from old albums, even those faded, brittle pictures fastened to album pages with yellowing tape. You'll need good, diffuse light and your macro lens. A macro lens allows you to shoot pictures from as little as an inch or two away from your subject. Most cameras now come with a built-in macro lens. If yours doesn't have one, you can buy an external macro lens that will allow you to shoot close-ups with any digital camera. With these two things—light and lens—you can expand your personal albums and spread the wealth of your family's past.

When you work with photo albums, the following tips will help you capture better images and reproduce photos at a higher quality:

- If you can, use a scanner. Okay, I know this is a book about digital cameras. But if your goal is to hold onto family treasures, any scanner will produce better results than a snapshot of a snapshot.

- Use good, indirect lighting. Many older photos have shiny (non-matte) finishes without any surface texture to spread light. Avoid reflections by lighting the photos with a diffuse light source.

- Turn your flash off. It will produce unwanted reflections and distort your results, if not wash them out entirely. In low-light conditions, you can cover your flash with some tissue paper to create more diffuse lighting.

- Always align your camera with the curve of the page. Pictures shot off-angle will turn out distorted. Although you can partially fix these distortions with certain image-editing software, good alignment will avoid distortions from the outset.

- Get in close. Don't waste pixels on the album pages and picture mounts. Use every bit of resolution you have on the pictures themselves.

◆ Take the pictures out of their plastic sleeves. Sleeves cause unnecessary reflections and may actually obscure picture detail. Just remember which sleeve each picture came out of!

N O T E   Looking for a challenge? How about fixing up old and damaged pictures? You might be surprised by the types of skill involved. RetouchPro offers a quasi-monthly game called the Photo Restoration Challenge (it's not a contest— there are no winners) that lets you test your photo restoration skills and learn from others. Anyone can enter and there's a chat board that lets participants share techniques. Stop by www.retouchpro.com/challenge to enter. There's a lot you can learn here about retouching and restoring antique images.

Share the Memories

The quality of a "picture of a picture" will never equal that of the original. Still, the emotional impact of looking at dear ones, especially those we have lost, will always be greater than simply knowing that such pictures exist with far-off relatives and friends. Using your camera to copy photos provides an important route toward sharing and spreading the wealth of our past. Consider the following ideas for enjoying and sharing your captured album pictures:

◆ Collect your pictures on a CD-R. Share copies with family and friends. This makes a marvelous holiday gift.

◆ Use the pictures for creating computer-generated greeting cards and picture calendars. (See number 39, "Feature Your Photo on a Calendar," and number 46, "You're Such a Card!")

◆ Upload your pictures to one of the World Wide Web album sites listed in the last section of this book and share your family album with the world.

◆ Print copies of your pictures and send them to your family and friends. You can upload your "pictures of pictures" to a photo-finishing site and create new photos from them. (See the "Some Day My Prints Will Come" part of this book.)

◆ Make copies for yourself and create your own "new" photo album.

N O T E   Does grandma have special "pinch-of-this/pinch-of-that" recipes? Use your digital camera to take pictures of the ingredients and amounts as she cooks. Capture secret family recipes so that they'll never get lost.

49   Make a Photo Mood Wheel

So what's your mood today? You can let the world know in a novel and strangely fun way. Use your digital camera to capture a whole range of your moods and collect them into mood wheel. Pin the wheel outside your office or your room. Let people know what they're about to face before they have to face you.

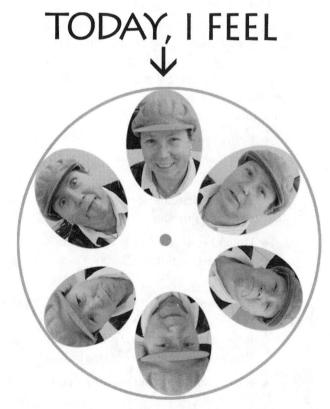

Here's how to create your own mood wheel:

1. Start by taking pictures of a number of expressions. Snap happy, sad, bewildered, angry, and tired. Transfer these pictures to your computer and print them on plain paper.

2. Grab your scissors, a paper plate, and a glue stick. Cut out each expression. Paste the photos around the outside of the plate. (Alternatively, create a file in PhotoDeluxe with all the faces on it. Add each face to a different layer in and use the Orientation ➤ Free Rotate command to orient them.)

3. Stick a thumbtack through the center of the plate, so you can rotate the plate. Add a down-pointing arrow and an appropriate caption (such as "Mood of the Day") above the plate, and you're set.

The fun doesn't stop with mood wheels. You can create all sorts of wheels. Create a chore wheel to distribute chores. Use your digital camera to shoot pictures of a broom, your toilet, and a feather duster. You'll be set to distribute sweeping, bathroom, and dusting duties to your children. Whose turn is it this week to have a special evening out with Dad? Create a wheel with pictures of your kids, and you'll know who's up next. Do you want to announce the best part of the dinner menu? Snap pictures of your vegetables and make a "wheel of roughage." Let your imagination soar!

50 New Materials for More Photo Projects

If you thought that creative ink-jet projects started and ended with glossy half-fold cards, think again. You'll be surprised by the amazing array of materials on which you can print your digital photos. Month by month, this list grows, as major manufacturers debut one new material after another.

NOTE The special materials covered here are available from many craft, office supply, and computer stores. I like to pick up my personal supplies from Michael's, Wal-Mart, Office Depot, CompUSA, and MicroCenter. Each store offers different vendors and products, so do shop around.

Window Decals

Are you looking for a novel project that will let you personalize your kitchen windows, bathroom mirrors, or candy jar? Pick up a packet of printable window decal blanks at your local office supply or craft store. This product allows you to print on a transparent, clingy medium that sticks to glass via static electricity. Just print, peel, and stick.

Ink-jet ink is very translucent. It allows light to stream through in beautiful colors. You can instantly transform the glass in your home into "stained glass" masterpieces. I love to use this product with smooth-sided mason jars. It clings like magic and makes a wonderfully unique jar, perfect for gift-giving.

NOTE When preparing window decal pictures, you might want to accentuate your photographic subject by minimizing the background. Follow the directions in number 33, "Alter Photo Backgrounds with PhotoDeluxe Tools."

Shrink Material

Shrinky Dinks were popular in the 1970s. You would cut out thin, plastic forms, decorate them with magic markers, and stick them into a toaster oven. The forms would shrink, becoming quite thick. The shrinky days are back! Use your ink-jet printer to print on print-and-shrink material, and then shrink it in your toaster or oven.

You might ask, "What good are they? Why would I want to print and shrink?" Outside the simple "coolness" factor, these shrinking craft sheets will help you make wonderful charm bracelets and necklaces. Just prepare your pictures with PhotoDeluxe, print them onto the sheets, and shrink 'em. Here's how you can make a collection of your family, your friends, your pets, or any of your favorite items:

1. Open a new 7.5 × 10–inch document in PhotoDeluxe at a resolution that matches the capabilities of your printer.

2. Add pictures of your family or friends, packed tightly onto the sheet, with just enough space for easy trimming and to accommodate a hole on top. Make sure to feather away all backgrounds (select Effects ➤ Feather) to leave just the main figures.

3. To leave space above each picture on your layout, use the Circle tool to add a hole of about ¼-inch diameter. Select Effects ➤ Outline to scribe the circle on your layout. Choose a very thick outline (say 10 or 12 pixels at least) to allow you to trim the outside while leaving space for a good-sized hole.

4. Print your pictures on the shrink material.

5. Cut out the individual pictures, making sure to include the hole on top. Trim as close to your subject's outlines as possible, leaving little extra material.

6. Use a hole puncher to remove the material within the circle to create the hole.

7. Follow the manufacturer's instructions to shrink the printed materials, transforming them into charms.

8. Wait until the shrunken charms have cooled completely before threading them to create your necklace or bracelet.

Jigsaw Puzzles

Did you know that you can print your photos as jigsaw puzzles? Just stick a special sheet into your ink-jet printer, print your photos, and peel the individual pieces away from the backing. You can make prints of the grandkids, of the dog, or of your close circle of friends.

After you've selected your puzzle photo, print it on the puzzle sheet. Then jumble the pieces up, place them in an envelope, and send them out to grandma or a special friend. They'll be in for a wonderful surprise when their mail arrives.

Adhesive Fabric

Adhesive fabric pages are a fairly new offering that show a lot of promise for crafting. The pages have a peel-and-stick backing. Unlike T-shirt transfers, which print onto stiff, ironable material, these pages allow you to print directly to soft fabric.

You can add artwork to a wide variety of projects, such as mouse pads, clock faces, photo-album covers, and so forth. Unfortunately, the fabric pages can't be laundered (use a damp sponge to clean them), so you can't apply them to clothes.

Magnetic Sheets

Make your own magnetic art and business cards with printable magnetic sheets. As you might suspect, you just print, cut, and use. You can make all sorts of projects:

Magnetic family   Trim magnetic pictures of your family members. Send these as gifts to far-away relatives.

Refrigerator reminders   Put a picture of a milk container, egg carton, and other grocery shopping items on magnetic backing.

Your calling card   Take a picture of yourself holding a large piece of paper with your phone number printed on it. Print several copies, cut them out, and give them to your neighbors.

Mr. Refrigerator Head   Print out family faces, all resized to approximately the same dimensions, cut them into parts—ears, noses, hair, and so forth—and make a magnet game for the young ones (or the young-at-heart).

Banner Paper

Banner paper allows you to print a several-foot-long sheet of paper with a single Print command. Just create the proper canvas size in PhotoDeluxe (File ➢ New lets you specify the banner size), add your pictures and text, and print. Follow the manufacturer's instructions for loading the banner paper, choosing an appropriate size, and printing.

Here are some ideas for photo banners:

◆ Print big panoramas. Follow the instructions in number 41, "What a Vista! Create Panoramas," to create your panorama.

◆ Make personalized "Welcome Back" signs. You can add pictures from the whole office.

◆ Create party greetings. Add photos appropriate to the occasion, along with the "Congratulations!"

◆ Produce extra-large baby announcements. You're not limited to "It's a girl!"—you can show her, too.

One of my favorite banner projects involves traveling around town with your digital camera. Snap photos of letters on signs wherever you go. Then build a "letter library" from these pictures. Photograph neon letters, slide-on letters, formal letters, and funky letters. When you're ready to make your banner, select individual characters from your library and add an eclectic touch to your artwork. It looks terrific, and once you've built up your collection, takes very little work to assemble.

Stickers

If your kids love stickers, you'll love print-on sticker blanks. These come in a range of sizes and shapes, including circles, rectangles, and full sheets. All you need to do is design your sticker, print to the sheet, and enjoy. Use these stickers to personalize mail, add to school projects, or whatever else you can think of.

PhotoDeluxe will let you print to most standard sticker-sheet layouts, particularly those made by Avery. Here's how to print stickers on Avery sheets:

1. Open the photo you want to make into a sticker in PhotoDeluxe. Click the Get & Fix Photo tab on the activity bar and select Print ➤ Print Multiple on a Page.

2. The Print Multiple dialog box will appear. Click the Change button.

3. Select Avery from the drop-down menu. Then select the sticker type and size you'll be using, such as 3113 - Kids Big Round Stickers (2.50" × 2.50").

4. PhotoDeluxe will automatically resize and arrange your pictures. You'll see a preview of the results. If the preview looks good, click the Print button.

5. Insert your blank sticker sheets into the ink-jet printer. From the Print dialog box, select the Best print quality and click OK to print.

Tattoos

If you're looking for the whole road hog or sideshow tattooed person look, but aren't ready to commit, ink-jet peel-off tattoos may be the answer for you. These print-on tattoo sheets offer skin-art without the risk of hepatitis. And if your children insist on decorating their arms, cheeks, or ankles with strange and exotic art, you can ask them to consider including pictures of you.

Follow these simple steps to make your tattoos:

1. As with all of the other art media, start by preparing your photos and artwork in PhotoDeluxe. Remember to keep your artwork small and sized appropriately to body parts, such as cheeks, ankles, and so forth.

2. Trim away all backgrounds and feather your selections to provide smooth edges. (Select Effects ➤ Feather.)

3. Print to the tattoo sheet and wait for it to dry.

4. Cut out each tattoo, peel it from the backing, and apply.

Wow, instant body art!

Digital Camera
Versatility

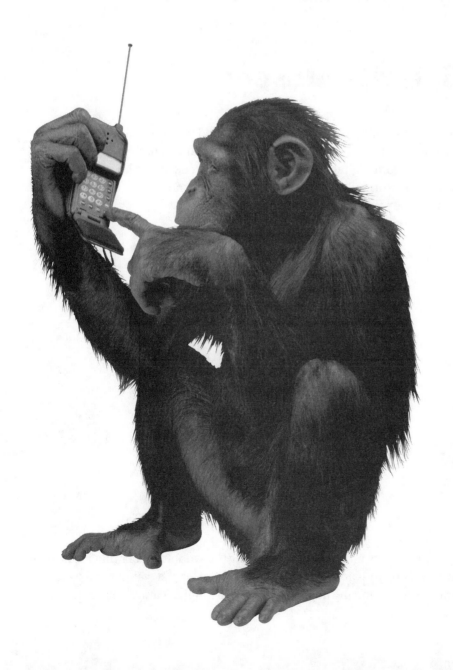

Who ever said that digital cameras were just for taking pretty pictures? You can use digital cameras for purposes you might never have imagined. These range from using your camera as a visual aid, to creating business presentations, to protecting yourself against fraud and monetary loss. The ideas presented in this part will get you started. And when you explore on your own, maybe you can teach me a digital camera trick or two.

51 See the Unseen

Your digital camera allows you to see beyond limits. Have you found that you can't fit behind a bureau? Do you wish that you had eyes behind your head? Let your digital camera come to the rescue. It can help you see things you normally could not. Just think, you can finally see a straight-on view of your own ear, as in the shot below.

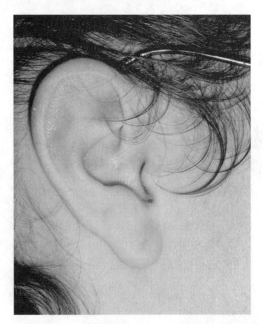

I am personally incapable of navigating the wobbly ladder that leads to our attic. When I'm searching for a particular box or just want to make a general survey, I send my husband up with the digital camera. By looking at just a few photos, I can tell him exactly what I want and where to find it. No longer do we carry on those insipid conversations. "Which box?" "The brown one, darling." "Which brown box?" "You know, the one with the tape on it, sweetheart." "Which brown box with the tape on it?" Think of your digital camera as a form of marital therapy.

Digital cameras also help out when your friend discovers something on your back. "There's something on your back." "What is it?" "I don't know something." "Does it look bad? Do I have to see a doctor?" "No, it's just a thing." "Well, take it off!" "I'm not sure I should." When your conversation reaches this level of precise description, you'll know that it's time to whip out the digital camera and have your friend take a quick picture of the part in question. (It's usually just a blemish.)

Here are some places you can let your camera do the looking:

◆ Do you want to know how your hair and dress really look from behind? Don't fuss with mirrors. Set the automatic timer on your camera, pose appropriately, and take a photo of yourself from the rear. Determine for sure if that dress really flatters your figure or if the saleslady is just being kind (and hoping for her commission).

◆ Did you hear something slide down behind the furniture, but you're not sure what it was? You can often use your digital camera to take a downward snapshot (with flash!) at an angle you could never achieve with your head. Use your camera to determine if you've lost another white sock (at least now all the rest are back to being pairs), or if you need to start fishing for your paycheck (how long did they say it would take to reissue it?).

◆ Digital cameras do a great job of seeing behind dust ruffles, too. Shoot a flash shot under the bed. See what sort of dust bunnies and third-generation slippers are creating new civilizations in your under-bed netherworld. This method works great for peeking under car seats, too.

◆ You can open up horizons in other ways, too. Use your digital camera with a magnifying glass, microscope, telescope, or loupe to explore other new worlds. That printed cotton shirt takes on a whole new look under a loupe, as you can see on the next page.

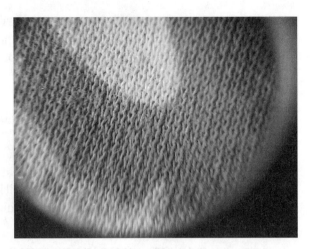

With instant viewing and no film cost, digital cameras make terrific "take-a-peek" tools for your daily life.

52 Acquire a Photographic Memory

Who needs to remember when you have a digital camera to remember for you? Your camera expands your personal memory and allows you to recall the most mundane facts without resorting to intensive brainwork.

From the merely informative to the truly treasured, you can snap all sorts of things to remember:

◆ Has a fixed-in-place map or schedule ever fascinated you? Instead of needing to abandon ready information when your bus or train arrives, snap a photo to study as you travel. Your digital camera can prove an invaluable aid when visiting strange cities and countries.

◆ Have you ever parked at a mall or an airport and forgotten where you left the car? Never forget again. Take a picture of the section and row sign, as shown on the next page, and then don't worry about it. When you're ready to return and look for your car, you'll have the parking information right at hand.

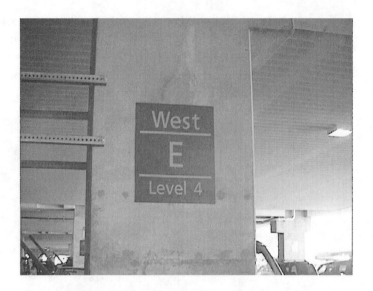

◆ Do you need to provide someone with directions to a location, but you're not sure that you remember precisely where the landmarks are? Have a family member or friend drive you to the location from the closest major highway. Take photos of landmarks along the way, and then update your directions to include these pictures. No one will miss the right turnoffs, because they'll recognize them at a glance.

◆ Have you ever been to a meeting where you came up with a terrific idea on the white board, but it was one of those old-fashioned boards that didn't make copies? Just pull out your digital camera, snap a photo or two of your notes, and make your copies back at the office. Don't let a good idea go to waste when your camera is on hand.

◆ Are you about to go grocery shopping? Take a quick snapshot of the insides of your pantry and your refrigerator. It can help you remember which items you do and do not have on hand as you're cruising up and down the store aisles.

◆ Have you ever been to a special place for the last time? Perhaps it will be sold or bulldozed. Maybe you are graduating and moving on, or maybe you're there for a once-in-a-lifetime opportunity. Let your camera capture memories for you.

◆ Does your child own a toy that looks like (or used to look like) the one shown below? Before allowing your child to play with a toy with many pieces, take a picture of the box with all the pieces in place. This has saved me many hours of head-scratching and bewilderment when faced with overly complicated toys and underlabeled boxes.

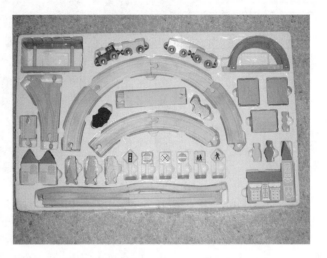

N O T E   Recently, my husband and I visited my mother-in-law's house for the final time after she passed away. We took several photos of the house, in particular the room that my husband grew up in. We knew that we would never again be able to step physically into that spot with the furnishings and memories in place. Instead, we trusted our memories to our handy digital camera so that we could share them with our family and hold onto them for the future.

53 Expanding Communication: Pictures Instead of Words

Pictures can say a thousand words. This proves especially important when communicating with the preliterate, illiterate, preverbal, and postverbal.

Whether dealing with youngsters, stroke patients, foreign nationals, or the senile, a picture can present important information in a way that language cannot. You can also use an array of photos on a single display to clearly offer choices to someone, as shown in the picture below.

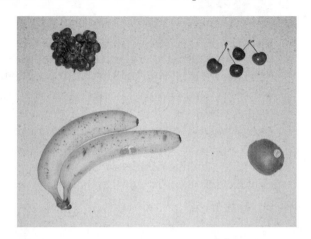

Digital cameras make it easy to transform everyday objects into visual imagery. Here are some suggestions for successful communication with your photos:

Be concrete   Make sure to photograph physical objects or realistic representations. Metaphor and abstractions work poorly in pictorial communication.

Be big   Make your pictures large and easy to recognize. Keep physical and optical limitations in mind when snapping your photos.

Be simple   Photograph objects on simple backgrounds that do not confuse or overwhelm the subject.

Ignore artistry   Communication, not elegance, is the primary motivation for these pictures. Confused tourists will not complain about inartistic snapshots of busses, taxis, and trains when seeking help at an information kiosk. Let your digital camera capture reality exactly as it is.

N O T E   People pictures are also very helpful for even the most literate and verbal. Mug-shot boards easily allow office visitors to identify department personnel. They're so simple to set up, too. Just snap a digital photo of each colleague, add a caption, print it, and pin it onto a bulletin board. These boards really help guests find the person they're looking for without unduly disturbing others.

54 Take Your Show on the Road

With your digital camera, you carry a portable presentation tool in your briefcase (or even your pocket). Most people think of digital cameras solely as image-acquisition instruments, without considering their image-display strengths. Most digital cameras can store and present graphs and slides just as easily as they can digitize images. Like personal computers, many digital cameras can connect to a variety of projection devices. Unlike computers, digital cameras are small and light. Whether you're on the road or at the office, your digital camera can make giving presentations simple and convenient.

N O T E   Are you coordinating a conference or another type of get-together? Don't overlook the photo "Hello My Name Is" badge. Adding digital photos makes it easy for participants to find their own badges. It also allows others time to browse over the badge table and connect names with faces.

Presentation Prerequisites

To give presentations, your digital camera must support both image download and display. Image download involves transferring data from your computer to either the digital camera itself or to its data card. For image display, you need either an LCD screen or a video-out port.

Image Download Support

If you can transfer pictures through a cable or write them onto a memory card and have your camera display them, you're probably set for downloading your presentation images.

Image download by cable is tedious and slow for the most part. In general, this involves hooking up your camera to your computer with a communication cable and downloading pictures one by one using the software included with your camera.

You can bypass the cable download procedure if your camera uses external memory cards or floppy disks. Just insert the cards or disks into your computer and transfer your images directly to these storage media. Make sure to follow your camera's naming protocols. Be aware that some popular digital cameras, such as the Nikon CoolPix series, require special image headers, called EXIF headers. These headers must remain intact and unmodified, just as they were saved by the camera, in order for your camera to "see" them.

Image Display Support

Your camera can support image display in either of two ways: through a built-in LCD monitor or through support for a video-out port. If your camera has either, you can drive a presentation.

LCD monitors provide convenient displays for intimate meetings with one or two others. However, the displays are small, so you'll usually need to pass the camera to each participant for a decent view.

Video-out ports, also called AV or media ports, allow your camera to create a video signal that can be displayed on a TV, a VCR, a projection system, and similar devices. Using the video-out port allows you to present to a much larger audience.

Whichever display solution you choose, it will be energy-intensive. If you intend to give presentations by camera, keep a good supply of power on hand.

N O T E   Video signals are country dependent. Current cameras support either NTSC or PAL formats, but few support both. That means the camera you use in New York City for a sales presentation may not work with Paris or Rome TV sets. The PAL format is used widely in western Europe, Japan, and Australia. Most other countries, including the United States, support NTSC. To paraphrase a government booklet on travel, "Know before you go."

Put Your Presentation Together

Preparing your presentation involves a number of steps:

◆ Create your show on a personal computer.

◆ Transfer it to your camera.

◆ Assemble your presentation materials.

◆ Practice, practice, practice.

All of these steps can take place before you ever leave your office. Together, they pave the way for smoother and less worrisome presentations.

Create and Transfer Your Slides

Create your slides using your favorite presentation software. Be sure to test your slides fully on your computer before you transfer data. Always assume that transferring the data to your camera will take substantial quantities of time, even when using memory cards. You don't want to do this more than once for your presentation. Adding and reordering slides may involve re-downloading the entire show. An ounce of preparation will save pounds, or at least hours, of downloads.

I like to create my slides in PowerPoint and Excel and save them in JPEG format, which my cameras support. To do this from PowerPoint, I select File ➢ Save As and choose JPEG File Interchange Format (*.jpg) from the Save As Type drop-down list. This allows me to save a single slide or an entire presentation as JPEG images. I rename them, copy them to my memory card, and I'm set.

N O T E   Do you have several similar but alternative presentations to give? Load each slide show onto a separate memory card. This allows you to choose just the right presentation for each audience while you're on the road.

Create a Checklist

Create a materials checklist to carry with you. This checklist should detail all of the hardware you will need for your presentation. Customize your own presentation "kit," and you will always be ready to go.

The following are some items you might want to include on your checklist:

◆ A video cable (and, perhaps, an extra one)

◆ Memory cards containing your presentations

◆ One or more power sources, such as extra batteries or a power cord

◆ An extension cord or two

◆ An alternative presentation (such as transparencies or a PowerPoint show on a floppy) in case of an emergency (like forgetting the last item on this list)

◆ A physical or a laser pointer

◆ A small, portable TV set (with batteries or cord)

◆ A camera remote control (if available)

◆ Your digital camera

The contents of a presentation checklist will vary from person to person. Some people may want to travel light; others will want the greater security and reassurance of backup hardware. No matter what your style is, making (and then checking!) a list of needed materials will prevent disaster when you are standing in front of your presentation audience.

NOTE Getting ready to pack? Don't forget your nonphotographic equipment. For example, you might want to bring a laptop computer and a portable printer. These provide you with mass storage, photo editing, communication, and printing capabilities on the road.

Practice!

Practice your presentation in a "safe" environment. You'll be surprised at how many gadgets and buttons there are on your digital camera. The correct power cords and buttons can play hide-and-seek, especially in low-light situations. Practicing with your camera will ensure that you know how to use it for your presentation and will help prevent mishaps.

Make sure to learn how to turn off your camera's image numbering and captions before giving your presentation. Captions—such as the picture number and the time and date the picture was taken—will obscure your pictures and distract your audience. Image numbers cover a large part of the image.

It's surprising how hard it is to gesticulate while holding a digital camera with cords poking out of it in all directions. Your tests may prompt you to use batteries rather than an A/C power cord, or encourage you to buy one of the manufacturer's remote control devices. These free up your hands.

55 Take Notes with Your Camera

Here's a common scenario: You're sitting at a doctor's office reading a magazine, and you come across an item that you want to remember. You consider reaching for your pen and notepad or your PalmPilot to jot it down, but then decide that maybe it isn't worth the effort. Here's where your digital camera can help. Take a picture of that article, quote, Web address, or other item of interest. Let your camera take notes for you. Later, when you're back at the office or at home, use an OCR (Optical Character Recognition) package to recover the text from your photos.

Yes, you can use digital snapshots with OCR. The snapshots will not match the quality of a well-scanned page, but with your digital camera, you can capture a paragraph or two of text.

OCR Test Results

I've tested the OCR method extensively, just to prove it can be done. My goals were to capture one to two paragraphs of text in either a newspaper or a magazine with a hand-held digital camera. I tried to simulate a traveler coming across a particularly interesting article with a few facts or a quote to archive. For my testing, I used a Nikon CoolPix 800 and a copy of Paperport Deluxe 6. After several hours of testing, here's what I found:

◆ Newspaper column widths worked better than that of magazine formats, such as those used in *Time*, *PC Magazine*, and *Newsweek*. I found it easier to snap close-in photos of a narrow column of newspaper text. Some magazines used whole pages, often spanning from the left to the right margins (this format is typically used for the beginning of articles).

◆ Newspaper fonts proved slightly larger and easier to read than those used in popular magazines.

◆ Basic text will work better with OCR than header material, which usually includes information about the article's author. These headers often use special fonts that OCR software may not understand. Rather than using OCR, you can just look at your photos to recover this information.

Generally, magazine OCR proved a little harder to accomplish because of the small fonts and shiny pages. Newspaper OCR, in contrast, was fairly easy and straightforward.

OCR Tips

Using OCR with your digital camera requires you to master a few techniques. These methods allow you to take clearer and more detailed photos from materials that naturally bend, reflect light, and contain distorting bindings:

◆ Put your magazine on a table or another flat surface. Do not hold it by hand. Weigh the edges down (you can use a coffee cup) to avoid the natural bend caused by bindings.

◆ You can hold a newspaper in your hand if you fold it and keep it from bending. However, it, too, may work better on a table.

◆ Shoot in landscape mode, not portrait. This provides greater pixel coverage for each column. You may need to take extra shots to fully capture the material, but you end up with better source images.

◆ Magazines are very shiny. Make sure to turn off the flash!

◆ Try to capture a single paragraph at a time rather than two or three. Less is better when you're working with OCR.

◆ Don't forget to take a picture of the page number, magazine cover with date, article title, and author name, if you want a complete reference when quoting.

◆ Turn your camera up to its highest imaging mode. More pixels produce better results.

With good focus, a flat surface, and reasonable lighting, you can easily capture a paragraph or two from a newspaper or magazine for later OCR recovery. I strongly encourage you to experiment with your camera and learn how well it works with this exciting technology.

56 Take Your Camera Shopping

Whether you're buying or selling, your digital camera can help you. Photos can guide you in making a major purchasing decision. They can also help someone else make the decision to buy one of your possessions.

Comparison Shopping with Your Camera

When you're ready to make an expensive purchase, let your camera do the shopping for you. Slow down and take photos of items before handing over your credit card. Ensure that your choice is the best one possible. Digital images help in several ways. They augment your memory, document an item's condition, and help you build consensus for a purchasing decision.

False Memory

Can you remember exactly what pattern that expensive sofa had? Will it match your curtains and fit into your décor? Take a picture. Then take the image home and compare it directly with the other elements. You've now moved the purchase decision-making process away from the store and into the comfort of your own home.

Like elephants, digital cameras don't forget. They capture important and small details that may sway you one way or another when you leave the showroom floor. And unlike traditional film cameras, you don't need to wait for the film to be processed or pay for prints to be made. Since most digital cameras have built-in LCD screens, you can quickly review your pictures on the spot. The bigger the item you plan to purchase, the more important it becomes to take photos and have them on hand to augment your memory.

For instance, suppose that you're shopping for a new home. You can't just visit each prospective house on a whim. Make the times you do visit each house count the most by taking a lot of pictures. Then you can review them later. If you're buying a car, you'll improve your negotiating stance if you take pictures and study them rather than returning time and again to the car lot.

Whatever the item, take a lot of pictures. While a single picture will help you remember the general look of the item, the more pictures you take, the more data you will have at hand. Take pictures inside the item and from different vantage points. If you're going to spend money on a big purchase, take the extra time to make sure you have a complete picture—or several complete pictures—of the item you may buy.

Building Consensus

Sharing pictures can help you come to a purchasing decision. Do you need to buy an out-of-state house? Does the sister who has excellent decorating taste live in another city? Do you want to get your friend's opinion before buying that $500 dress? Use digital images to build consensus and draw opinions from a shared pool of expertise.

Unusual Conditions

Use your digital camera to document the condition of an item you are about to purchase. Whether you're shopping for a car, a house, or furniture, once you have settled on a deal, you are entitled to receive the item in the same condition you last saw it. Protect yourself against problems arising from damage or alteration. Here are some examples:

- ◆ If furniture arrives with a large new scratch, prove it with pictures.
- ◆ If your house contract states that you own all built-in fixtures and the built-in microwave disappears before you move in, a digital image can bring proper compensation for the loss.
- ◆ Buying a new boat? You can prove the hull damage occurred after you purchased it (and before you took possession).

The larger the ticket, the more important it becomes to fully inspect and photograph your purchase. This not only protects your investment, but also creates a record trail that you may later need to use for police reports or insurance claims. However, you should be aware that the legal requirements for verifiably unmodified digital pictures are just now becoming established. Consider how easily digital images can be altered and enhanced. You may want to snap a few traditional 35mm pictures instead.

N O T E   The United States Department of Justice Web site offers a fuller discussion of the legal issues surrounding the use of digital photography for evidence. Stop by www.usdoj.gov/criminal/cybercrime/search_docs/sect8.htm for additional information.

If you receive damaged goods, take pictures of the carton and the contents to document the situation. Then go directly to the phone and report the damage. Don't just call the store where you bought the item, contact the shipping company, too. Sometimes, the delivery service, such as UPS or the post office, is at fault. Each shipper has its own policies for reporting damaged goods, but all of them have one feature in common: They expect you to report the damage immediately! If you cannot arrive at a reasonable accommodation with either the point of sale or the shipper, you may also want to contact your credit card company and contest the charge. No matter which route you take, a digital image taken directly after delivery will help prove your case.

Going Once, Going Twice—Online Auctions and Digital Photos

These days, online auction sites—eBay, Amazon, Yahoo!, and others—are becoming more and more popular. On these auction sites, you can put even the smallest items up for bid and often find a good buyer. You can use your digital camera to engage in selling your excess goods while cleaning up your house and reducing the overall clutter around you.

Most Internet auction sites allow you to include links to pictures of listed items. Take advantage of this opportunity to show your goods to their best advantage. Shoot at least one good, clean picture of your item, showing it in the best possible way. Make sure your image is well illuminated, and let the object fill as much of the frame as you can. The best pictures are the clearest and most depictive ones.

Do not, of course, try to deceive others by covering up flaws, either by taking deceptive photos or editing those photos before uploading them. A good photo will give your purchaser a true view of the condition of the item being offered.

Also, consider taking more than one picture of your lot. You can either post these directly on the auction site or send them to interested parties via e-mail. You may want to take pictures from different angles, show the back as well as the front, or show the object actually being used in different situations. Extra pictures may help to sell your item.

NOTE I recommend that you store your auction pictures on a different site than you use for personal ones. For example, if you use Ofoto for your family snaps, consider setting up a Zing album for your auction goods. This helps you protect your privacy while allowing others to view your sale items. See the "Field Guide to Online Photo Finishing and Album Sites" section for information about Ofoto, Zing, and other sites where you can share your photos.

57 Moving Day Made Easier

Looking for unneeded stress? Try moving. Moving can be one of the most unpleasant and troubling experiences in a person's life. But your trusty digital camera can help bring a little order into a disordered time.

What's in the Box?

Use your camera to take an inventory of what is in each box. It's always easier to search by looking through pictures than relying on memory or by opening every box. Don't be in the position where you're constantly asking which box some item or another is in. Look through your visual inventory and know right away. Your written inventory might simply say "box of books." Pictures will help you find which box has that all-important cookbook.

WARNING   Do not tape your visual inventories to your boxes. It acts as an invitation for theft by advertising the contents. Instead, store your inventories in another location.

Your worst fears may be confirmed when the mover calls and says, "We lost your box, Mrs. Smith. What was in it?" When a box is lost, don't depend on your memory to recall what it contained. Use your pictures to help file insurance claims for missing as well as for damaged items.

Hey! Don't Drop That!

If you think your movers are mishandling your possessions, do not hesitate to take out your camera and start taking pictures. At best, the movers will start acting more responsibly. At worst, you'll have valuable evidence of misconduct. And if your boxes arrive at your new location looking as if they've been stomped on, snap a picture, like the one shown below.

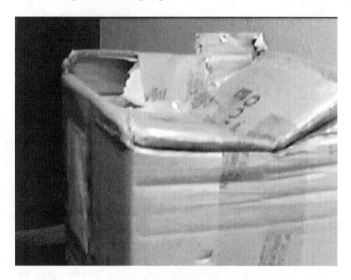

Use your camera to create a record of the conditions of all your belongings. Protect yourself by taking pictures of all your furniture and boxes. When a mover says, "that scratch was there before we moved it," you'll be able to prove that it was not.

58 Document Accidents

Taking photos can help enormously in the unpleasant event of an accident. Having personally used my digital camera after I was rear-ended by another car, I can assure you that having pictures is a great help when talking to the insurance agents. (Incidentally, the accident took place just outside of my favorite digital camera store.)

Consider these suggestions if you happen to have a camera on hand when an accident occurs:

- ◆ See the big picture. Take many pictures of the whole accident scene. Capture the positions of the cars. This will help prove who was at fault and protect you against lawsuits.

- ◆ Take pictures of the participants. Use your camera to document the health and general condition of the other driver and anyone else involved.

- ◆ Capture document information with your camera. Snap a picture of the other driver's license plates, driver's license, and insurance card.

- ◆ Record damage. Take complete pictures of damage done to the cars involved, as in the example shown below. You may also want to take a picture of the VIN plate in the other person's car.

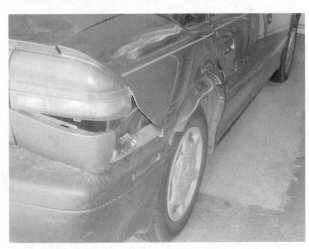

- ◆ Take pictures of any witnesses, even if you can't gather their names and phone numbers. If possible, also capture the license plates of their cars.

◆ If your camera has an optional sound-recording feature, this is a great time to use it. Capture the other driver saying, "I'm so sorry. It was all my fault!" before he goes home and changes his mind.

59 Create an Insurance Inventory

Did you know that your digital camera could help you create a permanent inventory for insurance purposes? You can take pictures of all your possessions and use those images in case of theft, fire, or storm damage.

It's almost impossible to remember what you have stored in each drawer of your house, but a digital camera can remember the important stuff for you. Take your camera for a tour through your house and your belongings. Be sure to cover the following areas:

Drawers   Go into every drawer in the house. Even little things cost you money, and you should be covered for them. Consider how much a drawer full of socks would cost you at the store and multiply that by all the people in your family. Just socks will set you back a bit! Be as thorough as possible and don't forget the closets, toy chests, and storage boxes.

Furnishings   Take pictures of the furniture in each room, but also take pictures of your window treatments, ceiling fans, and any other optional extras you have installed in your house. This includes wall treatments and rugs as well.

Garage   Don't neglect the garage when performing an inventory of your goods. Take pictures of your lawn mower, bicycles, and even your garden hose. You'll be surprised how many things you keep in your garage.

Outside   Take pictures of the home's exterior, including the patio and roof. Make sure to show the condition of any outdoor furniture, awnings, and so forth.

Valuables   Take pictures of any keepsakes you have around. You never know when you may lose a valuable piece of jewelry or a precious vase. Use the pictures to help the insurer appraise the true value of your loss. For some precious items, the weight of the item's metal is far less valuable than the craft and skill that went into making it.

Books, CDs, and software   Don't forget to photograph shelves of books, CDs, and software. These items are valuable, especially in terms of replacement costs. No matter what sort of collections you have, be sure to take pictures of them.

Once you've created a digital inventory, what do you do with the pictures? My suggestion is to make several copies of your pictures on CD-ROMs. If you do not have the CD-ROM burning equipment at your house, you can probably arrange to have it done for a small fee at a local computer store or a friend's house. CD-ROMs create a permanent record of your images, invulnerable to magnetic fields. In theory, the life span of a CD-ROM should exceed your own.

Store these CD-ROMs in a place other than your home. Keep them physically distant enough that damage to your home will not damage the CD-ROM. Put one set in a safe-deposit box. Leave another set at the house of a friend. Just be sure to have more than one copy of your records and to store them in more than one physical location.

These two things—performing a thorough inventory and using cautious storage—help reduce your risk for personal loss. Make sure you have your inventory on file before disaster strikes.

Review your possessions with your insurance agent. You might be surprised to discover that you are either over- or under-insured. Make sure your insurance needs are balanced by the actual value of your house and possessions. Take the time to sit down and discuss your true insurance needs by going through your digital images. You may actually save some money.

60   Fun and Games

You've learned about some practical digital camera applications. Now it's time for some fun. Here are some games you can play with your camera:

Beat the Clock   You can use your camera's automatic timer for "beat the clock" games. This is probably the silliest of all digital camera tricks. Just set the timer, press the shutter release, and say "Go!" Let the camera be the judge. Determine who built the biggest tower of blocks in the given time, or decide who really had more crackers in their mouths. Your imagination can be your guide.

Scavenger Hunt It's the old classic game, but with a twist. Don't bring a whole lot of junk back to home base; snap pictures of found items instead. Each team gets a list, a digital camera, and then they're off! When time runs out, the team that photographed the most items wins. It's a fun variation of an old-time pleaser.

Hide and Seek Have you ever been irritated by your camera's lag time between when you press the shutter release and when the camera actually snaps the photo? Be annoyed no more. Turn this latency into a fun and amusing game. To play, you need a bunch of rambunctious and hyperactive children. Hopefully, you've got a few already on hand that you can use—offspring, grandchildren, nieces and nephews, or kids borrowed from your neighbors. Set a timer for a minute or two. Say "go" and allow the youngsters to run around wildly as you try to snap photos of them with your digital camera. (You may want to play this game outdoors!) After the buzzer sounds, examine the shot's you've taken. Any clear photo of a child puts him or her "out" until the next round is over. This game is, incidentally, a terrific way to compare and evaluate cameras for ease-of-use as well as delay times.

Whose Is That? Here's a fun party game. Take pictures of people's ears, eyes, eyebrows, noses, and so forth. Your guests will guess whose part belongs to whom. Extreme close-up shots may prove harder to identify than you might think. The results can be hilarious, too. Make sure to use a macro lens for close-in photography and carefully label which nose belongs to which person. After all, it's no fun if after all the guessing, you cannot remember the answer!

Face Bingo This is one of those icebreaker games that allows near-strangers to meet under the auspices of friendly games. Face bingo works particularly well for large gatherings. Each person receives a "bingo" card with faces rather than numbers, then wanders around the crowd, trying to match the faces with real people. When they find one, they introduce themselves and write down the person's name. It takes five names in a row to win. You can prepare these cards well in advance. Just snap digital photos of the participants and randomly assign them to cards. Print them out, bring them along, and you're set. Even if a few people fail to show (and you know that's likely to happen), it won't stop the game. As with traditional bingo, each card allows 12 different ways to win.

I'm sure you can come up with variations of these games to suit particular occasions. In fact, you've probably thought of some other original game ideas (but pinning the boss's photo in the middle of the dartboard has been done before).

Some Day My Prints Will Come

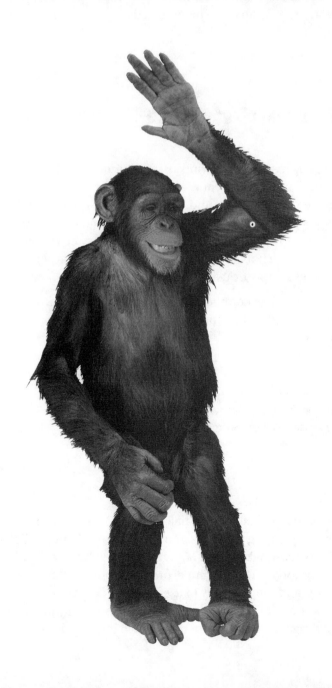

Your mother was right. You should share. Your digital camera captures great memories. Shouldn't you share them with friends and family? Sure, you could e-mail the digital versions, but a print is something tangible that doesn't require a computer to access. You can turn your digital photos into prints, either at home on your own printer or by using a finishing service. With only a few steps, you can make memories that really will last a lifetime or beyond.

61 Know Your Printer

These days, you can create terrific prints using your home printer. A home-based printer excels when you want to print just a few pictures at a time and you need rapid turnaround. The prints may not match the fineness and longevity of those from a photo finisher, but often you don't need those qualities. You may want to produce a birthday card, a poster, a business proposal, or a school assignment. For these projects, you can save time and energy simply by using your printer.

Ink-jet printers are the most common for home use, but there are several other types that can handle photo printing as well. Here's a quick summary of the top printer styles.

NOTE If you are still using a daisywheel printer, run—don't walk—to a computer store and buy yourself an ink-jet. Shame on you!

Ink-Jet Printers

Ink-jet printers are today's belles of the ball. These printers provide affordable and convenient printing solutions. You can pick up a high-quality ink-jet system for a very reasonable price. Many stores even bundle an ink-jet printer in with a computer. These printers produce good resolution and high-quality colors, and they are easy to use. Over the past few years, ink-jet quality has continued to climb higher. If you were put off by ink-jet quality in the past, look again. Today's printers are much improved.

Ink-jet printers work by squirting colored dyes onto paper. The paper absorbs these quick-drying inks to create your output. Ink-jets work well with both black and colored inks. This allows you to mix pictures and text on a single page. You can buy special-quality ink-jet photo paper, which works with your printer's dyes to produce professional-looking, glossy images. By picking the right paper (see number 62, "Know Your Paper"), you can create masterpieces without ever leaving your home.

On the down side, ink-jet printers have some disadvantages:

◆ They can be fussy. You must regularly clean their ink nozzles.

◆ If you print a lot of color pictures, you will need to refill your ink, and refills can be expensive.

◆ Ink-jets are notoriously slow, although more recent models can zip along nicely.

◆ Sometimes the paper-advance mechanism creates white lines within your picture.

◆ When you print a goof, you're stuck with it. You've lost the ink, paper, and the time it took to create that goof.

You may not want to use an ink-jet printer to create special keepsakes. For all other print jobs, it may be just the thing.

N O T E   Sometimes, after running your ink cartridges through a self-clean cycle, they may still seem clogged. You can use cotton swabs to clean the nozzles. Dip the swabs in rubbing alcohol and dab lightly at the nozzles to loosen and clear the ink. Avoid dripping the alcohol, and use care when dabbing.

Dye-Sublimation Printers

Dye-sublimation (*dye-sub* for short) printers are just starting to infiltrate the consumer market. Although expensive, these printers produce outstanding quality prints. Looking at a photo printed on a dye-sub printer, you might compare it favorably to a picture you see in a magazine.

Dye-sub printers work by heating ribbons of colored inks. The melted inks bond with the paper. The higher the heat, the more ink transferred and the more intense the color produced.

Dye-sub printers may produce great quality, but they do have their drawbacks:

◆ Along with the high cost for the printer itself comes the high cost for its supplies. Keeping your printer in ink can strain the wallet.

◆ They do not fare well at printing text. You can't replace your general-function printer with a dye-sub unit. At best, you can use it as a special-purpose second printer.

◆ Only the most expensive models can create full-size (8 × 10) output. Many dye-sub printers can create only small images.

N O T E I own a dye-sublimation printer that is a few years old. It creates 0.75 × 1.5–*inch* prints! Of course, today's dye-sub printers work with more standard output sizes, creating 3.5 × 5–inch or 4 × 6–inch prints.

Laser Printers

You can produce decent black-and-white prints using a laser printer. You probably won't want to frame these prints, but they work very well in school reports and business proposals when you don't need true color.

Laser printers approximate tone by using a technique called *dithering*. Darker areas print using more dots. Lighter areas use fewer dots.

Of course, if you really have the bucks to spend, you can pick up a color laser printer. These cost only a few thousand dollars.

62 Know Your Paper

Many people think, "paper is paper." They are wrong, at least when it comes to the paper for photo prints. Paper quality affects print quality. Often, the paper you print on can enhance or detract from your images. Today, you can purchase a vast range of paper types.

Plain Paper

Printing on "plain paper" offers both advantages and drawbacks. Paper cost is low; you can pick up a ream for a few dollars. On the other hand, the fibrous nature of the paper means that ink will spread to some degree before drying. The fibers wick the dyes as they are applied. Because of this, you can expect pictures printed on untreated paper to look a little fuzzier than those printed on special, photo-quality paper.

You can improve your plain-paper prints by purchasing bright, heavy stock. When shopping, look for key advertising phrases: Bright White, Brighter White, Heavy Weight, and Premium Grade. Brighter paper improves color quality and trueness. Heavier paper produces stiffer, more durable prints, with fewer curling problems. Avoid cheap, low-weight paper, because eventually the loose fibers can clog your printer.

There's one more tip for plain-paper printing: Purchase high-quality ink-jet paper from the same manufacturer that made your ink-jet printer. Each manufacturer fine-tunes its printer in different ways. You can be sure that each printer is tuned to produce the best results on its companion product.

Glossy Photo Paper

You can pick up ink-jet photographic-quality paper at almost any office supply store. This paper is very stiff (photo weight) and very bright. It is designed to avoid spreading ink and to produce a glossy finish after printing. Although prices are dropping, expect to spend up to a dollar a sheet for this product.

Here are few tips to keep in mind when using photo paper with your ink-jet:

◆ Print on the slightly rough/slightly glossy side. Although the way that you load paper varies by printer, you can always determine which side receives the ink. Orient the paper so that the photo will be printed on the rougher, glossier side.

◆ Avoid handling the paper. Keep fingerprints off the page, both before and after printing.

◆ Keep your paper dry and cool. Moisture and high temperatures can destroy both your prints and your paper.

◆ Don't mix paper types. In fact, I recommend you insert only one sheet of photo paper in your printer at a time. This avoids some jamming issues and ensures that you print your picture on the correct stock.

◆ Carefully adjust your printing dialog box settings. Make sure to specify a photo-grade paper and the best print quality before printing.

◆ Let your prints air dry, image side up, for an hour after printing. During that time, avoid touching or breathing on your paper. This allows your colors to set true. (Ambient humidity and ink quality will affect drying time.)

◆ You may stack your dried prints, but insert plain paper between each print. If any ink "bleeds," it will affect the inserts rather than the next print.

◆ As with plain paper, you should try to match your photo paper brand to your printer. You can be sure each manufacturer has fine-tuned its printer to work best with its own brand of photo paper.

◆ Photo paper is sensitive to ultraviolet (UV) light. When displaying your pictures, be sure to keep your photo out of direct sunlight and, if possible, use UV-blocking glass for the picture frame.

Special-Purpose Paper

Today, you can purchase an almost unlimited variety of specialty papers. These range from heavy-bond sheets to glossy print-to-the-edge cards. Check the paper section in your local office supply store or craft shop to get an idea of the range of product offerings.

Each package of specialty paper should contain instructions. Read these directions and follow them. They will help you to produce the best results with each paper type.

N O T E   If you're printing greeting cards, you can save a lot of money by buying bulk card stock rather than the pre-folded variety. Recently, I visited Wal-Mart and purchased a pack of 10 half-fold card stock (with envelopes) for about $8. At the same visit, I bought a pack of 150 (yes, that's right, 150, but without envelopes) unfolded card stock for $4. I consider 15 times the stock at half the cost to be a nice deal.

63 Print 'em Up

If you want to print some pictures on your new, expensive specialty paper (or even your cheap, plain paper), but find it's a pain to get the prints to look just right, you can let someone else do the hard work for you. Adobe PhotoDeluxe provides a variety of print styles and layouts. These help you conserve paper while printing one or more images at a time.

Before you begin, here's a tip to help you minimize your risk and conserve your specialty paper: Test print on plain paper before committing to your specialty stock. Sure, this consumes extra ink, but glossy or photo-weight stock usually costs a lot more per print than the ink.

N O T E For information about using Adobe PhotoDeluxe, see the "Enhancing Your Images with PhotoDeluxe" part of this book.

Print One

Okay, we're not talking rocket science here. We're just going to print one copy of a picture on one page. Can it get any simpler?

1. Launch PhotoDeluxe and open your picture.

2. Click the Get & Fix Photo tab of the activity bar. Then click Print ➤ Print Preview. This step allows you to preview how your picture will print before committing it to your printer. You will print everything within the large rectangle. When you finish examining the preview, click OK. You are now ready to print.

3. Click Print ➤ Print. The Print dialog box will appear, as shown below. Carefully set the options for your print job. Make sure to specify the proper resolution, print quality, and paper type. Also check that you've selected between black-and-white and color output.

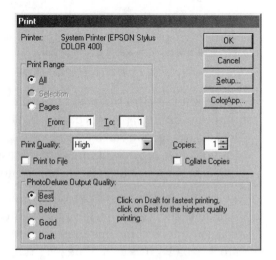

4. Select an output quality for your PhotoDeluxe image. Choose between Draft, Good, Better, and Best. When using specialty print stock, always select Best.

5. Use the Print dialog box to select the paper type and orientation.

6. After setting your print options and output quality, click OK to begin printing.

WARNING   Always set the correct orientation. Both PhotoDeluxe and your system's Print dialog box will let you choose between landscape or portrait prints. In the Print dialog box, simply click the appropriate icon. In PhotoDeluxe, choose File ➢ Page Setup or Get & Fix Photo ➢ Print ➢ Page Setup. Don't waste paper by forgetting this step.

Print Many

PhotoDeluxe allows you to print several copies of a photo on a single page. This both increases your printing efficiency (less wasted paper) and allows you to print on special-purpose stock. Your stock options (okay, forgive me, but it was an obvious pun) include such choices as sheets of labels, business cards, or stickers.

Here's how to print multiple copies on a single page:

1. Launch PhotoDeluxe and open your picture.

2. Click the Get & Fix Photo tab of the activity bar. Then click Print ➤ Print Multiple on a Page. The Print Multiple dialog box will appear. As shown below, this dialog box presents a preview of your print job, showing the maximum number of images that will fit on your page.

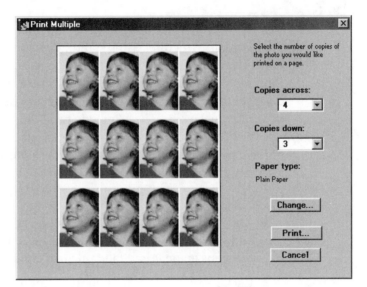

N O T E PhotoDeluxe does not resize your images. You will not be able to fit any more items on your page than shown in the Print Multiple dialog box without shrinking your picture.

3. If you want to print fewer copies than the maximum, reduce the number of copies in either the Copies Across or Copies Down box.

4. PhotoDeluxe assumes you will print on plain 8.5 × 11–inch paper. To print on another stock size, click the Change button, select your correct paper brand and type, and then click OK.

5. Click the Print button to continue. The Print dialog box will appear. As when you're printing a single copy (described in the previous section), set the options for your print job. Then click OK to begin printing.

After you've printed multiple photo copies on a page, you'll want to cut out the separate prints. See the "Cut It Out" section for some cutting tips.

Print Standard Sizes

When you print pictures using standard sizes, you can fit them into standard picture frames and photo album pockets. Unlike when you use the Print Multiple on a Page option, PhotoDeluxe's Print Standard Sizes option does not try to use every inch of the page. Instead, you select from a variety of print sheet layouts. These include two 4×6– inch prints or a 5×7–inch photo surrounded by a bunch of wallet-sized photos. If you've ever ordered pictures from a photo studio, these sheets will look familiar. You also have the option of printing different photos on the same page.

Here's how to print standard sizes:

1. Launch PhotoDeluxe. Click the Get & Fix Photo tab of the activity bar and select Print ➢ Print Standard Sizes. The activity bar will display the steps in the Print Standard Sizes guided activity.

2. Click 1 - Style ➢ Different Photos. (Choose this option even if you decide to use only one photo.)

3. Click 2 - Layout ➢ Choose Layout. Double-click one of the page templates.

4. Click 3 - Add ➢ Open File. Select your first image using the file browser. Click Open to confirm your selection. PhotoDeluxe will add your photo to the first standard print, automatically sizing it. Continue to find and open the file for each print on the page. Your page will look something like the one shown on the next page.

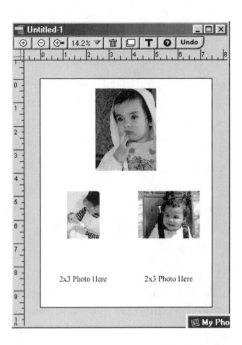

5. Click 4 - Print ➢ Print. The Print dialog box will appear. As when you're printing one or multiple copies, set the options for your print job. Then click OK.

6. Click 5 - Done.

Now you can cut out your standard prints, as described in the next section.

Cut It Out

Some paper stock arrives perforated, but most doesn't. When you print multiple images on an unperforated page, you'll need to cut it to detach the individual prints. Here are some tips to keep in mind for the best results:

◆ Avoid using scissors. Most people can't cut clean lines using hand-held scissors. (And if you do use scissors, don't run with them!)

◆ When possible, use a rotary paper cutter. This style of paper cutter creates more uniform and controlled cuts. The other, guillotine-style, paper cutter may rotate a page during cutting and unintentionally cut into your photos.

◆ Use scrapbook tools (such as circular cutters, crimping shears, and so forth) *after* separating the photos. This protects your other pictures from any tool-based errors such as slips and overcuts.

◆ Make full-page cuts first. Determine which cut lines completely bisect your page and perform these cuts before any others. Do not attempt a "halfway" cut. This usually results in overcutting into a picture or torn areas where cuts do not intersect.

64 Race to the Finish Line

Did you know that you can make real photos from your digital pictures? Over the past year, many photo finishers have added digital imaging to their product lines. These photos will last as long as "normal" photos, with the same durability, feel, and archival quality. In fact, they really are normal photos.

The photo finishers print your photos on real photo paper (traditional photo-quality silver-halide) and produce pictures that look nearly as good as 35mm prints. The difference is that instead of printing from negatives, they print using digital projection. Typically, a set of three high-resolution colored lasers draw on photo paper using complementary colors. Then the finisher develops the photo paper using a standard "wet" process.

Choose Your Finisher

You can find any number of digital photo finishers on the Internet. These sites offer many of the most exciting and innovative digital-imaging solutions around. They allow you to upload your pictures and order prints in a wide variety of styles and sizes, but that's not all. Most allow you to arrange your photos, annotate them, store them in albums, and share them with friends as well. Some sites support guest books; others offer slide shows.

Choosing between finishers can be hard. So many offer such wonderful deals and service that you may end up, like me, creating accounts on a dozen or more. Don't be put off by that. With a few exceptions, these sites provide free membership, generous storage allocations, and almost unlimited storage time. Recently, large megastores like Wal-Mart have entered the photo-finishing arena. The advantage here is that since these megastores are so ubiquitous, you can just drive over and pick up your order at their store, saving you a bundle on shipping and handling fees.

Expect to pay somewhere between a quarter and seventy-five cents for most 3×5–inch and 4×6–inch prints. On top of that, add a dollar or two or three for shipping and handling. Always check for specials before submitting your order. Some processors offer bulk discounts, especially when you order multiple prints of the same photo. Be sure to stop by the "Field Guide to Online Photo Finishing and Album Sites" section, located conveniently at the end of this book. This appendix includes descriptions and contact information for many online photo finishers.

Make the Cut

When you plan to use a photo-finishing service, you must keep two key things in mind: resolution and aspect ratio. The greater your camera's resolution, the better your prints will look and the bigger the prints you can order. The aspect ratio determines how your pictures work with standard print sizes. Before you order your prints, take the time to learn more about both.

Resolution

I'm sure you've heard the phrase "megapixel camera." This phrase refers to a camera's resolution—in this case, a camera that can capture more than a million picture elements, or *pixels*, at once. As the pixel count increases, so does the quality of your images and (not coincidentally) the camera price. Inexpensive cameras may capture images as small as 320×240 pixels. Other, very expensive, models might take pictures containing multiple millions of pixels. This is important because your camera's resolution determines how you can choose a proper print size.

Often, people order large prints from small images. This is a big mistake. These pictures will look rotten. Small images simply do not contain enough information to create a large print. The print will look blocky and fuzzy. Instead, use the following chart to determine the minimum print size for your images.

Print Size (in Inches)	Minimum Size (in Pixels)	Good Size (in Pixels)
3.5 × 5	640 × 480	800 × 600
4 × 6	800 × 600	1024 × 768
5 × 7	1024 × 768	1280 × 960
8 × 10	1280 × 960	1600 × 1200
11 × 14	1600 × 1200	1712 × 1368
12 × 18	1712 × 1368	2400 × 3600
16 × 24	1600 × 2400	3200 × 4800
24 × 36	2400 × 3600	4800 × 7200

This means that if you own a 640 × 480 camera, you should try to stick to 3.5 × 5–inch prints. If you own a 1280 × 960 camera, you might order prints in any size up to 8 × 10 inches. The 8 × 10–inch print may not look spectacular, but it should hold up to reasonable scrutiny.

In general, you can always select a smaller print size than your image resolution might suggest. In fact, print quality improves as you print smaller, because image density increases. You can see this phenomenon in a 35mm print. Use a magnifying glass to look closely at the print. The closer you look, the more details you see, because 35mm prints have very high image density. It works the same way with digital prints—the higher the image density, the finer the detail and sharpness in your print.

NOTE   I've recently developed what I like to call Erica's Photo Print Rule of 100's. (Catchy title, eh?) It works like this: When ordering prints, include at least 100 pixels per linear inch of height and width. When printing a 5 × 7, aim for at least 500 × 700 pixels. For an 8 × 10 print, nothing smaller than 800 × 1000 pixels will print particularly well. Of course, 200 or more pixels per linear inch will produce even better results. Most finishers consider 300 ppi to produce "best" quality prints. Keep in mind that this rule applies primarily to digital photography rather than scanned images. Always use higher resolutions for scanned sources because of quality loss introduced by the scanning process.

Aspect Ratios

An aspect ratio is defined by the ratio between your image's width and height. The following table shows print sizes and their aspect ratios.

Print Size	Aspect Ratio	Image Size	Aspect Ratio
3.5 × 5	1 : 1.43	320 × 240	1 : 1.33
4 × 6	1 : 1.50	640 × 480	1 : 1.33
5 × 7	1 : 1.40	768 × 512	1 : 1.50
8 × 10	1 : 1.25	1024 × 768	1 : 1.33
11 × 14	1 : 1.27	1600 × 1200	1 : 1.33

Sometimes, the aspect ratio of a digital image does not exactly match the aspect ratio of a print. When this happens, your picture's proportions will not precisely match those of the printed version. In this case, the photo finisher must choose between two approaches, which are illustrated below.

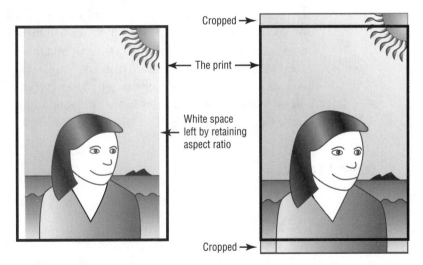

Choice 1: Leaving extra white space   Choice 2: Cropping to match aspect ratio

First, the finisher can retain the image's aspect ratio by leaving white space on one or both sides of the print. This allows you to cut off the excess paper and return your print to your original aspect ratio. Unfortunately, if you do so, your image may not fit in a standard size frame or photo album insert. Also, be aware that although the excess white space usually appears as a white color, some finishers digitally fill your picture with a black background, so the excess space may appear black. Results will vary by finisher.

Second, the finisher can adjust the image's aspect ratio by cropping the top, bottom, or both. This usually works great and produces a pleasing, standard-size picture. Unfortunately, sometimes things can go wrong—photos may arrive with missing heads or feet (or missing ears, when the "top" of a photo in portrait orientation is cropped). Also, by taking this chop-to-fit approach, the finisher changes the underlying composition. Although this method generally produces the most successful prints, sometimes it can create the biggest goofs.

So what can you do? Many photo finishers now allow *you* to choose which method you want to use for your images. By allowing the decision to rest with the customer, they increase satisfaction while limiting unpleasant surprises. If your finisher does not allow you to choose, make sure to determine in advance which method will be used. If you don't like their method, find another finisher.

Another thing you can do is to adjust your pictures in advance. PhotoDeluxe allows you to trim your photos to a standard size. With this feature, you control exactly how your pictures will turn out. Say you want to create a 5×7–inch print. You can create an image with a 1:1.4 aspect ratio before submitting it to the photo finisher. In this way, you can ensure that the print you order will visually match the image you upload. To size your images, follow the instructions in the "Print Standard Sizes" section in number 63, "Print 'em Up."

Just Do It!

When you're ready to order your high-quality prints from a photo finisher, just follow these steps:

1. Prepare your photos in PhotoDeluxe (see the "Enhancing Your Images with PhotoDeluxe" part of this book for details).

2. Select an online finisher (see the "Field Guide to Online Photo Finishing and Album Sites" section at the back of this book for a list of finishers). Determine that the finisher's pricing and delivery methods are satisfactory.

3. Upload your images to the finishing site. Several finishers now offer a variety of finish styles, including matte, glossy, and satin. Before you order, you may want to check if you can request a particular finish.

4. Place your order and wait. Your photos should be delivered within a week.

That's all you need to do. And you'll be amazed and delighted by the results. The ease and convenience of today's online photo finishing cannot be matched.

Upload Solutions

Each photo-finishing site provides one or more upload solutions, which vary by finisher. Make sure to determine which works best for you and with your computer. These include the following solutions:

Web page uploads Nearly every site offers a Web page that allows you to upload one or more images at once. Although this provides the most universal solution, this method has many drawbacks. Uploads proceed slowly and without any feedback. You must individually select each image for upload. You can't use drag and drop. Often, you can't upload more than five or ten images at once. Sometimes, you can't determine if your computer is merely busy uploading or has crashed.

Stand-alone applications Most sites now provide Windows-compatible (and, occasionally, Macintosh-compatible) programs that allow you to upload many pictures at once. These programs can run unattended, allowing you to send a large number of pictures without human intervention. Also, many of them allow you to select an upload folder so you don't need to add each photo individually.

Plug-ins Some sites offer Netscape or Microsoft Internet Explorer plug-ins. These expand the capabilities of your Web browser, allowing you to upload one or more images using drag and drop. The jury is still out on this upload method. Sometimes, the plug-ins can crash your browser or computer. Time will tell if this method proves popular or drops out of use.

E-mail upload A few finishing sites allow you to attach your images to e-mail. Just write a letter to the site, attach an image, and send the message. This method is tremendously convenient and avoids problems associated with software compatibility and browser types. In fact, this method opens up photo finishing to WebTV users who might not own a personal computer.

FTP Sites   Some sites have started to provide upload access through the file transfer protocol (FTP). This standard allows you to perform batch uploads using very common and standard FTP software. While this procedure targets more computer-proficient customers, it offers a number of advantages. You probably do not need to install yet another piece of software on your machine. An FTP program is already built into many operating systems and works with any site that supports FTP transfer. You can use FTP to transfer a large number of pictures at once, with a minimum of interaction. Most FTP programs work happily in the background as you turn your attention to other tasks. Finally, this procedure allows Linux users (and users of other non-standard operating systems) to access sites and purchase prints from finishers who might otherwise not be able to accept their business.

Disks by mail and walk-in   Some finishers allow you to stop by a storefront and drop off a disk or send a CD-R (recordable CD) or floppy disk by regular mail. Floppy disk acceptance, however, is dropping by the wayside. Some finishers that used to accept floppy disks (containing a Zip or Stuff-it archive of your images) now reject them because better cameras now produce larger pictures that, even when zipped, don't fit well or at all on a floppy disk. In contrast, CD acceptance continues to grow. To submit a CD, simply create a CD-R containing your images. Unless instructed to do otherwise, don't put your pictures into folders or subdirectories. Check ahead and see what image formats are supported by your finisher. Do not submit any pictures or files that your finisher cannot print. Keep things simple. Remember, the person receiving and processing your CD is, more likely than not, a part-time high-school student earning minimum wage.

Don't Look a Gift Horse...

Did you know you could order your pictures as gift items as well as prints? Most finishers offer photo gift items or have partnered with sites that do. You can order photos on items as diverse as mouse pads, tote bags, T-shirts, license plates, boxer briefs, and ceramic tiles. Be sure to check out the offerings on each finishing site to get some great gift ideas.

Share Your Pictures

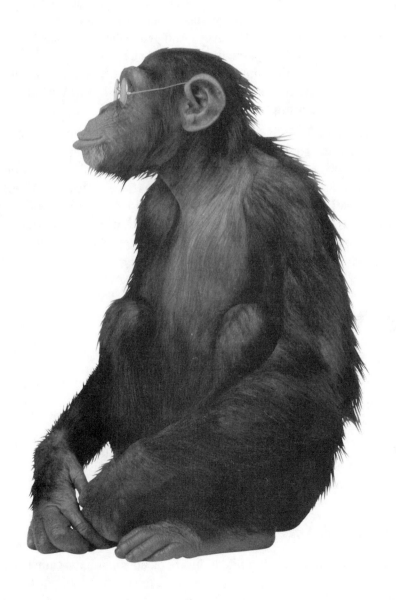

It's been well-documented: Today's global society isolates too many of us. Do you sometimes miss your friends and family? Do you wish you could share your pictures with them, even when you're hundreds or thousands of miles apart? Well, there are a lot of new and exciting ways to do so. From tapes and discs to the Internet, you can take advantage of any number of technologies.

VHS tapes, CDs and DVDs offer only some of the output media that provide exciting alternative to prints. With these, your slideshows can play back on computers, VCRs, or DVD players. And, while VHS and basic CD sharing have been around for years, new "Video on CD" and "DVD-R" how-to have just entered the consumer market. These discs offer many of the same features as the commercial Kodak Picture CDs, but with a bonus of easy consumer authoring.

The Internet adds even more alternatives to picture sharing. With e-mail, Web pages, and innovative solutions like the Internet-ready Ceiva frame, friends, family, and colleagues from all over the world can experience your digital photographs. The new Internet technologies have done an amazing thing: They allow people to share words and experiences, regardless of location or time zone. And if a picture is worth a thousand words, a shared picture must be worth millions.

65 Use Your Camera's Video-Out Port

If your camera offers a video-out port, you can use it in two very interesting ways. First, you can hook it up to a VCR. This allows you to become a moviemaker, recording your playback on tape and creating a video record of your pictures. Second, if you're a WebTV owner, you can use your camera's video-out port to take advantage of WebTV's photo e-mail capabilities.

I Want to Be in Movies

Digital cameras can make terrific videos. Just hook up your digital camera to your VCR and record your images on a videotape. You can send this tape to anyone who has access to a VCR (no need for a computer), and they'll be able to watch it. Many people can watch the video at once for that "whole family" experience.

Recently, out-of-town guests visited for a long weekend, during which I snapped a fair number of shots on my digital camera. The last night, I pulled out the camera, hooked it up to the VCR and played back a slide show (with music) for our departing friends. Unknown to them, I simultaneously recorded this on the VCR. When they left, they happily took a copy of the tape as a lasting souvenir of our time together.

When you make your video, you can easily mix live action with your digital camera still shots. You might also want to add music to enhance the image-montage effect.

When I make a video, I just hook up the digital camera to the video-in port and connect a nice album to the audio-in port. Then, with the camera captions turned off and VCR recording turned on, I present a slide show paced to the music. When I'm finished, I pop out the tape, and it's ready to send to the grandparents.

Follow these steps to make a video:

1. Load your images into your camera via card (such as compact flash or smart media) or cable (such as serial or USB).

2. Place a fresh tape in your VCR and set the VCR to Short Play (SP). This setting provides high-quality recording and playback for up to two hours, usually. I recommend that you select Short Play for all your image slide shows.

3. Connect your camera's video-out port to your VCR's video-in port, usually a yellow-colored RCA jack. You may use any cables supported by both your VCR and camera. The connection type varies by model.

4. Connect your sound device, such as cassette player or CD player, to your VCR's audio-in port or ports. Newer VCRs provide stereo recording, but older VCRs do not. Check the back of the VCR, looking for a pair of RCA jacks with red and white coloring. When in doubt, use the white RCA cord to connect for mono recordings.

5. Turn the volume up on your sound device. A higher volume works better because it provides a clearer audio track and allows your viewers to adjust down the playback volume on their TVs. (Do not, however, turn up the volume so loud that it distorts.)

6. Before proceeding, test your playback. Make sure the camera is connected correctly and you can see your images on a television connected to your VCR. Power on your sound source and make sure you can hear it through the television.

7. Set your camera to the first picture in your slide show.

8. Turn captions off on your camera. This function varies by manufacturer, but usually involves a "display" option in a menu or a special button. For instance, I press the "monitor" button once on my Nikon 800 to turn captions off.

9. Begin playback of your audio source.

10. Press Record on the VCR.

11. Slowly cycle through your camera's images.

12. (Optional) When the slideshow finishes, turn down the volume on your sound system to provide an audio fade-out effect.

13. Press the Stop button on your VCR, or if you plan to add to the video-tape, press the Pause button.

N O T E See number 54, "Take Your Show on the Road," for more details about creating business presentations and using slides with your digital camera.

Here are some additional tips:

◆ Go slow. People want time to really look at each picture before the next one appears. Display each shot for 10 to 20 seconds.

◆ Follow the music. Let the rhythm tell you when to advance your image playback. The closer you match your pictures to the beat, the more professional the video will seem to the audience.

◆ Get rid of bad pictures before you tape. Omit obvious flubs such as shots with closed eyes, embarassingly bad poses, and so forth.

◆ Keep as many "in between" shots as you can. These include views of people's backs, faces turning away, people getting ready to pose, or a group breaking up after the formal pose. These types of shots provide great transition material between posed shots and add to the total story.

I Want My WebTV

If your digital camera provides a video-out port, you can send your photos by WebTV e-mail. Here's how:

1. Connect your camera to WebTV's digital video-in port. (You must be using WebTV Plus. WebTV Classic does not support this feature.)

2. Compose a new e-mail message by selecting Write from your Mail List screen.

3. While writing your message, move the yellow box to Photo and press Return.

....

N O T E Make sure to turn off your captions and photo numbering before sending your pictures by e-mail. Otherwise these features will overlay your image and look ugly.

4. Select Video from the TV/Video toggle on the lower-left side of the video-capture screen. Move the yellow box to Video and press Return.

5. Make sure your camera is on and connected correctly. Your photo should display on your WebTV unit. If your unit says, "No video signal," check both your power and connections.

6. Select the Freeze button. Move the yellow box to the button and press Return.

7. Now add your image to your e-mail. Move the yellow box to Add to Message and press Return.

8. Send your message as you normally would.

66 Make a Video Using Screen Mirroring

Many newer computer video cards include TV-out ports. These cards allow you to use a TV as your monitor or hook up a VCR and record your screen.

This lets you create a computer-based slide show and record it directly to a VCR. Your video card will create the TV signal, making adjustments for screen size as needed. This provides an excellent way to create a video slide-show when your camera does not offer a video-out port.

N O T E   Video cards with TV-out ports cost about $30 or more. Stop by About.com's peripherals list (http://peripherals.about.com /compute/peripherals/cs/vidcaptvvendor/index.htm) for a fairly complete list of video-card vendors.

To create your video, you will need an image program on your computer that creates slide shows. There are many available, but my favorites include Graphic Converter (www.lemkesoft.com) for the Macintosh and CompUPic Pro (www.photodex.com) for the PC.

Follow these steps to use a TV-out port to record your slide show:

1. Connect your VCR to your TV-out port. You may use any cables supported by both your VCR and video card—coaxial cable, RCA plugs, or S-Video. The connection type varies by model.

2. Place a fresh tape in your VCR and set the VCR to Short Play (SP). This setting provides high-quality recording and playback for up to two hours, usually. I recommend that you select Short Play for all your image slide shows.

3. Load your pictures into your slideshow software.

4. Before proceeding, test your playback. Make sure you know how to start the full-screen slideshow feature of your software.

W A R N I N G   Take care. You may accidentally record computer artifacts, such as menus and your cursor. When you record too early, you'll capture screen shots before the playback. Instead, start recording just as full-screen slideshow begins.

5. Press Record on the VCR.

6. Begin playback (preferably full screen) on your computer.

7. Wait for your slideshow to play out, as the VCR records.

8. When the slideshow finishes, press the Stop button on your VCR, or if you plan to add more to the videotape, press the Pause button.

N O T E   In theory, you can mirror to a TV by hooking a USB-based video-out device to your computer. These devices are, however, notoriously slow and not recommended. A USB wire cannot transmit sufficient bandwidth to create good-quality video. One unit I tested tended to hang for a second in the middle of every other slide. This caused an odd and unpleasant presentation with half of the new slide on top and half the old slide on the bottom.

67 Create a Picture CD (and Web Page, Too!)

CompuPic Pro (www.photodex.com) offers a Picture CD creation tool that allows you to author CD-based photo albums, complete with playback software. Just add your pictures and let CompuPic Pro do the rest. You'll end up with a fully interactive CD solution. Registered users can freely distribute these CDs to friends, family and colleagues. This process also creates an Internet-ready set of Web pages that you can upload to your favorite hosting site.

W A R N I N G   You'll need a CD burner to create your Picture CD, obviously, but CompuPic only provides support for a limited number of burners. Stop by www.photodex.com/support/faqs/pro_cdr.html to find a list of supported hardware. If your hardware is not supported, skip to the next section for further instructions.

Creating a CD-based photo album proves pretty simple. Just follow these steps:

1. Select those files and folder you want to include on the CD. To do this, I click on my main folder, typically the "My Documents" folder, using the file browser on the top left of the CompuPic screen.

2. The contents of this folder will appear in the main viewing window on the right. Click on the first folder or file and then Ctrl + click on all the other materials. As a second Ctrl + click will remove an item from your list, you may toggle item inclusion back and forth with this method.

3. After selecting your files, choose Tools ➤ Picture CD ➤ Write Picture CD. This will open the Create Picture CD dialog box seen below.

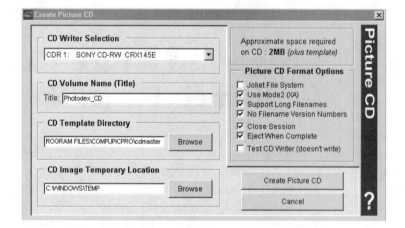

4. Select a CD Writer from the top pull-down menu. As you can see above, CompuPic correctly and automatically found my sole Sony CD-RW drive. For systems with multiple recording drives, this menu allows you to specify the one with which you wish to write.

5. Specify a CD Title. Although the title defaults to Photodex_CD, you may use any valid title by typing it into the Volume Name field.

6. (Optional) If desired, you may change the Template Directory and Image Location. The template directory points to a Picture CD "master", with all the autorun and readme files that CompuPic will place on your disc. The Image Location is used to create a temporary CD image file before burning. I strongly recommend you simply leave these alone.

7. Choose your Picture CD format options. These options offer standard CD-burning choices such as:

◆ Joliet file system (when unchecked, you use the default ISO-9660 standard instead)

◆ Use Mode 2 (an extended architecture that allows error correction)

◆ Long Filenames (longer, that is, than eight characters)

◆ Version Numbers (for ISO-9660 compatibility)

◆ Close Session (to prevent multiple writes and allow more CD-ROM drives to read your disc)

◆ Eject (a convenience option that opens your drive bay after writing your disc)

◆ Test (a feature that tests your disc without writing)

8. After choosing your options, click Create Picture CD. CompuPic will burn your CD, storing your pictures, a photo viewer program and an autorun file. This autorun file launches your album either when you start your computer with the CD inserted or, when CD notification is turned on, you load your CD into its drive.

Create a Picture CD with Unsupported Hardware

If your computer does not support Picture CD creation, despair not. It's fairly easy, albeit tedious, to create your Picture CD by hand. Follow these steps and you'll make a marvelous, shareable CD using the Picture CD software. This workaround allows you use CompuPic up to a point and then burn the CD manually.

1. Create a new folder to store your work. I usually place my folder in the "My Documents" directory and call it "PictureCD Work."

2. Create a subfolder named "Pictures." Inside the Pictures folder, create two more folders called THUMB and WEB. This exactly mimics how CompuPic creates the folders during the PictureCD creation process.

3. Navigate to the CompuPic Pro folder on your disk, typically C:\ Program Files\CompuPic Pro. Here you'll find a "cdmaster" folder. Open this folder.

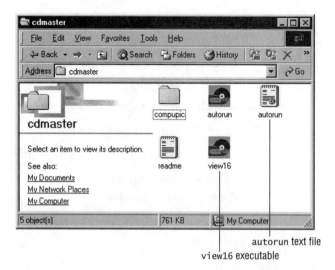

autorun text file

view16 executable

4. Copy the autorun text file and view16 executable to your work folder. Rename the view16 program to autorun. (Because the text file and executable are different file types it will not matter that they have the same names.)

5. Copy your photos to your Pictures folder.

6. Launch CompuPic Pro and use the navigator in the top-left corner to move to your folder. A list of your pictures, complete with thumbnails, will appear in the main window, to the right.

7. Scroll through your pictures and make sure they are the ones you want. You can delete pictures or move them to another directory if they don't fit.

　　◆ To move a picture to another directory, drag a picture from the right window to its new location in the top-left navigator.

　　◆ To delete a picture, right-click it and select Delete from the pop-up menu.

8. Check your orientations. If a picture is oriented incorrectly, either on its side or upside down, select Tools ➢ Lossless Image Modification and choose from the rotation options. You can rotate +90 degrees (a clockwise rotation), –90 degrees (a counter-clockwise rotation) or 180 degrees to turn an image around completely. These commands will change your actual files, but they will do so in a lossless way, so you do not lose resolution from your images.

9. Select all your pictures. To do so, click the first picture and then Shift+click the last one. This selects all the pictures between and including the first and last.

10. Select Internet ➤ Web Page Generator ➤ Create Thumbnail Web Pages. An interactive dialog box will appear.

11. (Optional) CompuPic incidentally creates Web pages at the same time it produces your thumbnails and other files needed for your Picture CD. If you plan to upload these generated Web pages to the Internet, you may pick themes for your thumbnail and main image pages from the pull-down menus on the right. When you select a theme, Compu-Pic will preview it for you in the left portion of the window.

12. Select Output options from the pull-down menu in the upper right corner.

13. Now you need to set the folder locations for the four output types. For each, click the Browse button on the right, navigate to the correct directory and click Select.

◆ Select your Pictures directory for the thumbnail pages.

◆ Select your THUMB directory for the thumbnail images.

◆ Select your WEB directory for both image pages and files.

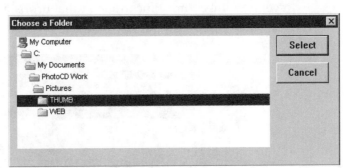

14. Deselect the Launch Web Browser When Complete option and click the Create button.

15. Leave CompuPic Pro and test your setup. Double-click the orange Autorun icon and determine if everything has worked correctly.

16. Launch your favorite CD burning program and start a new data disc. Copy the files from your work folder and burn them onto your CD, as seen here.

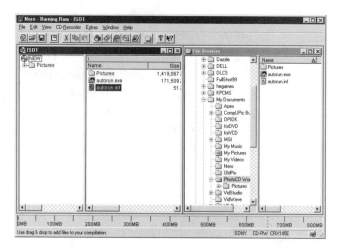

Run Your Picture CD Software

After burning your Picture CD, you're ready to share it with friends or enjoy it yourself. Take some time to survey the surprising power of this handy utility that you burned on the CD along with your pictures.

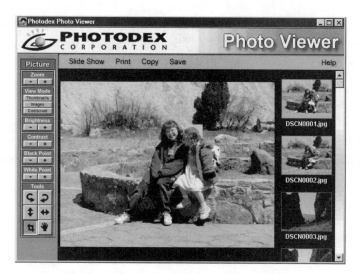

Run a slide show   Click the Slide Show link, found to the left on the top orange menu bar to begin your slide show playback. Once the show begins, this menu changes. Choose from Stop Slide Show to return to the main menu and slower or faster to change the playback rate.

Choose a picture   Scroll through the thumbnails on the right side of the main window to see the pictures stored on your Picture CD. Click on any picture to load it into the main viewing area.

Print, Copy, or Save a picture   The orange menu bar near the top of the screen allows you to choose from a number of options. Select print to create a hard copy of your currently selected image. Use the copy command to copy your selected image to the system clipboard. Save allows you to create a copy of the selected image from your CD to your hard drive.

Adjust your image   The controls on the left allow you to adjust the currently selected picture. Use these to change the brightness, contrast, orientation and zoom of the image. You can save this adjusted picture to disk as described above.

Upload Your Web Pages to the Internet

As discussed above, you created fully functional Web pages while manufacturing your Picture CD. You can send these pages to any Internet site. Simply upload the contents of your Pictures directory. Use `index.html`, found in the Pictures folder, as your main page.

NOTE   While Photodex's Picture CD remains fairly unique, CompuPic Pro's ability to create Web pages is not. Other image cataloging software, most notably Cerious ThumbsPlus (`www.cerious.com`) offers Web page generation capabilities.

68 Create a VCD Slideshow

Video CDs (VCD) offer a novel way for you to share and present your digital images. VCDs store pictures and video data on standard CDs that play back in many DVD players. VCDs are small, lightweight, and easy to copy and distribute. By burning your photo albums on VCDs, you can share your images in front of a TV rather than in front of a computer.

VCDs are new to America, but not to the world at large. Video CDs are extremely popular in Southeast Asia, where you can even buy stand-alone VCD players. In fact, VCDs have almost entirely replaced the videotape for movie rentals and sales.

The Video CD standard was created by JVC, Philips, Sony, and Matsushita (Panasonic) in 1993 as a way to store MPEG-1 video on CDs. In 1995, the 2.0 ("White Book") standard introduced slide show support. While this may seem like ancient history, it's only now that commercial DVD players have made inroads into the American consumer market, with players now providing VCD playback support.

VCD compatibility with any DVD unit is determined by two factors: format and media type. Of these two, format is the easiest to predict. It's on the box. If it says "VCD support," your player probably has it. Media type is another story. That's often a matter for trial, error, and a lot of experimentation. Some players accept CD-R (recordable CD) blanks. Most accept CD-RW (recordable *and* rewritable CDs). Stop by the terrific and informative VCD Help site (www.vcdhelp.com) to look up your player and see what formats and media types it supports.

N O T E   DVD players use red 635-nanometer or 650-nanometer lasers to play back DVD movies. CD-R and CD-RW weren't designed for lasers of these frequencies. CD drives on your computer use a 780nm infrared laser. The organic CD-R dyes and CD-RW compounds, designed to reflect 780nm light, might not reflect sufficient 635nm or 650nm light to create a clear signal. To fix this, some DVD players use two lasers to support VCD.

Using Nero 5.5 to Create a Slideshow

Nero 5.5 offers one of the most powerful and flexible CD-burning packages available on the market today. Among its other functions, it allows you to quickly and easily create a photo VCD that can play back on many DVD players. Most importantly, the VCD playback is reliable. The VCDs created by Nero have proven more consistent than VCDs created by any other general-purpose CD-burning software in conforming to the White Book standard. (For more information, go to www.nero.com.)

N O T E The Usenet group rec.video.desktop offers the latest and most informative discussions about all sorts of video editing and video CD-burning topics. You can search this group by using Google's new Usenet search engine (http://groups.google.com).

Prepare Your Pictures

VCD playback works best with properly sized images. Where possible, batch size your images in advance and do not rely on your DVD player to do the work for you. The following table gives the ideal size, in pixels, for your images. You'll find frame sizes for both standard video on CD (VCD) and super video on CD (SVCD). Many image cataloging and conversion programs, such as CompuPic Pro (www.photodex.com), Graphic Converter (www.lemkesoft.com) and Thumbs Plus (www.cerious.com) offer batch resizing functions.

VCD	Normal Quality	High Quality
NTSC	352 × 240	704 × 480
PAL	352 × 288	704 × 576
SVCD	Normal Quality	High Quality
NTSC	480 × 480	704 × 480
PAL	480 × 576	704 × 576

In my experience, smaller works better than larger. 1600 × 1200 images crashed my DVD player while less-than-ideal 320 × 240 images worked fine. I achieved the highest (subjective) image quality when using 704 × 480 pixel pictures.

Use CD-RW

If you can, start with CD-RW blanks. CD-RW blanks play back on more DVD players and you can experiment more, without throwing out discs, until you perfect your VCD burning technique. I found it took quite a few tries before I got my VCD slide shows to work just right. By using CD-RW, I saved some grief and minimized environmental impact from my discards.

Burn with Nero

Follow these steps to create and burn your own VCD slideshow with Nero.

1. Launch Nero 5.5 and wait for the Nero Wizard to appear.

2. Select Compile a New CD and click Next. Choose Other CD formats and click Next. Select Video CD and click Next. Then click Finish.

3. Use the file browser found on the right half of the Nero window to navigate to your images. Drag your images onto the left portion of the screen and add them to your slideshow.

4. By default, Nero adds an infinite pause after each image. This means that your slideshow cannot advance until you press the Next Chapter button on your remote control. You can change this, if you wish, to allow the slideshow to advance on its own. To do so, select one or all of the images and then double-click a selected image. The video properties window will appear. Select Seconds from the Pause settings pull-down menu and enter a number, such as 10, into the text field. Click OK to continue. Notice the file size in this picture, showing a Nero VCD slideshow, ready to be burned to disc.

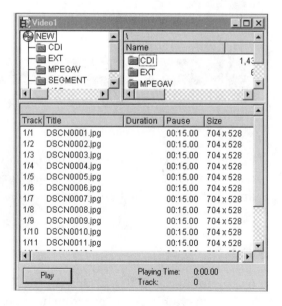

5. Select File ➤ Compilation Info. This will bring up the Info dialog box, where you can perform some fine-tuning.

6. Click the Video CD tab. Make sure the Encoding resolution is set correctly. My version always defaults to PAL. As I live in the United States, I must always change this to NTSC.

7. Click the Menu tab. You can, if desired, add a menu to your VCD. This menu will show thumbnails of the first 99 items in your slideshow. You may add more than 99 items to the show itself, but you cannot create a more detailed menu. To add a menu, select the Enable menu checkbox. Choose a layout from the Layout pull-down menu. These represent various ways you can structure your interactive menus. (I like the 9 and 12 thumbnail layouts in particular.) If desired, add a background picture and titles for the header and footer.

8. Click the ISO tab. I find that my disks work best when I select ISO level 1, with the DOS character set. I deselect Joliet and the two path options.

9. Click the Label tab. Enter any Volume name you desire. Since I use these disks on my DVD player rather than a PC, I usually stick to the default name.

10. Click the Burn tab. When I burn my VCDs, I choose the Simulation and Write options from the top set. As I own an older burner, I keep my writing speed slow, to prevent buffer under-runs.

11. Click OK to save your options and dismiss the dialog box.

12. Click the "burning disk" icon to open the Write CD dialog box. Choose either Test and Burn or Burn and click the Burn button to create your VCD.

N O T E   If you wish to burn additional copies of your CD at a later time, you can save either a compilation file, which contains all the file names and settings, or an image file, which is a binary image of the CD contents.

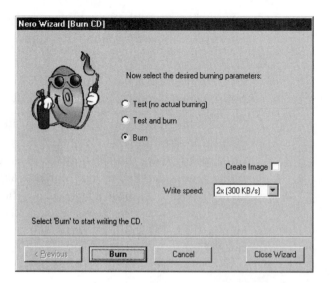

Show Your VCD Slideshow in Your DVD player

To play your VCD, insert it in your DVD player, just as you would a DVD. In general, VCDs will not automatically start playback. You probably need to press the play button to begin. You can stop playback at any time, using your DVD's stop button.

After your first picture loads, you can manage playback using your remote control. As each slide is stored in a separate "chapter" use the Next Chapter and Previous Chapter buttons to navigate through your slideshow. If you've entered a delay for each image, you won't have to use the remote at all once playback begins. After a certain number of seconds that you specified above, the slideshow will automatically progress to the next image.

69 Create Your Own DVD with iDVD

If you own a new G4 Macintosh with a SuperDrive, then congratulations. You have access to one of the coolest new technologies on the market today. SuperDrives allow you to create DVD disks in a new type of drive built by Pioneer, the DVR-103. What you may not know is that your Super-Drive and the free iDVD software that came bundled with your Macintosh offer a fantastic way to create slideshows with your digital videos.

To create your own slideshow DVDs, follow these basic steps.

1. Plan your DVD folders structure.

2. Build these folders in iDVD.

3. Import your digital photographs into your folders.

4. Set your folder icons.

5. Select a theme for your DVD.

6. Edit your titles and preview your disc.

7. Burn the DVD.

We'll go through each step in more detail below.

Plan Your Folders

Each iDVD screen allows you to include up to six items. These items include folders and slideshows. Folders can store slideshows or additional folders. Slideshows contain an arbitrary number of individual digital photographs.

For DVDs with six or fewer slideshows, you don't have to worry further about folder structure. However, when you create a DVD with more than six "rolls" of digital photographs, you need to plan how you will lay these out. For example, let's say you have a few dozen sets of images. You can break these down by months (Jan-Feb, Mar-Apr, etc.), by event (Baby Pictures, Sporting Events, etc.), and so forth. Each folder can contain subfolders, so you have a fair degree of flexibility despite the six-item limit.

Think your structure out carefully. Today it costs approximately $10 for a DVD-R blank from the Apple Store (www.apple.com/store). Good planning can avoid regrets. Write your notes down. You'll need this information for the following section.

Build Your Folders and Slideshows

Follow these steps to create your folders in iDVD.

1. Launch iDVD and select New Project from the introductory splash screen. Navigate to where you wish to save your new project. Name the project and click Save.

2. Your new project workspace will look something like the screen shown here.

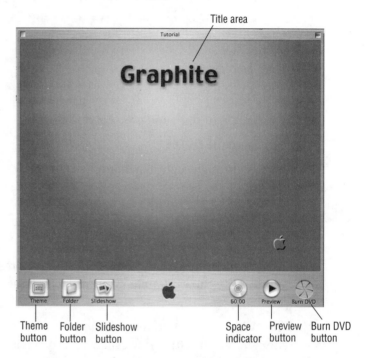

Title area

Graphite

Theme   Folder   Slideshow   Space   Preview Burn DVD
button   button   button   indicator button   button

Take a few seconds to locate the following items:

- The DVD title appears in bold letters at the top of the screen. The default title is Graphite, because that is the name of the default theme.

- The Theme, Folder, and Slideshow buttons are on the lower-left side of the screen. These buttons offer one-click access to the most commonly used layout items.

- The disk space used/free indicator, Preview button, and Burn button are on the lower-right corner of the screen. These items let you plan, test, and burn your DVD.

3. Refer to your plan and add your top-level folders and slideshows in order. Click the Folder button to add a folder and the Slideshow button to add a slideshow. In the example shown next, I've added three folders.

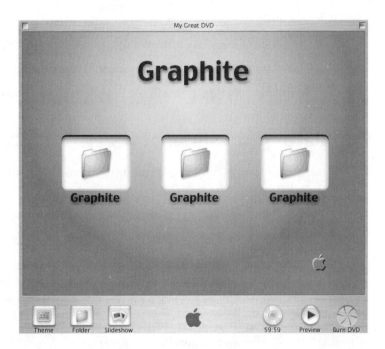

4. Double-click a folder to move down into it. From there you can add more slideshows and folders. In this example, I've added two slideshows to a folder. Note the double left angle-bracket. Click this to return to the previous level.

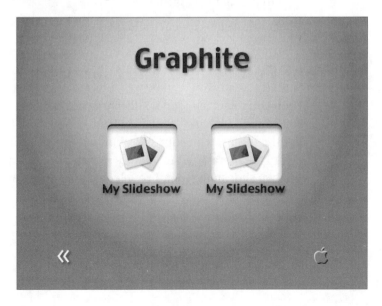

5. Label your folders and slideshows by clicking on the default text below each icon. Enter a new label and press return.

6. Create a full skeleton of your folders and slide shows.

In the next section, you will see how to add your pictures.

Populate Your Slideshows with Pictures

After creating your folder structure, you're now ready to add pictures to the individual slideshows. To do so, follow these steps.

1. Double-click any slideshow to see the contents list.

2. Drag your pictures for this slideshow onto the list.

3. Select Picture Duration from the pull-down menu at the bottom of the window. Choose from 1, 3, 5 and 10 seconds or pick Manual to force viewers to click a button to progress to the next screen.

4. (Optional) Select Display <> on Image if you want to had helpful reminder arrows for navigation.

5. From this screen you can drag any slide to a new position or select it and tap Delete to remove it from the slideshow.

6. Click the Return button on the lower-right of the window to return to the main layout screen.

Repeat these steps for each slideshow on your DVD.

Set Your Folder and Slideshow Icons

When you select a folder or slideshow, a slider bar appears over the icon. Move this slider to select an icon from the content of that folder or slideshow. Start with your slideshows at the lowest levels and move your way up the hierarchy. The picture shown on the next page reflects a folder with two slideshows in it. I've selected an icon for each slideshow.

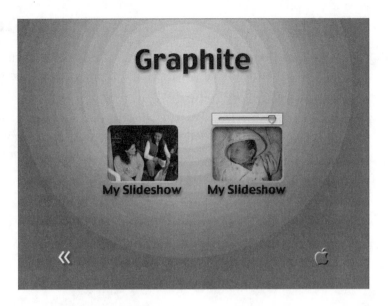

Please note that folder sliders work with folder contents. You can only pick from those icons set on the subfolders and slideshows that they contain. At any time, you can select from a maximum of six icons for any folder, even if the slideshows in that folder contain dozens or even hundreds of images.

Select a Theme for Your DVD

iDVD offers a number of prebuilt themes for your DVD. These lend a particular style to your DVD menu structure. To choose a theme, follow these steps.

1. Click the Theme button in the lower-right corner of the iDVD window.

2. Scroll through the choices and click on the theme you like. The main display will automatically update with this theme.

3. (Optional) If you're feeling adventurous, choose Custom from the Theme pop-up window. By doing so, you reveal a number of control panels that offer fine tuning of your theme.

Keep in mind that you can set the theme for each menu (folder) on your DVD. Changing the look of the main menu will not affect any subfolder.

Edit Your Titles and Preview Your Disc

Before continuing, make sure to set a title for each folder. Just click on the default title (usually "Graphite" from the default theme) and replace it with a more appropriate word or phrase.

To test your iDVD project, click the Preview button (at the bottom of the screen, just to the left of the Burn button). By choosing this option, you can try out your DVD as if it were playing in a stand-alone player. iDVD provides you with a handy remote-control to use.

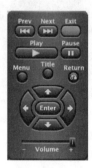

Go ahead. Enjoy. There's no one to fight with for the remote and you can lean back in your comfy chair and rule the video world. When you're ready to return to design mode, click the Preview button again.

Burn Your DVD

When you've fully laid out your DVD and are ready to burn your blank, click the Burn DVD icon (on the bottom-right corner of the screen). Watch it open to reveal a pulsating yellow-and-black button. Click the button and let your SuperDrive burn your DVD-R blank. (It will probably take a bit of time to do so. The SuperDrive is notorious for taking its time to burn your DVD-Rs. You may wish to go get a cup of coffee.)

After burning your DVD, it will automatically eject. It's now ready to play back on any commercial DVD player. Your DVD should play universally, on any unit you have available to you, without the uncertainties that come with VCD technology.

70 Create a Slideshow to Share over the Internet

Real (www.real.com) offers a terrific little utility called RealSlideshow. This free program allows you to create an Internet-based slide show using a technology called RealPix. This software is easy and quick to use.

NOTE Be aware that RealSlideshow does not create a "video" of your slides. It uses Real Picture technology to load your images and synchronize them with the sound track. If you wish to create an actual Real video (.rm), then skip to the next section.

Follow these steps to create your own Internet slideshow.

1. Launch RealSlideshow.

2. Drag your images onto the RealSlideshow window. Drag the slider to the right and make a note of how long your Slideshow will last.

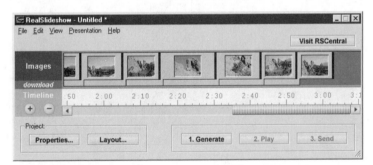

3. Insert a music CD into your drive. Select File ➢ Add Background Music.

4. Choose a track from the pull-down menu. This allows you to choose from the various selections offered on your CD.

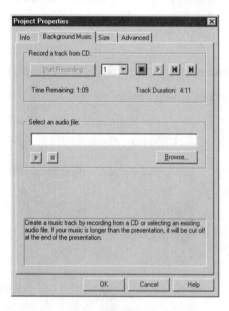

N O T E   If you plan to share this slideshow with others on the Net, make sure you use royalty-free tracks. You may use copyrighted material so long as you retain your slideshow for private use. Posting a slideshow to the Internet is considered public exhibition and is strictly forbidden in the case of copyrighted music.

5. Click the Start Recording button. RealSlideshow will caution you about copyright issues. Read this warning and click Accept. Your recording will begin.

6. When you've recorded enough music, click the Stop Recording button. Acknowledge that you must save the file by clicking OK. Navigate to where you wish to save your new WAV file and click Save. Click OK again and RealSlideshow will load your file into the music track.

7. Click the Properties button. Enter any pertinent information including Title, Author, Copyright Notice, etc.

8. Now you can generate an actual slideshow. Select Presentation ➢ Generate or click the 1. Generate button. If RealSlideshow complains that you have not entered sufficient information, click Ignore.

9. Navigate to where you will save the slideshow. Be sure to save it in a folder—RealSlideshow will create a huge number of files! Enter a file-name (with no spaces or odd characters) and click Save.

After following these steps, you'll have created an entire set of images and Real files. Let's go over what's in this folder:

Image Files   You'll find a complete collection of image files, sized to fit within a small player window. There will be one file for each original image.

Web Page   RealSlideshow creates a convenient Web page from which you can launch your slideshow. Your Web page ends with a .htm extension.

SMIL Files   SMIL (pronounced "Smile") files refer to the multimedia elements that create the presentation surrounding your video. Files include the main SMIL file (with a .smil extension), and supporting files with the Real Text (.rt), Real Media (.ram), Real Player (.rm) and Real Pix (.rp) extensions.

To play your slideshow back, load the main .htm file in your Web page and follow directions. You may upload your entire folder to your favorite Web site to allow general Internet access to this page and to your slideshow.

Create a Narrated Slideshow with Ulead VideoStudio

If you happen to own a copy of Ulead Video Studio, you can quickly and easily create a streaming slideshow with narration. While other video edi-tors offer slideshow capabilities, in my experience VideoStudio stands apart with its ability to integrate narration over slides as they play back. Follow these steps to create your narrated slideshow with Ulead VideoStudio:

1. Launch VideoStudio and click the New Project Icon in the upper left corner.

2. Navigate to where you wish to save your work and enter a name for your project, such as "SlideShow." You may add, if you wish, a subject and a description. Select AVI 720x480 DV NTSC from the Available Project Templates pull-down menu and click OK.

3. Select the Storyboard step.

4. Turn your attention to the lower left hand portion of the screen and click the Insert Media Files button. Choose Add Image... from the pop-up menu that immediately appears.

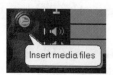

5. Choose your slide duration and enter it in the fields at the bottom of the dialog box. This value defaults to 3 seconds. I prefer longer delays of 5, 10, or even 15 seconds for narrated slideshows.

6. Navigate to the folder where you've stored your images. Select all your images at once and click Open. VideoStudio will load your images and add them in order to your movie.

7. Choose the Voice step. Make sure you've attached a microphone to the mic-in port of your computer.

8. Move the video play head to the very start of your slide show, all the way to the left. The play head is the green-colored downward arrow found among the time codes, just above the storyboard timeline.

9. Look at the Controls panel. Just under the Record button, you'll find an option called Record with Preview. Make sure this option is checked.

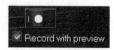

10. Click the Record button at the very top of the controls area.

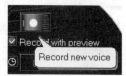

11. Make any volume adjustments using the level meter provided in the pop-up window, then click Start.

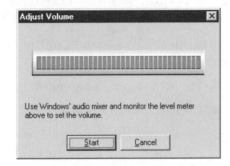

12. Start speaking, narrating your pictures. The secret here is to watch the video playback window as you narrate. Discuss what's happening and try to keep an informal, interesting tone. After finishing your narration, click the Record button again to stop recording.

13. (Optional) If desired, click the Music step and add a music track to your video. (Check your VideoStudio manual for specific instructions on how to do this.) If you plan to exhibit this video outside your immediate family or on the Internet, make sure to use royalty-free tracks.

14. Select the Finish step and Click the Make a Movie icon in the upper left corner.

15. Select from any of the following four options: High Quality RealVideo, Low Quality Real Video, High Quality Windows Media and Low Quality Windows Media. Navigate to where you wish to save your streaming video and click Save.

Share Your Streaming Media over the Internet

Several sites, like iClips (www.iclips.com), allow you to store and share your streaming video over the Internet. iClips offers Real media streaming, while other sites provide video hosting for QuickTime and Windows

Media. Each site varies in its offerings and pricing—many, like iClips, offer both free and pay accounts. iClips' free account offers a full 20MB of video storage and 56Kbps streaming. You can upgrade to 100MB of storage and broadband streaming for $10 per month.

Sign up for an iClips account and follow these directions to upload your Real media video.

1. Log in to your iClips account.

2. Click Upload an Existing Real Media File from the main window.

3. Locate Step 1 and click the Browse button. Navigate to your file and click Open. Click either the Continue>>> button on the top-right or on the lower-right of your Web browser window.

4. Locate Step 2. Confirm that your name and e-mail address are correct. Add a title and description of your video. Again, click one of the Continue>>> buttons.

5. Locate Step 3. Choose how you want to share your video, either by e-mail or for Web pages.

6. Click Done to begin your upload. A progress window will appear as the upload commences.

71 Protect Your Pictures

Any picture you snap with your digital camera belongs to you. It is your creation and your expression of how you see the world around you. By default, you own the copyright to your own work and thus have the exclusive right to produce, exhibit, and reproduce that material in print or on the Internet. Only you have the right to change your photos and create what's called a "derivative work" from those photos. All of these rights automatically belong to you and cannot be taken away or forced from you unless you decide to assign those rights to others.

While only a lawyer can give you specific details regarding issues pertaining to copyright law, there are a number of important Web sites that you might want to investigate. These include the following:

United States Copyright Home Page
(http://lcweb.loc.gov/copyright/) The main Library of Congress site.

Copyright Office's Recording and Deposit System

(http://lcweb.loc.gov/copyright/cords) From here, you can download forms to fill out, but as of this writing you couldn't submit them electronically.

1971 Bern Convention

(www.law.cornell.edu/treaties/berne/overview.html) Cornell's coverage of the 1971 Berne Convention treaty to provide international protection to intellectual property.

Watermarks

It used to be that you could hold up most good quality paper to the light and reveal faint marks, lettering, and patterns. These elements were known as *watermarks*, and were invented by Italian papermakers around the twelfth or thirteenth century. To create the marks, they pressed designs over wet pulp. As the paper dried, the marks "disappeared" except when held up to light. These hallmarks worked in much the same way as those you'd find on silver, porcelain, or other handcrafted products: they identified the maker. Over time, watermarks became a crucial part of document security, particularly in the creation of currency. Today, an electronic form of watermarks helps identify ownership and copyright of digital images.

Digimarc (www.digimarc.com) offers today's premiere digital watermarking product. Using proprietary technology, a marked image offers instant identification of the true creator. Most importantly, it doesn't degrade the quality of your picture. To use Digimarc's technology, you sign up for one of three services offered: ImageBridge, ImageBridge Plus, or ImageBridge Pro. Fees vary by the number of images you watermark and the level of service you choose.

After signing up, you'll be assigned a creator identification code to use when watermarking your pictures. This identifier links to an identifying Web page. From there, anyone can view the copyright information associated with an image.

The basic service offers a free trial where you may watermark up to 99 pictures per year. ImageBridge Plus service adds greater Web page customization, allowing you to add more information about yourself and your organization. ImageBridge Pro service provides full Web customization and greater tracking information. You'll be able to monitor individual transactions and provide image-specific links for information and ordering.

To embed a watermark, you must use a plug-in built into many image processing and cataloging products. These products include Adobe Photoshop, Cerious ThumbsPlus, Corel PhotoPaint, Extensis Portfolio, Jasc Paintshop Pro, and Ulead PhotoImpact. (Stop by the Digimarc site for a full list.) The embedding function works much the same in each program. For example, here are the instructions to embed a watermark in Adobe Photoshop. The only difference between these steps and the steps for another software title lies in the menu under which you find the embed and detect functions.

1. With your image open, select Filter ➢ Digimarc ➢ Embed Watermark.

2. The following dialog box appears. Notice how it's customized to my Digimarc ID (799051). When you register for your service, you'll be assigned an ID and a personal identification number.

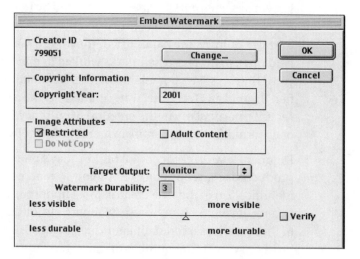

3. Enter the year for the copyright, select the watermark durability, and click OK. Your watermark will automatically be added to your picture.

4. Save your picture.

After saving, you may now detect the watermark you created.

1. Load your picture in Photoshop.

2. Select Filter ➢ Digimarc ➢ Read Watermark to open the Watermark Information dialog box.

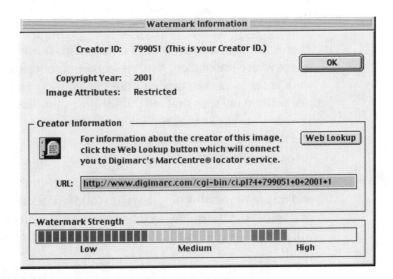

3. Click OK if you simply wish to see the creator ID. Otherwise, click Web Lookup to connect to Digimarc's locator service. The copyright and contact information will appear in your Web browser, looking something like this:

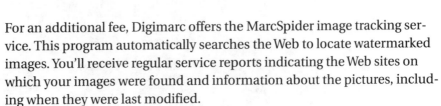

For an additional fee, Digimarc offers the MarcSpider image tracking service. This program automatically searches the Web to locate watermarked images. You'll receive regular service reports indicating the Web sites on which your images were found and information about the pictures, including when they were last modified.

Visible Watermarks

There's another way to use watermarks. This involves overlaying your image with a translucent pattern. Photographers who wish to display their work yet protect their originals use this method. You'll find these watermarks on many sites that sell publishing rights like news photo services. The idea works like this. You see the picture you wish to use. You pay a fee and then you're given access to the original (without watermarks) for your magazine, newspaper, or other publication.

You can easily create a watermark like this in Photoshop and other higher-end image processing programs. Just add a pattern layer over your image and adjust the transparency down to about 25 percent. Your original image will show through clearly, yet it's quite difficult to remove the markings that result.

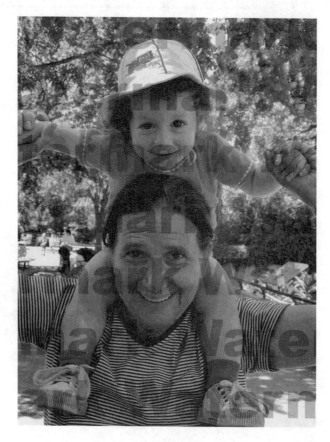

Clever Content

Alchemedia (www.alchemedia.com/) offers an innovative way to protect your images. "Clever Content" thwarts unauthorized use of digital images by preventing copying, printing, and screenshots. This enables you to post your digital pictures on the World Wide Web knowing they're nearly impossible to duplicate. To view a Clever Content image, you need a special viewer, freely available for download for both PC and Macintosh platforms (www.alchemedia.com/products/install.html).

With Clever Content, your image automatically hides itself. When someone attempts to duplicate your image, they will copy a logo screen instead, as seen below. This is an actual screen shot, taken from a normal-looking photograph. When the viewer detects the screen shot function, it covers the image with this pattern until the capture has finished. Then it redisplays the original picture.

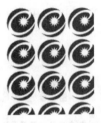

Clever Content protection is not limited to digital photographs. With it, you can protect text and Adobe PDF files as well.

Subject Waivers

In general, when you want to publish your pictures in any way, including on the Internet, your subjects should sign a waiver. This allows you to use their image and name and protects you from lawsuits. Whenever I go out to shoot pictures, I carry a number of blank waivers with me. Subject waiver forms don't have to be complex; in fact, all you really need are the following elements:

Granting the right to use an image and name   The subject gives the photographer (and his or her licensees, successors in interest, legal representatives and heirs) the irrevocable right to use his or her name and picture.

Approving alterations   The subject must acknowledge that the picture may be altered for any lawful purpose. He or she waives any right to inspect or approve the alterations.

Holding harmless   The subject promises to hold the photographer harmless (except where malice occurs).

Acknowledging copyright   The subject acknowledges that copyright belongs to the photographer. He or she waives any claims based on how the photographer uses or sells the pictures (so long as they're not used for defamation or associated with pornography or other prurient interests).

Binding agreement   The agreement must be binding under a state or the District of Columbia.

Consent for minors   If the subject is a minor, the parent or guardian must sign the release.

Signature   The subject must sign and date the release and provide basic contact information.

72 Ceiva Picture Frames: Sharing with the PC-Less

Every now and then, a gadget comes along that makes your heart run fast, your palms sweat, and thoughts of the Tenth Commandment run through your head. The Ceiva Internet-connected picture frame is one of them. With a Ceiva frame, you can share your digital photos with people who don't even own a PC.

N O T E   You can pick up your own Ceiva for just under $200. The price includes a one-year service subscription. Stop by www.ceiva.com for more information.

The Ceiva looks more or less like any picture frame, as you can see in the graphic below, except that it arrives with an A/C adapter and a phone cord. Plug your frame into the appropriate wall jack and it springs to life, displaying your digital image. You can show just one picture continuously, or present a slide show of up to ten images. Once a day, the Ceiva dials into a special account and checks for new pictures. When it finds them waiting, it automatically downloads them to your frame and displays them. With a Ceiva, not only can you display your digital images on grandma's night-stand, you can update them from day to day or week to week.

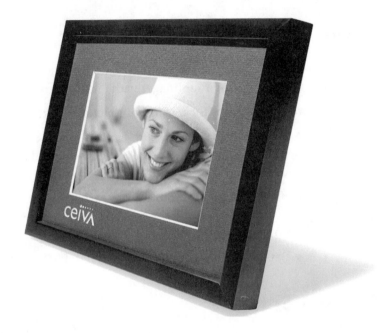

Each Ceiva system actually consists of two parts: a special Web site and the picture frame receiver. The Ceiva Web site stores incoming pictures and allows you to upload new ones. The receiver connects to this site, down-loads pictures, and displays them.

The Ceiva unit receives new pictures by "calling home" once a day. It picks an off hour, usually near midnight, and connects to the Ceiva Web site via the phone line. This connection occurs without sound and should not dis-turb anyone in the house. (If the line is busy, it will try again later.) The unit scans the Web-based inbox. When it finds new pictures waiting, it down-loads up to ten of them. These pictures displace any images already on the unit, transferring them to your "recently removed" outbox. At the same time, your Ceiva also downloads any new settings. Each call lasts approxi-mately 5 to 10 minutes. After the download process concludes, the Ceiva will begin to display the new pictures.

N O T E   Ceivas make great presents for people who don't own a PC. When you send friends or family a receiver, you can transmit your latest and greatest pictures directly to them. (But remember, you'll be managing their Ceiva Web account yourself.)

Picture Prep

With a few exceptions, prepare your pictures according to the instructions in the "Enhancing Your Images with PhotoDeluxe" part of this book.

Here are some tips for getting your pictures ready for the Ceiva frame:

◆ Make sure to select pictures with good contrast. The picture quality on early Ceiva models can best be described as "iffy." The better the contrast, the better your images will appear.

◆ Keep in mind that your images should not exceed 640 × 480 pixels. Typically, this works out to about 64KB per image. In no case should you upload any image larger than 3MB.

◆ Save your images in BMP, JPEG, PICT, PSD, TIFF, or GIF format.

Account Setup

I recommend that you set up both the frame and Web site before commencing regular use. I learned this lesson the hard way. My Ceiva arrived configured for California, across the country from my location. (The nice folks at Ceiva set up the account for my publisher, who is located in California.) For the first two weeks, my Ceiva unit made daily long-distance calls. Had I first set it up correctly, I could have avoided a few dollars in long-distance charges. Although I strongly doubt this will happen to you, a few moments of preparation can almost always prevent an unpleasant surprise.

To set up your Ceiva account, follow these steps:

1. Point your browser at www.ceiva.com and log in according to the instructions in your Welcome letter that arrives with your frame.

2. Click Ceiva Settings. The Settings page will appear.

3. For the Slide Show Interval option, specify the duration between showing each image. You can select from 5 seconds to 1 minute.

4. You can set the Picture Off option to turn off the picture to save energy and keep the room dark. Picture Off times run from 6 P.M. to 2 A.M. You can also choose Never to leave the picture on at all times.

5. If you specified a time to turn the picture off, set a Picture On time to specify when to turn the picture back on. You may select from 4 A.M. to 11 A.M.

6. In the Your Phone Number field, make sure you enter your phone number correctly. Your area code will determine the local access number.

7. In the Dialing Prefix field, enter any prefix needed to dial out.

8. Click Update to complete the account setup process.

Picture Posting

Your Ceiva frame can hold up to ten pictures at any time and arrives with ten "factory-wrapped" images onboard. Most of us have a least one family member who will insist on knowing who "those strange people" are. Sidestep the whole issue by preloading ten pictures of your own.

Here's how to add your pictures to the Ceiva frame:

1. Visit your Ceiva home page at www.ceiva.com by logging into your account. Locate the Send a Picture section and click To My Frame.

2. Wait for the next page to load, then click Send Multiple Pictures. (I use this page, which I have bookmarked, to perform all my Ceiva uploads, rather than using the single Send a Picture page.)

3. Choose your Ceiva from the list and click the right-arrow button.

4. Click Browse and select an image from your computer. You can upload just one image or as many as ten at a time.

5. Click Continue, and then go get a cup of coffee. Uploading images can take a lot of time.

This process adds pictures to your Ceiva inbox. The next time your unit connects, it will download your images from your inbox to your frame.

Ceiva Tips

If you're lucky enough to own your own Ceiva, the following tips and tricks can help you make the most of your unit.

Set the Slideshow in Motion

Your Ceiva unit can display either a single picture or a slideshow of multiple photos. You can move between these two modes at any time. When you wish to activate the slideshow, press and hold the white button for about 5 seconds. Release the white button when you see the message "Let go now to start the slide show."

Update Your Pictures

You never have to wait until tomorrow when you want to see new pictures today. At any time, you can press and hold the white button to tell your frame to check for new pictures. Hold the button for about 10 seconds, until your unit says "You can let go now, I'm connecting." A progress bar will appear at the bottom of the screen to show how the call proceeds.

Manually Select a Picture

To select a specific picture, tap the white button. At each tap, your Ceiva will advance to the next image. When you select a picture in this manner, you exit the slideshow mode.

Adjust Brightness

To adjust the brightness, tap the black button. This button will cycle through the eight levels of brightness supported by your Ceiva. If you push once too often, fear not. Just push another six times, and you're set.

Lock a Picture

Do you have a picture that you absolutely love? You can "lock" it. This allows it to remain on your unit after your Ceiva downloads the next set of images. Here's how you can lock a picture:

1. Point your browser at www.ceiva.com and log in to your Ceiva account.

2. Click Now Showing. You'll see a page similar to the one shown below. From this page, you can lock and unlock photos, send pictures, and remove pictures.

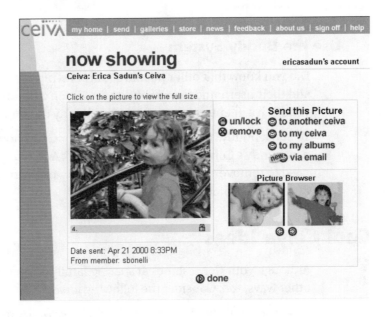

3. Click the arrow buttons to navigate to the picture that you wish to lock.

4. Click the picture you wish to lock, and then click Un/lock to toggle the locking mode.

5. Click Done to complete the process.

Pick an Orientation

You can use your Ceiva in portrait mode as well as landscape mode. Just flip your unit on its side. Of course, you must make sure you rotate your images correctly. Use counter-clockwise rotation, or the frame won't stand up correctly. In PhotoDeluxe, rotate your portraits to the left. The first time I tried this, I chose the wrong option. My children ended up on their heads.

NOTE See the "Enhancing Your Images with PhotoDeluxe" part of this book for information about rotating pictures.

Whether you decide to upload landscape or (rotated) portrait pictures, be consistent. Once you decide on one or the other, make sure that every picture on your Ceiva has the same orientation, especially when you use the slideshow mode.

Use the Buddy System

Did you know that other people could send pictures to your Ceiva? Just add their username to your buddy list. When a buddy sends a picture to your Ceiva, it enters your inbox, just like any other image.

To add a buddy, click Buddy List from your Ceiva home page. Enter your new buddy's Ceiva site username and click Add. Then click Done. If you need to remove a buddy, just select your ex-pal from the buddy list, click Remove, and then click Done.

Cool Ceiva Ideas

Although your Ceiva shines at sharing family photos, you can use it in other ways, too. Consider the following ideas:

◆ Send a birthday card to a friend's Ceiva or a Mother's Day card to your mom's Ceiva. Your buddies will feel special when they wake up to see your greeting card on their Ceiva.

◆ Send a series of visual "clues" to your special buddy to hint at a special gift or get-together. Don't forget to label them as "clues."

◆ Send an invitation for a special night out. In fact, why not send a picture of a dozen roses, too?

◆ Send a good joke. Combine a picture of yourself laughing with a great pun and upload it to your buddy's inbox.

◆ Is your buddy forgetful? Why not send a helpful reminder or a grocery list?

◆ Try "animating" your Ceiva. Use your digital camera to take a series of pictures moving closer and closer to your subject. Don't forget to upload the photos in the correct order!

You can also use your Ceiva in your business. For under $300, you can place a unit at your point of sale or in your store window. These ideas only begin to suggest how you can showcase your special offerings or services:

◆ Set up your Ceiva at the front of your restaurant and upload pictures of today's specials.

◆ Place a Ceiva on your hotel's reception desk and have it cycle through today's weather report, activity schedule, welcome for convention members, and so forth.

◆ Place a Ceiva in a locker room to demonstrate the stretch-of-the-day and remind your clients to stay hydrated.

◆ Set up a Ceiva to show off the latest fashions that have just arrived at your store.

◆ Place a Ceiva at your teller windows and sell "advertising" space to local businesses.

The ideas go on and on.

Upcoming Ceiva Features

Ceiva continues to grow, develop and introduce creative sharing solutions. Over the next year or so, look for the following products to debut:

Modem Cameras   The Polaroid Modem camera (PDC640, `www.polaroid.com`, $249.99) uses software created by Ceiva to share your pictures. Simply connect your camera to a phone line. You can upload to your Ceiva account or e-mail the picture or pictures to an address that you specify. The camera captures 640×480 pixel images at any of three compression levels. Each picture takes about 30 to 60 seconds to upload, using a 56k built-in modem. You can call from anywhere. The camera dials a toll-free number, uses caller-id technology to determine your location, and provides a list of local access numbers for your area. Ceiva's dial-in network covers approximately 98% of the U.S. with local call access.

PDAs   Soon, you'll be able to share your Ceiva pictures on PDAs, such as the Palm Pilot, as well as electronic frames.

Integrated Printing Cevia is working to integrate your frame with a number of printing solutions. Soon they'll offer wireless printing to connect with your Ceiva frame. In addition, they've partnered with online photofinishers to create silver-halide prints from your Ceiva images.

Ceiva TV Due for release next year, Ceiva TV will allow you to share pictures with friends and family using regular television sets rather than a special-purpose frame. This should relieve those people who could never find the "right place" for a Ceiva frame.

Ceiva 2 Watch out for the next generation of Ceiva picture frames, offering expanded memory and better picture resolution, to debut sometime in 2002.

Field Guide to Online Photofinishing and Album Sites

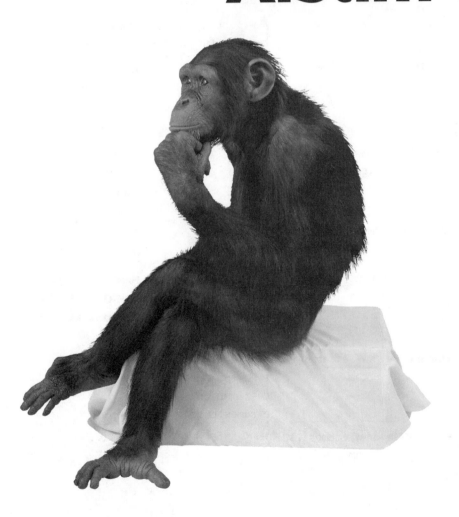

Service	URL	Contact	What's Offered
AltiPlano	www.altiplano.com	support@altiplano.com	**Albums and finishing. Membership. European.**
Big Nose	www.bignose.com	**1-877-672-4466,** info@bignose.com	**Poster processing, both digital and film.**
Black's	www.blacks.ca	**1-800-668-3826 (toll free in Canada only),** smile.centre@blackphoto.com	**Finishing. Can pick up at any Black's store.**
Cartogra	www.cartogra.com	www.cartogra.com/home/contactus.asp	**Photo sharing.**
Club Photo	www.clubphoto.com	**1-408-557-6740,** support@clubphoto.com	**Album & photo finishing. Regular and premium memberships.**
Color Mailer	www.colormailer.com www.colormailer.com.au	info@colormailer.com	**Finishing. Switzerland and Australia.**
DigitaalFoto	www.digitaalfoto.nl		**Albums & prints. Netherlands.**
DotPhoto	www.dotPhoto.com	http://dotphoto.custhelp.com/cgi-bin/dotphoto/people	**Finishing. Accepts CD-ROMs, Zip, Superdisk, and Orb.**
Eframes	www.eframes.com	**1-877-370-7000, 1-415-401-9211,** customerservice@eframes.com	**Framed prints, albums, finishing.**
EMemories	www.ememories.com	**1-310-586-4040**	**Prints & gifts.**

Service	URL	Contact	What's Offered
EZPrints	www.ezprints.com	1-888-584-7040, ezprints@ezprints.com	Finishing. Panoramic and Large (20 x 30) prints. Accepts CD-ROMS.
EZShots	www.ezshots.com	email@ezshots.com	Albums.
Fotango	www.fotango.com	+44 20 7251 7920, 9am-6pm, M-F, help@fotango.com	Finishing, reprints, gifts.
Fotofun	www.fotofun.be		Finishing. Belgium.
FotoTime	www.fototime.com	support@fototime.com, feedback@fototime.com	Albums, finishing.
FujiFilm	www.fujifilm.net	webmaster@fujifiilm.net	Finishing, albums. Membership.
Futureshop	www.futureshop.ca	1-888-785-8384, service@futureshop.ca	Finishing.
GatherRound	www.gatherround.com		Album sharing, gifts.
GinPhoto	www.ginphoto.on.ca		Service center, including overhead slides, prints.
Image Station	www.imagestation.com	1-877-488-2880, support@imagestation.com	Storage, sharing, prints.

Service	URL	Contact	What's Offered
IPrint	www.iprint.com	1-650-298-8500, Customer_Service@ iprint.com, Customer_Support@ iprint.com	Business and gift production.
Michael's Camera Store	www.michaels .com.au	(03) 9672 2224	Finishing. Australia (Melbourne).
MotoPhoto	www.motophoto. com	1-800-733-6686	Finishing.
MyPhotos-Now	www.myphotosnow .com		35mm to online photos.
Mystic Color Lab	www .mysticcolorlab .com	1-800-367-6061, cservice@ mysticcolorlab .com	Finishing.
Ofoto	www.ofoto.com	1-877-986-3686, support@ofoto .com	Finishing. Now a subsidiary of Kodak.
PhotoAccess	www.photoaccess .com **and** www .photoaccess .co.jp	1-206-264-2488, then push 0, support@ photoaccess .com, info@ photoaccess .com	Finishing.
PhotoBox	www.photobox .co.uk **and** www.photobox .ie	020 7691 1208, info@photobox .co.uk	Finishing and gifts.

Service	URL	Contact	What's Offered
PhotoChannel	www .photochannel .com	**1-604-893-8955,** support@ photochannel .com, info@ photochannel .com	**Finishing.**
PhotoIsland	www .photoisland .com	**1-800-762-8657,** support@ photoisland .com	**Albums, image processing fun. A tremendously entertaining site.**
PhotoLoft	www.photoloft .com	**1-800-480-2582,** support@ photoloft.com	**Finishing, albums. Membership.**
Photonet (Kodak)	www.photonet .com	**1-888-299-9576**	**Partnered with many sites.**
PhotoPoint	www.photopoint .com	help@photopoint.com	**Albums. Membership.**
PhotoWorks	www.photoworks .com	**1-800-445-3348,** **1-800-FILMWORKS,** info@filmworks .com	**Finishing. Formerly Seattle Filmworks.**
Print Room	www.printroom .com	**1-510-413-1200,** support@ printroom.com	**Finishing, albums. Partnered with** www.saycheese.com.
Shutterfly	www.shutterfly .com	customerservice@ shutterfly.com	**Finishing.**
Signature Color	www .signaturecolor .com	**1-512-445-0256,** cs@signaturecolor .com	**Finishing. Customer service hard to reach.**

Service	URL	Contact	What's Offered
SnapFish	www.snapfish .com	**1-304-420-5615,** service@ snapfish.com	**Finishing.**
The Digital Fridge	www. thedigital- fridge.com		**Albums.**
Top Photo	www.topfoto.com/ digital_print_ service.htm		**Finishing.**
Wal-Mart	www.walmart.com		**Finishing. Store pickup available.**
Wolf Camera	www.wolfcamera .com	**1-800-643-9653,** wolfstore@ wolfcamera.com	**Finishing. Panoramics available.**
Yahoo	http://photos .yahoo.com	yahoo-photos@ shutterfly.com	**Finishing, albums.**

Glossary

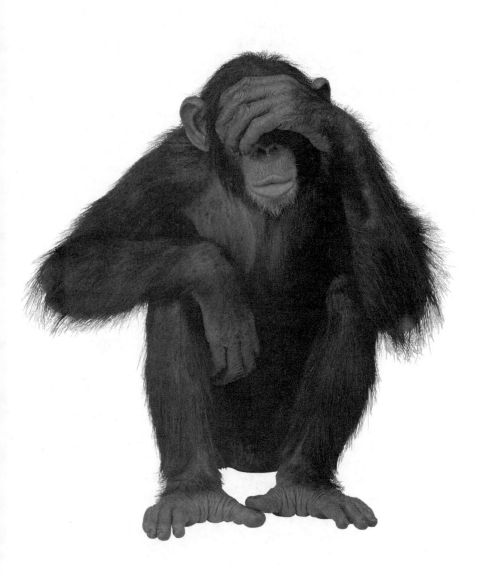

A

A/C adapter

An adapter that allows you to plug your camera into a wall outlet. Your camera's manufacturer usually provides this adapter at an additional cost.

ADC

See *analog-to-digital converter*.

aliasing

The jagged effect produced on lines, characters, and so forth when the resolution of the display is not sufficient to capture fine image detail.

alkaline battery

A type of non-rechargeable battery that can be used in your digital camera. Alkaline batteries drain very quickly under the demands of most digital cameras.

analog-to-digital converter (ADC)

A device that translates analog data (typically voltage data) to a digital value that may be used by a computer. Charge couple devices (CCDs) are ADCs that translate light signals to image data.

anti-aliasing

The technique that smoothes jagged effects in images caused by aliasing. Anti-aliasing combines image data from a higher-resolution image or model into adjacent pixels and produces cleaner, more natural lines.

aperture

The size of the camera's lens opening. A small aperture provides a larger depth of field while letting in less light. A large aperture lets in more light at the cost of a narrower range of focus.

artifact

An unintentional image element produced in error by an imaging device or as a byproduct of inaccurate software.

aspect ratio

The ratio between an image's width and height. Typical ratios include 3:2, 4:3, and so forth. The first number refers to the image's width and the second refers to its height. As in mathematics, an aspect ratio of 1.5:1 is identical to 3:2.

ATA adapter

A type of adapter that allows you to read data from a digital camera using the computer's PCMCIA ports. You insert your memory card into the ATA adapter and place the adapter into your port. It appears on your computer just like any other hard drive, ready to be read and provide rapid data transfer.

auto-focus lens

A camera lens that automatically chooses the proper settings to create a sharp picture.

AV port

See *video-out port*.

B

backlight

An image effect that occurs when the sun or another light source shines too close to your subject's back. Backlight tricks your camera into thinking it is taking a picture of a very bright object. Your camera adjusts its light levels too high. Instead of picking up the light levels from your subject, it picks them up from the background.

banding

The "layered" effect produced in images when smooth gradients are displayed or printed with a smaller number of hues than demanded by the image. Similar hues are printed with different colors because they fall to either side of a threshold and produce a visual discontinuity.

barrel distortion

Image distortion that spreads the center of the image.

bitmap

Strictly speaking, a black-and-white image constructed of arrays of black-and-white pixels. However, in common usage, the term *bitmap* (incorrectly) refers to arrays of pixels of any colors.

blooming

Image distortion caused by overexposing a CCD camera to light. A white area will appear to bleed from light sources such as a window or lamp.

blue

One of the three base colors of light. Adding blue, red, and green light produces white. Cameras tend to "cheat" when capturing blue in images, because the human eye is less responsive to blue compared to other colors.

blurring

A loss of image detail caused by incorrect focus or camera motion. Blurry pictures can be partially corrected with sharpening filters and deconvolution techniques.

BMP

A file format for Windows. It stores images as an uncompressed matrix of pixels.

brightness

The amount of light detected at each picture element by the camera's CCD.

C

capture

To acquire digital data through a camera or other scanning device.

CCD

See *charge couple device*.

CF

See *compact flash*.

charge couple device (CCD)

A light sensor used in digital cameras to sample light intensity for gathering image data. CCD sensors produce more accurate images than CMOS sensors. A CCD array consists of a series of CCD sensors arranged in the digital camera to capture many points of light at once.

cloning

In photo-editing software, a feature that allows you to copy a part of a photo and use that copy to replace another part of the photo. Cloning is typically used to hide flaws and undesirable features.

CMOS

See *complementary metal-oxide semiconductor.*

CMYK

The color standard for professional printing services. Instead of printing in red, green, and blue, this standard uses cyan (C), magenta (M), yellow (Y), and black (K) ink.

color temperature

The temperature, in Kelvin, of a light source. The lower the temperature, the redder the light. The higher the temperature, the more blue. Candlelight clocks in at about 2,000 Kelvin and sunset at 3,000 Kelvin. Daylight and flash photography both register at about 5,000 Kelvin.

compact flash (CF)

A type of removable media used in some digital cameras. Compact flash cards are built from banks of flash memory and a controller embedded in thin plastic.

complementary metal-oxide semiconductor (CMOS)

A light sensor used in digital cameras to sample light intensity for gathering image data. CMOS sensors produce images with more noise and errors than do CCD sensors. However, CMOS sensors are available at a lower price than CCD sensors.

compression

Techniques used to store image data in the smallest amount of space. GIF and JPEG images both use image compression.

continuous tones

Arbitrary image tones. Digital cameras cannot produce continuous tone because they must approximate colors and shades within fixed-byte values.

contrast

The ratio in brightness between the darkest and lightest elements of an image. Natural scenes should contain moderate contrast, unlike printed text, which should be highly contrasted.

cyan

One of the three base colors for printing. Adding cyan, magenta, and yellow ink produces black.

D

depth of field

The area in front of the camera that appears in sharp focus within a scene.

digital

Made up of binary information, readable by a computer.

digital accuracy

How close pixel values match the colors and shades of the physical qualities of the item being imaged.

digital camera

A film-free camera that uses a CCD array or CMOS sensors to capture images in digital form.

digital camera speed

The time during which light is allowed through the digital camera's lens to fall upon the sensor. The faster the speed, the less likely the image will be subject to motion blur. Digital camera speed is analogous to traditional shutter speed, although some digital cameras do not come equipped with true shutters.

digital film

See *removable media.*

digital zoom

Magnification of an image by means of software within a digital camera. Digital zoom does not increase resolution and creates a lower-quality image by interpolating between pixel values.

digitization

Converting analog "real-world" data into digital form.

dithering

The technique of placing a series of monochromatic dots in a small area to simulate a range of tones and colors.

dye-sublimation printer

A type of printer in which a thermal print head transfers ink from a roll or ribbon onto paper. The color intensity of the dye is controlled by the heat level of the print head. Dye sublimation produces the best quality prints for home use, but at a substantial cost.

dynamic range

The difference between the darkest and brightest light that a digital camera can capture and reproduce.

E

equalization

A technique for distributing image data across a greater range of pixel values. Typical equalization techniques include gamma correction and adaptive histogram equalization.

exposure compensation

The mechanism that overrides a camera's automatic exposure sensors to manually select a longer or slower exposure.

exposure meter

The system that sets the speed and aperture of a camera. Using the segment-metering system, the image is divided into segments, each of which is evaluated by the camera's light meter. With the center-weighted-metering system, the meter gives greater importance to the light values at the center of the image.

F

feathering

In photo-editing software, a feature that allows you to soften the edges of a selected area so you can gently blend it with other picture elements.

fill-in flash

See *forced flash*.

filter

A camera accessory that allows you to customize the light entering your camera. You can accessorize your digital camera with optical filters to create a variety of special effects. In photo-editing software, a feature that allows you to alter image quality. Software filters can produce artistic, distorted, blurred, sharper, and many other versions of an image.

Firewire

A cable connection standard that promises even faster data transfer rates than USB cable connections. Currently, Firewire connections are expensive.

first-curtain flash

A camera mode in which the flash fires at the moment the shutter opens.

fish eye

A lens that produces a distinctive distorted view. Elements at the center of a fish-eye view occupy proportionately greater space than elements that lie towards its edges.

fixed-focus lens

A wide-angle lens that provides good focus over a wide range of distances from the camera. Fixed-focus lenses do not require your camera to provide auto-focusing.

FlashPath

A type of adapter that allows you to transfer data from a digital camera into your computer. A FlashPath adapter looks like a 3.5-inch floppy disk. FlashPath systems transfer data from 2 to 15 times faster than serial cable connections.

focal length

The distance between the lens and the point where light rays focus behind the lens when light enters the lens in parallel lines. The longer the focal length, the greater the magnification that the lens will provide.

forced flash

Forcing the flash to fire when the camera does not sense that it is required. Also called fill-in flash.

fractals

Mathematical representation of images. An image converted into fractal representation is resolution-independent. Fractals are composed of scalable textures rather than pixels, so you can create images ten times as large as the original or bigger.

G

gamma correction

The distribution of image data to match the mathematical gamma curve that enhances details and generally lightens the image in a visually "natural" manner.

GIF

See *Graphics Image Format*.

GIF89a

The standard for GIF image support for animation.

Graphics Image Format (GIF)

One of the two most common formats of digital pictures. The GIF format was copyrighted by CompuServe. GIF pictures store images in a lossless format, using at most 256 colors.

grayscale

A colorless image consisting of black, white, and gray elements. Grayscale images are similar to black-and-white photos.

green

One of the three base colors of light. Adding blue, red, and green light produces white.

H

horizontal resolution

The greatest possible number of pixels that a digital camera can produce along the width of an image.

hue

The color (as opposed to the brightness) of a pixel.

I

infrared-block filter

A type of camera filter that reduces some of the infrared light entering your camera, while allowing regular visible light to pass through.

ink-jet printer

A printer in which colored dyes are squirted from cartridges onto paper. Ink-jet printers create color intensity by dithering.

IR-block filter

See *infrared-block filter*.

J

Joint Photographic Experts Group (JPEG)

An image format for digital pictures. JPEG pictures use efficient compression algorithms and averaging techniques to minimize image size at a slight accuracy cost. JPEG pictures can capture an arbitrary number of colors, providing greater color sensitivity than GIFs.

JPEG

See *Joint Photographic Experts Group.*

K

Kelvin

A temperature measurement system used for light sources. See also *color temperature.*

L

landscape

A digital picture whose width exceeds its height. Landscape is also a paper-orientation option for printing.

laser printer

A type of printer that uses a laser to set electrical charges along a print drum. Toner (an ink mixture) is drawn to the charged areas of the drum, and a heating element fuses the toner from the drum to paper.

layer

In photo-editing software, a feature that allows you to isolate your picture elements so you can work on each one individually.

LCD

See *liquid crystal display.*

liquid crystal display (LCD)

The screen on the back of your digital camera that allows you to preview and review your digital images. LCDs consume a large percentage of your battery's power. New advances in LCD technology, particularly in passive-matrix LCD displays known as DSTN, produce brighter screens with sharper colors. Many cameras support two types of LCD displays: one icon/character-based for displaying camera status and one pixel-based for use as a viewfinder.

lithium battery

A type of one-time-use battery that provides greater power and endurance than alkaline batteries. Some new lithium batteries can be recharged.

lossless compression

Any compression scheme that, when decompressed, produces an image identical to the original. For example, TIFF compression is lossless.

lossy compression

Any compression scheme that, when decompressed, produces an image not identical to the original. Usually, colors have been blended, averaged, or estimated in the decompressed version. For example, JPEG compression is lossy. Each time you load and resave a JPEG image, you may lose valuable image information.

luminance

The intensity (as opposed to the color) of a pixel.

M

macro lens

A camera lens that allows you to shoot pictures from as little as an inch or two away from your subject.

magenta

One of the three base colors for printing. Adding cyan, magenta, and yellow ink produces black.

media port

See *video-out port*.

megapixel camera

A digital camera that produces images of at least one million pixels.

memory card

A type of removable media used in digital cameras. Flash memory cards include compact flash, smart media, and stick memory. They use solid-state memory chips to store your pictures indefinitely and without power.

Memory Stick

See *stick memory*.

moire

A photo artifact consisting of bands of diagonal distortions.

N

National Television Standards Committee (NTSC)

Refers to the video standard for television signals used in the United States, American Samoa, Barbados, Bermuda, Bolivia, Canada, Chile, Columbia, Costa Rica, Cuba, Democratic People's Republic of Korea, Dominica, El Salvador, Equador, Guam, Guatemala, Haiti, Honduras, Mexico, Micronesia, Myanmar, Nicaragua, Panama, Peru, Philippines, Puerto Rico, Suriname, Taiwan, Trinidad, Tobago, and Venezuela.

NiCd battery

See *Nickel-Cadmium (NiCd) battery*.

Nickel-Cadmium (NiCd) battery

A type of rechargeable battery that provides excellent camera operation. Because NiCds (pronounced "nigh-cads") contain the heavy metal cadmium, they promote concerns about proper disposal.

Nickel-Metal Hydride (NiMH) battery

A type of rechargeable battery that provides excellent camera operation, long effective life, and fewer environmental concerns than alkaline or NiCd batteries. NiMHs (pronounced "nimms") also have fewer "memory effects" than NiCd batteries do. You do not need to drain them each time before recharging.

noise

Random, unintended image values added to and distributed across a digital picture. See also *artifact*.

NTSC

See *National Television Standards Committee*.

O

OCR

See *Optical Character Recognition*.

Optical Character Recognition (OCR)

A technology that allows a computer to recognize printed or typed characters. It's possible to use OCR packages with digital camera images.

optical zoom

Magnification of an image by means of an optical zoom lens. Optical zoom does not lower resolution and creates the same quality image as an image taken without optical zoom.

P

PAL

See *Phase Alternation Line*.

panorama

A series of images joined together to produce a composite image of arbitrary size.

PC card

Any media you can insert in a PCMCIA slot in your computer. A few digital cameras use PC cards to store photos.

PDD

Adobe PhotoDeluxe's proprietary format for image files.

Phase Alternation Line (PAL)

The video standard for television signals used in Western Europe, Australia, Japan, and other countries that do not specifically support the NTSC standard.

photographic-quality paper

Printer paper that is very stiff, or photo weight, and very bright. It is designed to avoid spreading ink and to produce a glossy finish after printing.

PICT

A file format for storing uncompressed pictures.

pixel

A picture element. A pixel is the smallest part of an image, which when placed into a two-dimensional array with other pixels forms a picture.

polarizing filter

A type of camera filter that uses circular polarization to allow or deny access to certain types of light.

portrait

A digital picture whose height exceeds its width. Portrait is also a paper-orientation option for printing.

Q

quilt

A two-dimensional panorama. Quilts are made up of photos snapped in two dimensions, both rows and columns.

R

red

One of the three base colors of light. Adding blue, red, and green light produces white.

red-eye

An effect that appears to make a person's eyes glow red. Red-eye occurs when light from flash photography reflects from the blood-vessels (or *choroid*) directly behind a person's retina. Animal retinas reflect light, too. However, many animals have an extra layer inside their eyes (known as a *tapetum lucidum*). Unlike humans, this layer is not composed of black pigment but some other color and can produce all sorts of red-eye variations, including green-eye.

red-eye reduction mode

A solution for red-eye built into some digital cameras. In this mode, the camera flashes twice. The first flash causes people's pupils to quickly contract. This allows less light into the eye, and thus produces less reflection when the light flashes a second time to actually take the picture.

removable media

Any of the many types of storage devices that can be inserted into your camera and read from your computer. Removable media are often called "digital film." Media include floppy disks, compact flash cards, smart media cards, and Clik! disks among others. Removable media allow you to transfer pictures to your personal computer without using cables. Using removable media, you can expand your camera's memory by replacing a full card or disk with a fresh one when needed.

resolution

The number of pixels that a display or printing device can control. Each pixel must be "addressed" for writing or reading. Resolution also refers to the pixel density.

RGB

The standard set of colors used by computer monitors to create images on your screen. RGB stands for red, green, and blue.

S

second-curtain flash

A camera mode in which the flash fires just before the shutter closes.

serial cable transfer

A method used to transfer images from a digital camera to a computer. This method uses software packaged with the camera and serial cable plugged into the camera and the computer's serial port. Serial cable transfer is very slow. Speedier transfer methods are available for cameras that use removable media.

silver-halide paper

Traditional photo-quality paper, typically used by photo finishers for prints.

slow-synch flash

A camera mode that captures both a dark background as well as a well-illuminated foreground. This technique combines a long exposure with a short flash. This allows the camera to create a well-exposed image of the background and add it to the flash photography of the foreground.

smart media

A type of removable media used in some digital cameras. The actual name for this type of memory is Solid-State Floppy Disk Cards (SSFDC). These cards consist of a flash memory chip embedded in thin plastic.

solar power pack

A type of power supply for digital cameras that uses the sun as its energy source.

stereo images

A pair of images that, when viewed through a special viewer, produce a three-dimensional effect. The two photos approximate the location of our eyes. The left image and right images are taken at exactly the same height and orientation, but offset horizontally by about 2.5 inches.

stick memory

A type of removable media used in digital cameras. The Memory Stick product, developed by Sony, is a form of flash memory that shares many of the same features of compact flash cards.

T

Tagged Image File Format (TIFF)

An image format used to store high-resolution images. Although TIFF images are often uncompressed, this format does support some proprietary compression algorithms. TIFF images are lossless. This makes TIFF a good choice for storing your pictures while you are working on them.

telephoto lens

A magnifying lens with a very high focal length. The opposite of wide-angle lenses, telephoto lenses provide images with a narrow angle of view. Telephoto lenses take pictures of a smaller area of the scene.

Use a telephoto lens when you cannot get close to your subject, such as in wildlife photography.

U

ultraviolet (UV) filter

A type of camera filter that helps cut through fog and creates clearer pictures in misty conditions.

Universal Serial Bus (USB)

A cable connection standard that provides quick and efficient data transfer. Most newer computers provide USB ports. Some digital cameras have started to support USB transfer in place of, or in addition to, the more traditional serial cable transfers.

USB

See *Universal Serial Bus.*

UV filter

See *ultraviolet (UV) filter.*

V

vertical resolution

The greatest possible number of pixels that a digital camera can produce across the height of an image.

video-out port

A port on a digital camera that allows you to create a video signal that can be displayed on a TV, a VCR, a projection system, and similar devices. Also called an AV or media port, this port typically creates NTSC or PAL signals, or sometimes both.

vista

A type of panorama that shows images aligned in a row. To produce a simple vista, you stitch together a linear series of pictures.

W

white balance

A feature that allows you to manually adjust how your camera reacts to different light sources with differing color temperatures. When a camera is balanced for one temperature of light and used to photograph another temperature, it creates colors that are not true.

wide-angle lens

A lens that allows your camera to capture a wider image. The opposite of telephoto lenses, wide-angle lenses provide greater depth of field. Wide-angle lenses take pictures of a larger part of the scene.

Y

yellow

One of the three base colors for printing. Adding cyan, magenta, and yellow ink produces black.

Z

zoom
See *digital zoom; optical zoom.*

zoom lens
A lens that provides a magnification effect by changing your camera's focal length.

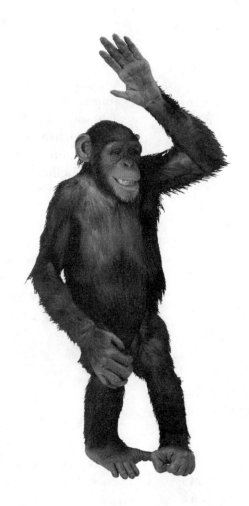

INDEX

Note to the Reader: Throughout this index **boldfaced** page numbers indicate primary discussions of a topic. *Italicized* page numbers indicate illustrations.

Z

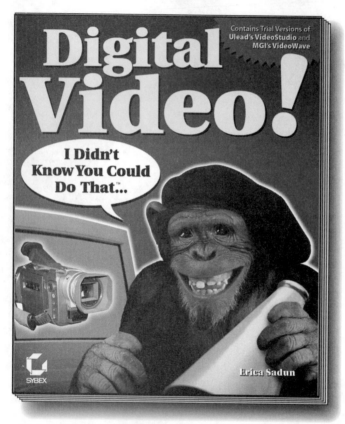

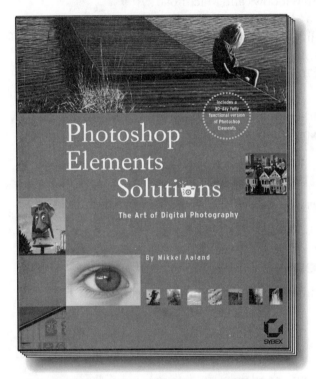

About the CD

Wow, are you lucky! That CD just to the right of this page is packed with software and goodies. Best of all, you'll find an absolutely free, fully licensed version of Adobe PhotoDeluxe 3.1 (for both Windows and Macintosh systems). This terrific image-processing software is a $49 value. With PhotoDeluxe, you work your way through guided activities that let you fix, enhance, and play with your photos. But that's not all. This book will show you how to unlock Photo-Deluxe's secret "power mode" to access features you would expect to find only in expensive image-processing packages.

But wait! There's still more. Your CD contains many other demonstrations and shareware programs. Here's a list of what you'll find on the CD:

Adobe PhotoDeluxe Home Edition 3.1

Edit and manipulate your digital images with tons of projects and tools. (PC and Mac, free)

Adobe Photoshop Elements

The new and exciting consumer-grade image processing solution from Adobe. (PC and Mac, demo)

JASC Paint Shop Pro

Paint Shop Pro offers one of the most popular and powerful image editing packages on the market today. (PC, trial)

Ulead PhotoImpact

PhotoImpact offers image editing that's specialized for Web page creation. (PC, trial)

Ulead GIF Animator

Quickly and easily create animated GIFs. (PC, 15-day trial)